T0199210

The Typewriter Is Holy

The Complete, Uncensored History
of the Beat Generation

The Typewriter
Is Holy

Bill Morgan

COUNTERPOINT

BERKELEY

First hardcover edition published by Free Press, a Division of Simon and Schuster, Inc., July 2010.

Library of Congress Cataloging-in-Publication Data

Morgan, Bill, 1949–
The typewriter is holy: the complete, uncensored history of the beat generation/
Bill Morgan
p. cm.
ISBN 978-1-58243-738-5
Includes bibliographical references and index.
1. Beat generation. 2. American literature—20th century—History and criticism.
I. Title.
PS228.B6M58 2010
810.9'0054—dc22
2009042224

Cover Design by Domini Dragoone

Printed in the United States of America

COUNTERPOINT
2560 Ninth Street, Suite 318
Berkeley, CA 94710

www.counterpointpress.com

To the memory of Alan Ansen
the unknown Beat

Contents

The typewriter is holy the poem is holy the voice is holy the hearers are holy the ecstasy is holy!

–Allen Ginsberg (*Footnote to Howl*)

Acknowledgments

Jack Kerouac and Allen Ginsberg had a way of calling everyone they liked an angel. From Jack's "desolation angels" to Allen's "visionary Indian angels," they showed their attachment to the people around them through that designation. I was never more proud than when Ginsberg included me in this club by referring to me as his "bibliographic angel" in an inscription. Following that tradition, I'd like to acknowledge all the angels who have helped in the preparation of this book.

First and foremost, I'd like to thank my literary agent, Sterling Lord, for his enthusiasm from the outset. Sterling was not only my agent but also Jack Kerouac's, and his firsthand knowledge of the era helped me get it right. His confidence in this project brought it to the attention of Free Press. Their editorial staff, Martin Beiser in particular, as well as Leslie Meredith, Donna Loffredo, Alexandra Pisano, and Philip Metcalf, then dedicated themselves to making the book into what you find before you. Their many suggestions and recommendations resulted in a much more polished story.

As always, the people at the Allen Ginsberg Trust, Peter Hale and Bob Rosenthal, have been generous and helpful, never failing to answer my questions or add their knowledge. John Sampas of the Jack Kerouac estate helped steer me away from common mistakes several times, and James Grauerholz of the William Burroughs estate entrusted me with invaluable information that only he would know.

A host of poets, scholars, and librarians have greeted me warmly at every turn and assisted in ways too numerous to count. I appreciate especially the help of Michael Aldrich, David Amram, Gordon Ball, Carolyn Cassady, Ann Charters, Neeli Cherkovski, Diane Di Prima, Lawrence Ferlinghetti, Bill Gargan, Jacqueline Gens, Jack W. C. Hagstrom, Jack Hirschman, Michael Horowitz, Hettie Jones, Larry Keenan, Bill Keogan, Shelley Kraut, Joanne Kyger, Robert LaVigne, Michael and Amy McClure, Kaye McDonough, Judith Malina, Tim Moran, Peter Orlovsky, Nancy Peters, Barney Rosset, Ed Sanders, Steven Sandy, Ben Schafer, Michael Schumacher, Steve Silberman, Gary Snyder, Robert Sutherland-Cohen, Steven Taylor, John and Mellon Tytell, Joan Wilentz, and Bob Wilson. Libby Chenault at the University of North Carolina's Wilson Library, Isaac Gewirtz at the Berg Collection of the New York Public Library, and Tony Bliss at the University of California's Bancroft Library have been extremely helpful during years of research.

Appreciation is also owed to all the angels past, who gave of themselves and upon whom all the following is based: Alan Ansen, William Burroughs, Lucien Carr, Gregory Corso, Allen Ginsberg, Jack Kerouac, Edie Kerouac-Parker, Timothy Leary, Carl Solomon, and Philip Whalen. Each was an inspiration in one way or another.

For permission to use photographs, I especially would like to thank Gordon Ball, Carolyn Cassady, Ann Charters, Chris Felver, Larry Keenan, and the Allen Ginsberg Trust.

Finally, I'd like to thank my wife, Judy, who has truly earned her angelic wings in so many ways. Only through her encouragement, support, and wise counsel have this and other projects been possible.

Introduction

Recently Anthony Daniels concluded his review of John Leland's book *Why Kerouac Matters* with a parody of the opening line of Allen Ginsberg's *Howl*. "I have seen some of the most mediocre minds of my generation," wrote Mr. Daniels, "destroyed by too great an interest in the Beats." The ridicule came as no surprise; I've been reading examples of the same sort and worse for the past fifty years, but I am amazed that the ire of conservative critics can still be raised by the mere suggestion that the Beat Generation was anything but a bunch of juvenile delinquents.

Not so long ago Roger Kimball wrote the following about the same group. "They were drug-abusing sexual predators and infantilized narcissists," he said, "whose shamelessness helped dupe a confused and gullible public into believing that their utterances were works of genius." Mr. Kimball seems to be making the not-so-subtle point that if you take pleasure in reading the works of Jack Kerouac, William S. Burroughs, Allen Ginsberg, and their ilk, you are no doubt a member of this confused and gullible segment of the population. This is the very same tactic that literary critics have used since the first reviews of *On the Road, Naked Lunch,* and *Howl* appeared in the 1950s. In those days Norman Podhoretz dubbed the Beats as "know-nothing bohemians," and Robert Brustein declared them leaders of "the cult of unthink." Even Al Capp's *Li'l Abner* comic strip featured a character named Ginzbird, "the most irritable unidentified flying object on earth." The trail of insults became more ridiculous with each passing year. Now that the first books by the Beats are widely considered modern classics, those same harsh critics who denounced their initial work point out that the later books by Beat writers were not up to the standards of their earlier writings.

When I tell people that I write books about the Beat Generation, I generally receive one of two reactions. One group will stare at me blankly, having no idea what I'm talking about. Perhaps they think I'm referring to a whole segment of the population who grew up eating nothing but beets. Members of the second group will acknowledge complete understanding and be familiar with the most intimate details of at least one member of the Beat canon. There appears to be no middle ground: either a reader knows a good deal about the lives of these persons, or they are not familiar with them at all.

When I first proposed the idea of a history of the Beat Generation to Martin Beiser, my editor at Free Press, he suggested that the book be aimed at readers who have little or no idea about who the Beat writers were or why their books remain important to us today. For people who already are familiar with the Beats, this book outlines the many ways these unique writers are interrelated. In the course of my research, I've studied dozens of biographies of individual Beat authors such as Kerouac, Burroughs, Ginsberg, Ferlinghetti, and the rest, but stories that focus on a single writer sometimes obscure the overall Beat chronology and make it difficult to see exactly how their lives intersected. For example, when Burroughs was experimenting with his cut-up method, what was Kerouac doing? Or where was Ginsberg when Ferlinghetti was standing trial for the publication of *Howl*? Or what were they all doing while Cassady was locked in a San Quentin prison cell?

As a model for this book, my editor recommended that I take a close look at Susan Cheever's *American Bloomsbury*, about the social circle of the Transcendentalists of the mid-nineteenth century in Massachusetts, which was published in 2006. As I read her book, I noted the strong parallels she drew between those Transcendentalists and the people of the period many of us of a certain age remember vividly as "the sixties." Quoting Ms. Cheever, "In many ways, the period of the late 1830s and '40s was a time like the 1960s when individual adventure was prized and all the old rules suddenly seemed corrupt." After reading her book, I found that I couldn't agree more with Ms. Cheever's comparison, yet I would go one step further. I've always felt that the cultural changes that society underwent during the nineteen-sixties were a direct result of the example set still earlier in the forties and fifties by the group I knew as the Beat Generation.

There were several passages in *American Bloomsbury* to which one could add a hundred years to the date and find the same ideas being embraced by the Beats. "The new generation of Concord intellectuals was intoxicated with freedom, with leisure, and with the possibilities of life devoted to thought and pleasure," she wrote. That is a perfect way to summarize the spirit of the tiny group of friends who first met around the Columbia College campus in the mid-forties, too.

There is one important distinction between the story that Cheever tells of the Transcendentalists and the one I'll tell about the Beat Generation. The history of the Transcendentalists seems to be a spaghetti bowl of personalities, each strand nearly equal in importance to the finished dish. In contrast, I would compare the story of the Beats to a freight train, with Allen Ginsberg as the locomotive that pulled the others along like so many boxcars. The Transcendentalist Movement wouldn't have been as tasty without Emerson, but the Beat Generation would never have existed without Ginsberg.

My association with the Beat writers dates back to my own college days during the sixties. One evening I attended a poetry reading given on campus by Lawrence Ferlinghetti, not knowing quite what to expect. The packed auditorium cheered, laughed, and listened attentively as Ferlinghetti delivered his poems from a well-worn copy of *A Coney Island of the Mind*, his slim collection that was selling like hotcakes in college bookstores across America at the time. It was unlike any poetry that I had heard before, and I bought my own copy the next day. Later, while working on my library degree, I was assigned to compile a bibliography of the work of a living author and I selected Ferlinghetti. When my professor suggested that the university press publish the bibliography, I wrote to Lawrence asking him a few more questions to fill in some of the gaps. I was disappointed when Lawrence wrote back saying that he was too busy to answer questions via mail. However, he suggested I come to San Francisco for a week or two, where I could go through his files, ask questions, and stay in the apartment above the City Lights publishing company office. That began a friendship that has lasted for more than forty years now, one that has led from San Francisco to New York to Athens to Benares, constantly on the trail of the Beats. Although I arrived on the scene too late to meet either Cassady or Kerouac, I have been fortunate enough to meet and work closely with nearly every other member of the Beat pantheon in the intervening years.

In particular, for the last two decades of Allen Ginsberg's life, I assisted him daily as his bibliographer and archivist. During that period, I managed to track down nearly everything that he had ever published and a good deal of what had been printed about him. It was a mammoth task. Every day, as I walked to the apartment that served as both Allen's home and office, I wondered what new treasures I'd uncover, but the true rewards came through working with Allen himself. As everyone who ever met Ginsberg knows, he was the great "introducer" of the twentieth century. He loved to initiate relationships among his many contacts, and so it was that he introduced me to all his friends. After I sold his archive to Stanford University for a million dollars, Allen referred everyone with questions about their papers to me. In this way I came to work with people like Lawrence Ferlinghetti, Anne Waldman, Diane Di Prima,

Abbie Hoffman, Timothy Leary, and Larry Rivers on their archives. Through Allen I became friends with Alan Ansen, Lucien Carr, Michael McClure, and of course, Peter Orlovsky. One day while sitting at his kitchen table cataloguing translations of poetry in Urdu and Tamil, Bianca Jagger ducked under the laundry drying on clothesline strung in the hallway. She was there to discuss the political situation in Nicaragua, and of course, Allen introduced me as a "genius" of bibliography, and later Keith Richards called me about his papers. And it continued that way until the very day that Allen died in his apartment, surrounded by friends and celebrities like Patti Smith, Philip Glass, and Francesco Clemente, each of whom considered him their hero, too.

The history of the Beat Generation is really the story of this one man's desire to gather a circle of friends around him, people he loved and who could love him. What united these people was not only a love of literature, but also Ginsberg's supportive character, a trait that often verged on obsession. It was their friendship that they shared and not any one common literary style, philosophy, or social theory.

Study other movements in art, music, and literature and you'll find a common style or a shared attribute that appears in the work of the various members. In the early Cubist paintings of Picasso and Braque, it is difficult to distinguish which artist created which picture, so similar are they in composition. The Surrealist and Dadaist movements were made up of artists and writers who adhered to their group's manifestos. Often their works are hard to tell one from another, but no one could ever mistake a piece of writing by Burroughs for one by Kerouac, or a poem by Corso for one by Ginsberg. Lawrence Ferlinghetti's work is as unlike Gary Snyder's as Longfellow's is from e. e. cummings's. Friendship held these writers together as a group more than style or ideology, and at the center of all those friendships was the strongly cohesive glue that was Allen Ginsberg.

Once the press began to identify those writers collectively as "the

Beat Generation," some within the group began to struggle with a definition for the word *beat*. Since it was Jack Kerouac who had originally coined the phrase, he was asked repeatedly what he meant by it. Initially he said that the Beat Generation was composed of people who had been beaten down, worn out, and exhausted. As time passed, he refined his definition to emphasize the beatific, blessed, or sympathetic qualities of his generation.

A decade after Kerouac first mentioned the term in a conversation with John Clellon Holmes, he was still trying to explain his thoughts on the subject. He wrote to Allen Ginsberg on March 24, 1959, "*American College Dictionary* sent me their big square definition of 'beat generation' and wanted to know if I would revise, emend or make a new one. Theirs was awful, 'certain members of the generation that came of age after World War II who affect detachment from moral and social forms and responsibilities, supposedly due to disillusionment. Coined by John Kerouac.' So I sent in this: '*beat generation*, members of the generation that came of age after World War II–Korean War who join in a relaxation of social and sexual tensions and espouse anti-regimentation, mystic-disaffiliation and material-simplicity values, supposedly as a result of Cold War disillusionment. Coined by JK.'"

Over the years countless others have tried to identify the literary or philosophical qualities that might be common to all Beat writers. As a student of semantics himself, William Burroughs once told friends that art was merely a word and it meant whatever the person who used it wanted it to mean. Paraphrasing his idea about art is appropriate for the term *Beat,* because it also can mean whatever you want it to mean. In this respect it is of importance to note that many of the writers we commonly think of as quintessentially Beat didn't consider themselves members of the Beat Generation. Lawrence Ferlinghetti, Philip Lamantia, Gary Snyder, and several others repeatedly denied that they were members of the group. From a stylistic perspective, their opinions are correct. However, they were all close friends of Allen Ginsberg, and by applying my definition they are linked to the genre by that friendship, and that alone qualifies them for Beat-hood status whether they like it or not.

The problem of devising a workable definition extends to those scholars who try to write about the Beat Generation. In the 1966 Monarch Notes study guide entitled *Beat Literature*, author Gregor Roy included Charles Farber, Paul Dreyfus, Mark di Suvero, Chandler Brossard, and Anatole Broyard as good examples of Beat writers. Other surveys have included writers as diverse as Charles Bukowski, Barbara Guest, Charles Olson, and Paul Blackburn in the roster of Beat writers. Perhaps the most egregious inclusion occurred recently in the Gale Critical Companion Series's three-volume set, *The Beat Generation*, which includes San Francisco poet Jack Spicer. Spicer hated the Beats so much that he refused to allow Lawrence Ferlinghetti to sell his own books in the City Lights Bookstore for fear of being somehow tainted by the volumes of Beat poetry on nearby shelves.

These various rosters are neither right nor wrong, because they all depend entirely upon how the theorist defines his subject. The only definition that truly holds up to serious scrutiny is this: The Beat Generation was essentially a group of friends who gathered around and interacted with Allen Ginsberg. Among themselves they formed smaller groups and merged with other literary circles from time to time. Many of the groups split and reformed, but each of them at one time or another was included in the fellowship of Ginsberg's immediate circle.

Using friendship with Ginsberg as the common criteria, it is possible to include writers who were kindred spirits and are widely considered to be Beat whether they themselves acknowledge that label or not. Therefore, even friends who wrote very little, such as Neal Cassady, Carl Solomon, and Peter Orlovsky, and those who did not publish at all, like Lucien Carr, Joan Adams, Bill Cannastra, and David Kammerer can be considered part of the Beat Generation.

This definition might upset readers who believe that Jack Kerouac, often referred to as the "King of the Beats," was the most important writer in the group and try to build a definition around his spontaneous method of writing. Although I also subscribe to the belief that Kerouac's work has had the greater influence on the world, I do not think that he was the force who created the group or held it together. Jack might have been the person who named the generation, but until Ginsberg's death in 1997, Allen was the vortex of the Beat phenomenon. Ginsberg attracted interesting and talented people through the power of his inclusive, supportive nature and nurturing personality. No other member of the group had the ability to bring so many diverse people together.

Jack Kerouac and/or the Beat Generation first came to the attention of the public when Gilbert Millstein's review of *On the Road* hit the stands in the September 5, 1957, issue of the *New York Times*. Millstein called the publication of Jack's book "a historic occasion" and said that it was "the most beautifully executed, the clearest and the most important utterance yet made by the generation Kerouac himself named years ago as 'beat.'" Millstein's rave review was to be one of the last good things that Kerouac read about himself for quite a while. It was soon followed by reactionary articles with titles such as "The Innocent Nihilists Adrift in Squaresville," "Epitaph for the Dead Beats," "The Know-Nothing Bohemians," and "Beatniks Just Sick, Sick, Sick," all aimed at attacking and denigrating the writings of Kerouac and the Beat Generation.

No one was more outspoken in his criticism of the Beats than the conservative writer Norman Podhoretz. Ironically, he was once a college classmate and colleague of Ginsberg and Kerouac and knew them all personally. In one of his first essays castigating the new group, he wrote, "this notion that to be hopped-up is the most desirable of all human conditions, lies at the heart of the Beat Generation ethos." He criticized Kerouac for "his simple inability to express anything in words," a terrible insult to hurl at any writer. In his vicious article he declared the Beats to be "young men who can't think straight and so hate anyone who can." He concluded with the statement that he believed "the spirit of the Beat Generation strikes me [Podhoretz] as the same spirit which animates the young savages in leather jackets who have been running amuck in the last few years with their switch-blades and zip guns."

Podhoretz's statements are examples of the type of conservative backlash that grew more widespread after readers began to take an interest in the Beats. Critics defined who the Beats were and what they represented to suit their own agendas. For whatever their reasons, they felt the need to pigeonhole everyone into a single category. It was Ginsberg who really decided to take advantage of the situation, using the pulpit that the Beat moniker bestowed on him to promote his own work and the work of his friends.

At one time or another most of the Beat writers commented on the definition of the Beat Generation. Gregory Corso once said that "three people do not make a generation," and even at the beginning of a book about the Beat Generation it has to be acknowledged that any statement cannot be applied to an entire generation of people. The Beat Generation began as a very small group of friends, and even as the years passed and their numbers increased, they remained a relatively tiny circle. The remarkable thing is that such a small group was able to transform our culture in so many ways.

The Typewriter Is Holy

Chapter 1

Friendship and Murder

It was in the spring of 1943 that the story of the Beat Generation really begins. That's when a chain reaction of events began to unfold. Following a suicide attempt, Lucien Carr, a good-looking eighteen-year-old boy from St. Louis, spent some time recuperating in Chicago's Cook County Hospital. There he received little therapy for the depression that had made him put his head in an oven in the first place. When the doctors determined that Carr was no longer a threat to himself, they released him into the care of his divorced mother, Marion Gratz, then living in New York City. Underneath all their rude banter, Carr and his mother maintained a loving, if somewhat volatile, relationship. They quarreled continually, and during the worst arguments Lucien resorted to calling his mother every nasty name he could think of, from the commonest epithet to vulgar displays of his immense and obscene vocabulary— a vocabulary that he had honed during his years away in boarding schools. On such occasions, he might refer to her as a *hetaera* (a high-class whore) or a *coprophiliac* (someone who eats excrement). Carr filched money from her purse whenever he needed it. Eventually, to escape from her watchful eyes, he enrolled as a second-term

1

freshman at Columbia University, transferring the few credits he had earned in a number of schools around the country. Carr appeared to be a man on the run, but it wasn't clear even to him whether he was running away from something or in search of something.

Lucien was blessed to be one of the most handsome students in the incoming class at Columbia that year. Women fell in love with him on sight, and to be honest, so did many men. He had a youthful charm and possessed an amiable aspect that made him seem even younger than he was. In spite of his youth, by the time he arrived in New York he had already managed to acquire an adult drinking problem.

That fall, Columbia's incoming class of tuitioned students was much smaller than usual. To aid the war effort, the college had given over most of its space to the Navy College Training Program. A majority of the classroom seats were filled with V-12 cadets who were studying to become commissioned officers. America had been at war for nearly two years, and most of the men were bound for active duty, so not many of them were devoted to the lectures on English literature offered by legendary professors like Mark Van Doren, Raymond Weaver, and Lionel Trilling. In that way, Carr fit in perfectly, for he wasn't much interested in the established curriculum either. He was far more absorbed in the exciting, colorful, and even lurid lives of the people he was meeting in the city, beyond the wrought-iron fence that surrounded the campus. His classroom became the bar stools and booths of the West End, a dingy tavern directly across Broadway from Columbia's main gate.

During Christmas break, Carr stayed on in his room, preferring the solitude of the empty dormitory to his mother's company. One afternoon while Carr was listening to Brahms on his record player, his door opened. Curious about the music echoing down the deserted hallway and wondering who besides himself had chosen to spend the holiday in the dorm, in walked seventeen-year-old Allen Ginsberg, another Columbia student.

Ginsberg had grown up across the Hudson River in nearby Paterson, New Jersey, where he had lived in a series of apartments with his parents and older brother. His father, Louis, taught high school English in Paterson, raised two sons, and wrote poetry in what little spare time he had left. Allen's mother, Naomi, suffered from increasingly severe schizophrenia and had spent many of the previous years in mental hospitals. It was the expense of those hospitalizations that had kept the family on the move, continually looking for cheaper quarters. Ginsberg's older brother, Eugene, who had been studying to become a lawyer, was serving in the army for the duration of the war.

The Ginsberg family was Jewish in name only, and both of Allen's parents were fully agnostic; they were much more active in leftist politics. Louis usually supported socialist candidates for office while his wife was a devoted communist. She had often taken her sons with her to party cell meetings before her mental condition deteriorated to the point where the local chapter expelled her. Allen, their youngest son, absorbed it all, but being immature for his years, tended to live in a world of naïve dreams. He was not an attractive boy; his ears stuck out from his head, and his complexion was pale from spending all his time at his studies. His lips were large, and he wore heavy, dark-rimmed eyeglasses that made him look like an egghead. Although not overweight, he was not athletic either. In short, he was the very image of a nerd before that term became common.

Ginsberg and the affable Carr hit it off immediately, and before long Lucien invited Allen to meet some of the people he knew. A few days before Christmas 1943, Allen found himself riding the subway down to Greenwich Village to meet Lucien's friends. That get-together would lead to a lifelong relationship that was to change Ginsberg's life and alter the course of American literature and culture forever. Lucien took Allen to the Bedford Street apartment of William S. Burroughs, the grandson of the inventor of the modern adding machine. Burroughs, a St. Louis native like Carr, knew

Lucien through a mutual Missouri friend, David Kammerer, who was also visiting Burroughs that night. This gathering of young men was the first assembly of the group that would grow over the next fifteen years to become the literary circle known as the Beat Generation.

Always at the center of this circle was the sociable impresario Ginsberg. Allen would be the adhesive that held it all together, for he became the proselytizer, the networker, the agitator, and the driving force who brought the group to the public's attention more than a decade later. Before the Beats emerged in the fifties, a network of friends took shape in the forties.

As a result of Carr's buildup, Ginsberg was expecting a lot when he met Burroughs and Kammerer, and he wasn't disappointed. They were intelligent, imaginative, and demonic, all at once. In Allen they saw an awkward, unpolished bookworm, but nonetheless they found his natural curiosity about their homosexual innuendoes during conversations encouraging.

Burroughs and Kammerer were each more than ten years Ginsberg's senior. They'd been around and knew the world in a way that Ginsberg had only experienced through the pages of his books. In St. Louis, Burroughs had led a life of privilege, born into a household that employed a nanny, maid, cook, and gardener. He had graduated from Harvard, studied in Europe, and before the war had married a woman to help her escape fascism. By the time Allen met him, Bill had already cut off a part of one of his fingers in a fit of gay angst after a lover rejected him. That Van Gogh–like act had led him straight to a psychotherapist's couch. Burroughs already possessed the macabre sense of humor and gentlemanly charm that would win many friends in the future. Being twelve years older than Ginsberg, Bill had life experience that Allen envied, and before long he was mentoring his young associate.

The other man Ginsberg met that night, David Kammerer, was also from a well-to-do St. Louis family. He had graduated from Washington University and became a teacher and scout leader who had fallen disastrously in love with one of his teenage charges, Lucien Carr. When Lucien left St. Louis, Kammerer followed him from one school to another hoping to seduce the stubbornly heterosexual lad. For his part, Lucien was ambivalent about his relationship with David. He considered him both a nuisance and a welcome mentor and accomplice. It was uncertain how far he would go to string Kammerer along, for he seemed to enjoy the attention that was lavished on him by the older man. "Kammerer had everything going for him; intelligence, money, physique—but he was blind when it came to Lucien. He acted like a groupie around some superstar," Edie Kerouac would later say in her memoir, *You'll Be Okay*.

It was into this backdrop that a shy, inhibited Allen Ginsberg stumbled. He had been secretly gay for as long as he could remember and painfully shy when it came to all things sexual. In high school, he had experienced a deep crush on another boy in his class, but when he hinted of his desire, he was rebuffed and soundly reminded that those kinds of feelings were not appreciated. In fact, it was in pursuit of that same boy that had brought Ginsberg to Columbia with the hope that something would happen, but the boy had been drafted, and nothing ever came of it.

Since Ginsberg's mother was mentally unbalanced, Allen worried that his homosexual tendency might be the warning sign of his own insanity. At that time, being gay was considered a form of mental illness in itself. The new trio that Allen was about to become involved with played beyond the limits of what was socially acceptable at the time. During that first night, they all drank heavily, which inspired Lucien and David to try to compete with each other in outrageous behavior. It came to a head when Lucien broke off bits of his beer glass with his teeth and, bleeding badly, challenged David to do the same. That prompted Burroughs to bring a tray of razor blades and lightbulbs from the kitchen "as hors d'oeuvre." Initially gay sex was not discussed outright, but the innuendoes that both Kammerer and Burroughs made were unmistakable, even to the inexperienced Ginsberg.

In the months that followed, Allen began to spend more time off campus with his new friends and less time with his college classmates. Carr's circle also included other interesting people, each one determined to live life in the fast lane. They were generally not the dedicated scholars on "career paths" that Allen had been associating with during his freshman year. Drugs and alcohol played an important role in the lives of some of these outsiders, and Ginsberg was eager to experiment, first with liquor and marijuana and then with a wide range of narcotics. Allen was always studiously curious about the effects of various substances on his brain and even the first time he got drunk, he did so with pen and paper in hand. Minute by minute he described his state of mind as he became more and more inebriated. He would follow this practice for the rest of his life whenever he explored new areas of consciousness by using drugs.

One of Carr's female friends was a flirtatious, sexy blonde named Edie "Frankie" Parker, who described herself accurately as an almost wealthy girl from Grosse Pointe, Michigan. She was gorgeous, and people sometimes mistook her for a young Barbara Stanwyck. Edie had come to New York ostensibly to study art, but actually she just wanted to escape the boredom and limitations of living with her mother in suburban Detroit. She dreamed of having a free and independent life against the sophisticated backdrop of the big city. Edie had been living with her grandmother near the Columbia campus when she first met Lucien, but by the time Allen came along, she had taken a room in an apartment with a young war bride, Joan Vollmer Adams. Joan loved Edie's wild streak, and her outgoing personality made her fun to be around.

Adams had been a student, too, but was now pregnant. Her husband was serving overseas, and Joan found that she could not visualize herself as either a devoted wife or a mother. Like Edie, Joan had grown up in an affluent suburb and now wanted to pursue her own freedom. She was not comfortable with the restrictions that society silently placed on her as a married woman and was looking for a little excitement of her own.

Parker's good looks and carefree nature had already attracted many male suitors. One of them was Henri Cru, the son of a well-respected French professor at City College. Edie thought Henri romantically dangerous, and his black hair and eyes gave him a certain swarthy charm that she found appealing. Cru had gone to the prestigious Horace Mann School in the Bronx before being expelled for selling condoms and pornographic pictures to his classmates. Now he was as intent on putting his stuffy academic background behind him as Edie was determined to escape her privileged one. Cru decided to see the world as a merchant marine and was torn between his need to be with Edie and his desire to travel. Cru decided to introduce Parker to a classmate of his from Horace Mann by the name of Jack Kerouac. Henri's idea was to hook Edie up with Kerouac, someone he felt would not try to seduce her. By appointing his own "safe" replacement, Henri thought she would still be waiting for him upon his return.

Whatever Cru's reasoning for the introduction, he was wrong about Jack's being harmless; before long, Jack and Edie were sleeping together. For Edie this wasn't a bad thing, as she enjoyed the company of men, and Jack was even more handsome than Cru. She found that Jack's natural shyness only added to his sexual appeal. When Parker, still in her teens, became pregnant, she wasn't certain if the baby was Henri's or Jack's. A backroom abortion put an end to her pregnancy but caused tension between Edie and both her men. Finally, she picked Kerouac as her steady boyfriend, much to Henri's disappointment.

One day after class Parker introduced her fellow classmate, Lucien Carr, to Kerouac at the West End Bar. While relaxing over a few beers, the two men struck up a conversation and swapped stories. Kerouac came from a working-class family but hoped to become a writer. He told Lucien that he had been a star football player back in his hometown of Lowell, Massachusetts, but he had been injured during his second year on the Columbia team. He quit the team, dropped out of school, and was now determined to find subjects worth writing about on the streets of New York. It was Kerouac's belief that he didn't need a college degree to become a great writer.

Jack's French Canadian heritage was a far cry from Carr's Waspish background, but they both had the same lust for adventure, booze, and intelligent conversation. Celine Young, Lucien's girlfriend at the time, had already become best friends with Edie and Joan. When they weren't sitting in the West End Bar, they were at the girls' apartment at 421 West 118th Street, just a block away from campus.

One night that winter Ginsberg was talking with Carr at the bar and by chance met Edie and Celine. They invited him over to their apartment to meet Kerouac, whom they described as a writer and a sailor, both careers that seemed romantic to Allen. To Ginsberg, Kerouac personified the ideal author. Edie told Allen that Jack had already written more than a million words of prose but hadn't been able to find a publisher for his work yet. At the time, Ginsberg was planning to become a labor lawyer, but he considered himself to be an amateur poet as well. It was something that he saw himself doing more or less as a hobby, like his father. He was fascinated by Kerouac's idea of writing as his calling in life.

After walking up five flights of stairs to Edie's apartment, Ginsberg found himself face to face with one of the most handsome men he had ever met. Nearly four years older than Ginsberg, twenty-one-year-old Jack Kerouac struck Allen as the very epitome of masculine beauty. At their first meeting Kerouac didn't think very highly of Ginsberg and later described him as being a "spindly Jewish kid with horn-rimmed glasses and tremendous ears sticking out . . ." Jack was mostly hanging around, working at temporary jobs while gathering friends and experiences to use in future books. He had already given up his original plan of getting his degree, but he needed subjects to write about. His association with Edie exposed the more reserved and inhibited Kerouac to a wide range of offbeat and colorful people.

Although Jack recognized that Allen was bright, he could also see that he was something of an odd duck, full of neuroses. On the afternoon they met, Allen had the chutzpah to ask Jack to help him move all his belongings from his dorm to another room about ten blocks away. Begrudgingly Jack agreed. As Allen locked the door to his old room for the last time and walked down the hallway carrying his few possessions, he turned and said, "Good-bye, door." At the first landing he paused again. "Good-bye, stairs," he said and continued in that vein all the way out of the building. It was at that moment that Jack realized that he and Allen were kindred spirits, because he often said good-bye to physical things when he left one place for another.

Once Ginsberg had gotten to know Kerouac a little better, he and Lucien brought William Burroughs up to Edie's apartment to talk to Jack about the ins and outs of merchant marine service. That winter Burroughs had decided that he should earn some money by going to sea as Cru and Kerouac had been doing. What he needed was practical advice on how to go about it. In 1944 it was lucrative, albeit dangerous, to work on American ships resupplying the troops in Europe and North Africa. Kerouac had already served on some convoys and he was happy to give Bill a few pointers. In the end Burroughs didn't follow up on the idea, but like the others, he became a close friend and confidant of Kerouac.

In those days, wherever Carr went, Kammerer was sure to follow, and by spring the new gang, which now included Ginsberg, Kerouac, Burroughs, Carr, Kammerer, Parker, Young, and Adams, could usually be found either in a bar on upper Broadway or in the girls' 118th Street apartment. There was an undercurrent of sexual passion that seemed to tie the group together in a tangled web of unspoken desire. Allen had fallen in love with Jack, David was crazy about Lucien, Bill thought Allen looked like a promising partner, Jack wouldn't have minded getting into bed with the flirtatious Celine, and so on.

An emotional disaster of one sort or another was inevitable given the volatile atmosphere.

As spring turned to summer on Morningside Heights, the women worked odd jobs to pay the rent while the men talked and traded reading lists and made suggestions for one another's independent study. They were interested in everything from literature and philosophy to art and anthropology. In his role as the older and wiser professor, Burroughs often dominated the motley group with his theories about how to enjoy life, and he took pleasure in introducing them to important ideas and literary masterpieces. Oswald Spengler's *The Decline of the West* offered them a chance to discuss the future of civilization itself, and Alfred Korzybski's ideas about semantics as expressed in his *Science and Sanity* played a major role in their discussions. Burroughs gave Ginsberg a copy of Yeats's *A Vision* as an example of what great poetry should be. They debated various aspects of their personal philosophies at length and tried to develop a new theory of truth and love achievable only through art. They wanted to apply this model to their immediate circle of friends, even dubbing it "the New Vision," but they never quite got around to completing a formula acceptable to everyone.

At the time, only Ginsberg and Carr were Columbia students, still attending classes daily. Kerouac was writing and spending a good deal of his time in the new Butler Library reading whatever struck him as worthwhile. His parents had moved from Lowell to an apartment in Queens, so each evening he would retreat to his mother's kitchen table to write. In the stillness of the night, far from the merrymaking of his friends, he wrote family sagas patterned after the exuberant autobiographical novels of Thomas Wolfe. By using his own life as his inspiration, he wrote many of the stories that would be published posthumously as *Atop an Underwood*.

By the summer of 1944, Lucien Carr had wearied of David Kammerer's obsession with him. Lucien had just turned eighteen and wanted to travel the world on his own. He certainly did not want to be tied down to a thirty-three-year-old homosexual like Kammerer whose one-track mind, fixated on Lucien, threatened to smother him. David was stalking Lucien more than ever and had even taken to climbing into Lucien's room from the fire escape to stare at him while he slept.

Kerouac, although not as eager to leave Edie, also craved an opportunity to travel. That summer's news of the Allied invasion at Normandy had inspired both Jack and Lucien to escape. Unbeknownst to Kammerer, Kerouac had helped Carr obtain his seaman's papers and together they made plans to sign on to a ship bound for France. Once there, with Jack acting as interpreter, the pair planned to jump ship and make their way to Paris as soon as it was liberated from the Nazis. In Paris, they imagined, they would live a bohemian life on the Left Bank, enjoying French wine and Parisian women. Lucien's more immediate goal was to sneak away from Kammerer.

With their union cards in hand, they were able to sign on to a ship about to weigh anchor on the Brooklyn waterfront, but a hitch dashed their plans at the last minute. At the dock they had a run-in with the ship's chief mate known for his temper, and decided to postpone their departure to await a more congenial assignment. The delay was to prove fatal.

David Kammerer discovered their plan that night at the West End Bar where he informed Carr that he would join them on their trip, invited or not. Over the course of the night, the two continued to drink heavily until the bar closed, and then they walked over to Riverside Park to finish off a six-pack of beer. There, in the early hours of the morning on August 14, 1944, Lucien stabbed David in the chest and dumped the body in the nearby Hudson River. At the time, Lucien believed he had killed David with his pocketknife, but the coroner's report showed that Kammerer's death was due to drowning, that he had still been alive when Lucien pushed him into the river.

As dawn broke and Carr began to sober, he first sought out Burroughs and then Kerouac, asking each for advice. Bill's suggestions were practical. He told Lucien to find a good lawyer and turn himself in, but the less-experienced Kerouac helped Lucien discard the evidence. A day or so later Carr went to his mother's lawyer and following his advice, confessed to the police.

Jack and Bill were held as material witnesses to the murder, since they had not reported the crime, and modest bails were set. Bail for Carr and Burroughs was posted by their respective families, but Jack's father felt disgraced and wanted to have nothing to do with his wayward son, especially if it would cost him money. On the phone he told Jack that he could "go to hell" and hung up. Jack was thus remanded to the Bronx County jail to await Lucien's trial. His only companion there was a copy of Gogol's *Dead Souls*. Under the circumstances, Jack turned to his girlfriend, Edie, for financial help. Ever since the abortion, the couple had been talking about marriage, and they had even taken their blood tests earlier that same week. So with a judge's permission Kerouac was escorted in handcuffs to city hall for a civil wedding ceremony. Edie was then able to borrow the necessary bail from her trust fund, and her new husband was released pending the trial.

Chapter 2

The Lumpen World

Columbia University did not want to be entangled in scandal, so in the weeks that followed the murder, the college used its considerable influence to downplay the crime. The administration promoted the theory that Carr, having fallen into the clutches of a homosexual predator, was merely acting as any innocent heterosexual student would act under the circumstances. That enabled Carr's lawyers to depict the crime as an honor slaying, and Lucien was able to avoid serious prison time. He spent the next two years upstate as a resident of an Elmira reformatory. Later, even Lucien's closest friends would say that he had "gotten away with murder." The truth behind the sexual nature of his and David's relationship will never be known.

The calamity of Kammerer's death temporarily scattered the gang that hung out at Edie and Joan's apartment. When Carr was sentenced for manslaughter in early October, Burroughs was in St. Louis in his parent's custody. Kerouac and Edie were living in Edie's mother's house near Detroit, where her father helped Jack land a job in a nearby ball-bearing factory. Joan Adams had gone to stay with her parents in Loudonville, New York, where she gave birth to a daughter, Julie. Lucien's girlfriend, Celine Young, returned to her parents in Pelham, New York, and began to date other men. For a while only Ginsberg remained in the city, where he attended his classes while battling a case of jaundice. The scattering gave each member of the cast time to reflect on the aftershock of the tragedy.

Slowly, over the next few months the circle of friends began to drift back to Morningside Heights. Kerouac stayed in Grosse Pointe only long enough to repay Edie for the loan of his bail money. After Carr was sentenced in October, the charges against Jack and Bill were dropped. Feeling trapped and out of place with Edie's wealthy family, Jack left Detroit to ship out with the merchant marines. This time the chief bosun gave Jack trouble. By the time the ship reached Norfolk, Jack was fed up with the bosun's unwanted sexual advances. He jumped ship and returned directly to New York. Embarrassed by what had happened, Kerouac decided not to tell either his family or his new bride that he had quit. Secretly he got a room at the Warren Residence Hall near the Columbia campus where Ginsberg was living at the time, and supported himself by operating the switchboard in the lobby. Once again he devoted himself to his work, determined more than ever to become a great writer.

After being deposed by the court, Burroughs had marked his time in St. Louis. Once Carr was sentenced, Bill felt it was safe to return. By then Joan had come back with her baby and found an apartment large enough for all of them to share, this time in the Cragsmoor, a building on West 115th Street, a few blocks south of their old apartment. Joan had already told her husband that he was not the baby's father, and he was happy to give her a divorce. To help make ends meet she decided to rent out some of the rooms in the apartment, and so it was that Haldon Chase moved in just before Christmas 1944.

In spite of her marital status, Joan had already been dating Chase off and on. He was a handsome young Columbia student who resembled Lucien Carr in both appearance and demeanor, so he fit in easily with the group. Hal had come to Columbia University from Denver on the recommendation of an older alumnus named Justin Brierly. Brierly was a well-known lawyer, educator, and patron of the arts in Colorado who often helped deserving young boys get into good schools. Chase was working toward his degree in anthropology when he moved in with Adams and her friends. Quickly he made friends with Jack, Bill, and Allen and joined in their all-night philosophical discussions that were frequently fueled by amphetamines and marijuana. Before long, Hal was also recommending books for them to read. Together they discovered André Gide's masterpiece *The Counterfeiters* and were so impressed by it that they acted out scenes from the book. Many of the characters in the book were either bisexual or homosexual, and that, combined with the narrator's direct address to the reader, made it unusual for the period.

Night after night the group debated the fine points of what they were reading. The gatherings were abuzz with intellectual discussion. During that winter, Burroughs decided that he would psychoanalyze both Kerouac and Ginsberg for an hour each day. Bill had no training for this, so the therapy was amateurish at best. A few years later Ginsberg's own doctors would tell him that it had actually been harmful. Each session consisted of the "patient" lying on Burroughs's couch, talking about himself and his problems for an hour. Occasionally "Doctor" Burroughs would add a comment or make a suggestion. Even if it wasn't good therapy, it did give them the opportunity to talk about their own lives and to communicate their ideas to one another. Through this process they were able to refine their own personal mythologies.

The only one of the group with a religious background at all was Jack Kerouac, who had been raised a Roman Catholic in Lowell's French Canadian community. As an adolescent, he hadn't thought much about his religion, but as he grew older, spiritual life became a primary interest. While in high school, he studied the Gospels, but he had also become fascinated by other literature, the works of

Thomas Wolfe and Shakespeare in particular. All these things became the recurrent topics for his sessions with Burroughs.

Ginsberg was much more interested in the social and sexual aspects of his own life than the spiritual. It was easy for Burroughs,
who made no secret of his own homosexuality, to bring some of Allen's repressed desires to the surface. Possibly inspired by Kerouac's
persistent journal writing, it was during this period that Ginsberg
started to keep his own diary. Until the murder, Allen had sporadi-
cally written poetry and kept a journal, but now he considered it a
part of his own therapy. For the next fifty years, he faithfully kept a
journal of his thoughts and activities. Those journals were the beginning of Ginsberg's career as a writer.

Ginsberg continued to plug away perfunctorily at his class work,
but the intellectual stimulation of his friends inspired him more.
In his journal Allen recorded the details of their conversation on
the "The Night of the Wolfeans," as he and Kerouac came to call
it. Kerouac and Hal Chase, a personable young man, took a position in the argument that favored the more romantic philosophy of
Thomas Wolfe, whose American narratives of self-examination were
extremely popular in the forties. Burroughs and Ginsberg felt that
truth could best be found not in American but in European models
like the bitter reality of Gide and Rimbaud. Their philosophy was
an outgrowth of the "New Vision" discussions they had begun when
Carr was still around. Ginsberg was inspired to write an epic poem
he titled "The Last Voyage," in a grand attempt to put their new
philosophy into words. Through his labors on that long poem, he
realized that he held within him the promise of expressing himself
seriously as a poet. He was smart enough to realize that his poems
were merely derivative of the academic poetry he had been studying
in class, but until he discovered how to express himself in his own
voice, it was enough.

Burroughs, who had once tried to write a book with his old friend
Kells Elvins, was inspired by Kerouac's example to take up his pen

again. The two decided that they would take turns writing alternating chapters to tell the story of the Carr-Kammerer tragedy. Originally titled *I Wish I Were You,* in homage to the fact that Kammerer worshiped Carr, the final manuscript was renamed *And the Hippos Were Boiled in Their Tanks.* The new title came from a radio report that Burroughs overheard about a fire in a zoo. The fire had nothing to do with the story, but it struck them as a great title for a book.

The book wasn't published during their lifetimes for two reasons. First, it was offensive to Lucien, who didn't want to be remembered as a killer. And second, it was not, to be blunt, well written. Bill himself labeled it as "undistinguished." For Kerouac it became an exercise in writing, but for Burroughs it reinforced his belief that he didn't have the talent to become an author. While the two of them were working together, Ginsberg began to outline and write his own novel based on the murder. Since Allen was still a student, he thought it would make a great class project and submitted a draft to his English professor for comment, who in turn gave it to Assistant Dean Nicholas McKnight. It was then that the dean, fearing that the book would resurrect the nearly forgotten case and cause new embarrassment for Columbia, asked Allen to discontinue working on it. Allen, who had come to an impasse of writer's block on the project anyway, agreed without argument.

Then, on March 16, 1945, while being analyzed by Burroughs on the sofa in his apartment, Jack and Bill had a long conversation about Kerouac's dependency on his mother. Bill told Jack—with great prescience—that "if you continue going back to live with Memère [his mother] you'll be wound tighter and tighter by her apron strings till you're an old man." He urged him to break free emotionally. Burroughs's opinion upset Jack so much that he went directly to Ginsberg's dorm room to get his opinion. The two talked all night and as dawn approached, Allen suggested that Jack sleep there and not make the long subway trip back home to Queens.

A few hours later, Allen awoke to a knock on the door and found that the director of student-faculty relations, Dean Ralph Furey, wanted to inspect his room. Hoping to shame the maid into washing his filthy windows Ginsberg had written obscenities on the windowpane with his finger. Instead of cleaning the windows, the maid had complained to her boss, so the dean was there to investigate her complaint. Not only did he find the offending words, but he also found Kerouac sleeping in bed, a violation of dorm rules governing unauthorized overnight guests. Ginsberg found himself expelled from Columbia for the dual infractions.

Having nowhere else that he would rather live, Allen moved into Joan's apartment at the Cragsmoor on West 115th Street for the rest of the season. Without classes to attend, he had plenty of free time to spend in intellectual debate, self-analysis, and drug experimentation with his friends.

When classes were over, Hal Chase returned to Denver for the summer, leaving the others in the sweltering heat of the city. Most of the residents on West 115th Street found temporary employment to pay the rent and support themselves while Joan busied herself with her baby. Germany had just surrendered to the Allies and the war in the Pacific was coming to a violent end, so Ginsberg decided to enter the Maritime Service Training Station in Brooklyn for advanced training in order to secure a better job. A few weeks later Burroughs made plans to join him there, but just as Bill was scheduled to arrive on the base, the United States dropped the atom bomb on Japan, and the war was over. As a result, there was little need for additional sailors, so Bill never began his training. Soon the country was flooded by the returning troops, and jobs were harder than ever to come by.

One day, hoping for some ready cash, Burroughs tried to sell an old shotgun and some morphine syrettes to a petty criminal he knew in Brooklyn. Always fascinated by crime, Bill thrived on meeting characters on the wrong side of the law. Rooming with this proposed buyer was another small-time crook named Herbert Huncke.

Bill's deal didn't go down in large part because Huncke thought that Burroughs, wearing his trademark tie, trench coat, and hat with a turned-down brim, was too clean looking and therefore must be a cop. With a surplus of unwanted morphine on his hands from this failed business transaction, Bill began to use the drug himself, and before long, he was hooked.

Huncke was a con artist, junkie, and hustler who operated mainly on the seedier edges of Times Square. He knew the ins and outs of the squalid neighborhoods in the city better than anyone the group had ever met before. In no time, he was taken into their circle and became something of a sallow-skinned mascot. As a curious footnote, Huncke was procuring interviewees at the time for Alfred Kinsey's scientific study of male sexuality. As a result, Burroughs, Kerouac, and Ginsberg soon were subjects in Kinsey's landmark survey.

Huncke seemed like a romantic character to add to the group, completely unlike anyone in their sheltered college crowd on Morningside Heights. They had all been pampered and protected by their families for most of their lives, and in Herbert they found someone who quite literally lived by his wits on the streets. By the time they met him, Herbert already had been in and out of prison several times. In fact, shortly after meeting Burroughs, Huncke found himself back in jail on Rikers Island for another three-month stint for burglary. There he met a crook from Philadelphia named William Garver, whom Herbert would later introduce to the group. Garver's income came from an overcoat scam he had perfected. It was a simple modus operandi: wearing a worn-out jacket, he would walk into an elegant restaurant and exchange it in the cloak room for an expensive, well-tailored coat. Then he would casually walk out and head directly for the nearest pawnshop.

The advantage of knowing Huncke was that he was able to score just about any drug anyone wanted. A felon, Huncke knew all the right people, and it was much easier for him to find a connection than it was for the more conventional Burroughs, Ginsberg, and Kerouac. This ability made him indispensable to the group. Despite his drug connections, no one was more down on his luck than Huncke, and Ginsberg always had a soft spot in his heart for the downtrodden, so he frequently shared his apartment and money with Herbert.

The ready availability of drugs became a problem. Joan Adams and Burroughs had developed addictions at the time, and too much benzedrine contributed to a flare-up of Kerouac's phlebitis. Meanwhile, Huncke's own problems with the law made him undependable. Shortly after his release from Rikers, he was arrested again, this time for car theft.

Now that he had a habit, Burroughs needed a dependable source of drugs. Without Huncke to score for him, Burroughs decided to do it himself. In the spring of 1946, Bill was arrested for trying to pass a forged prescription at a local pharmacy. Again the courts released him on probation into the custody of his parents in St. Louis, a turn of events that led to the dissolution of the group around Joan's apartment. Ginsberg was still not allowed back into Columbia, but he had recently applied for readmission. In order to earn tuition money, he had signed on as a ship's messman working the East Coast. Although he still kept his clothing and books at Joan's, he wasn't around much. Kerouac was spending most of his time at his mother's in Queens, and without a job he could not afford to help Joan pay the rent. He had recently been hospitalized with phlebitis in his leg and had gone home to recover. There he found his father, Leo, suffering from stomach cancer, a painful condition that would lead to his death in May 1946. From then on, Jack was the man of the house and felt a renewed responsibility for his mother. There would be no opportunity to cut the maternal apron strings, as Burroughs had counseled.

In the summer of 1946, after two years in the Elmira Reformatory, Lucien Carr was released. He returned to the city and took a job as an office boy for the United Press at minimum wage. Still on probation, Lucien kept his distance from his old crowd, wanting to avoid any situation that might send him back to jail. But eventually, over the next few years, he slowly became an integral part of their social lives again. Lucien shied away from the narcotics that his friends were taking, but liquor continued to be his weakness. He returned to alcohol with even greater enthusiasm than he had before prison. When drinking, Lucien became more belligerent, argumentative, and self-destructive than ever.

Ginsberg was still in love with Carr and was distraught when Lucien initially refused to see him. Even as a boy, Allen Ginsberg had erotic fantasies about men, never women. Since society in those days looked upon homosexuality as insanity, his orientation bothered Allen considerably. Because of his mother's mental problems, he feared that his own love of men meant that he was near the tipping point in his own struggle against insanity. As a result, he kept his feelings in the closet and under control throughout high school and into his early years at Columbia.

Allen practiced self-discipline to a greater extent than many of his new friends. They frequently acted on impulse, without much thought to the consequences. In fact, their spontaneity was one of the things that appealed most to Allen. In the fall of 1946, he was sitting at the Hotel Astor bar, a noted gay hangout, when he met a man and went back to his room with him. Allen was twenty at the time, and this turned out to be his first sexual contact with anyone, male or female. After he lost his virginity, he realized that being intimate with someone was not the horrible thing he had both feared and desired.

Following the court-directed probation period with his parents in St. Louis that autumn, Burroughs had visited the southern Texas town of Pharr, where his oldest friend, Kells Elvins, had purchased a farm. Kells convinced Burroughs that farming was an easy way to get rich with minimal effort. They discussed various agricultural methods that relied on cheap Mexican labor and government subsidies. Bill borrowed some money from his parents and began shopping for farmland of his own.

While in Texas looking for property, Bill received word that Joan Adams had suffered a severe breakdown in New York due to her abuse of amphetamines. Her parents had taken custody of her baby, and she was locked up in Bellevue Hospital, where New York City's drug and mental cases were commonly put away. Sympathetic to her plight, Burroughs decided to rescue her. Normally, Bill was not interested in women and more than any other in the group, was steadfastly misogynistic, but he liked Joan and wanted to help her. Later he would say some pretty shocking things about women being naturally evil, and he even suggested that the female of the species was a mistake of nature. However, at that moment he saw Joan not as a woman, but as a friend and fellow spirit in need of help. She was one of the few people he knew who could hold her own with him intellectually, and during the previous few years in New York, they had become close. Now that she was in trouble, he was determined to help, so he drove to New York from Texas and secured her release from the hospital. Before leaving town, they spent the night in a cheap Times Square hotel and even had sex, a rare occasion for Bill. As luck would have it, Joan became pregnant with a boy who was to be Burroughs's only child. Later Joan would flatter Bill by saying that although he might not like women, he was as good as any pimp in bed.

Not aware that she was pregnant, the two made plans to work a farm together in a remote part of Texas. There they believed they would have complete freedom to pursue whatever vices they desired without legal hassles. Burroughs painted an idyllic picture of a rugged frontier where their nearest neighbors would be miles away, and everyone minded his own business. Soon Bill located an isolated farm of ninety-seven acres, twelve miles from the sleepy crossroads town of New Waverly.

Bill and Joan, now living together as husband and wife and expecting a baby, moved into the rat-infested cabin at the edge of the bayou with Joan's daughter, Julie, and immediately wrote to Herbert

Huncke, who was finally out of jail. They asked him to come down and help them farm the land, but more important, they wanted him to bring marijuana seeds to plant as their primary crop. Instead of bothering with legitimate crops, they had decided to grow poppies and hemp in the backwoods. If they harvested the plants and sold them in New York City, they stood to make a tidy profit. All they thought they needed were the seeds and someone who knew how to sell the crop. Nature would take care of the rest.

Back in New York, Ginsberg was trying to finish his undergraduate course work at Columbia. Emboldened by his sexual initiation at the Hotel Astor, he finally revealed to Lucien that he was gay. Carr, who had been through all this before with Kammerer, was not happy to hear Allen's revelation, although he must have suspected it for years. Allen had always been eager to learn about other people's sex lives, even though he appeared to have no experience himself. Underlying everything was Ginsberg's despairing loneliness and forlorn gay isolation. Allen might have pressed his yearnings toward Carr more at that moment if something else hadn't happened to distract him. At the end of 1946, a new arrival in town was to replace Ginsberg's angst with a severe case of unrequited love.

Chapter 3

The Adonis of Denver

Ever since the group had first encountered Hal Chase, he had regaled them with tales of a young Lothario he knew in Denver by the name of Neal Cassady. The man who had persuaded Chase to attend Columbia, Justin Brierly, was also Cassady's mentor in Colorado and had introduced Chase to Cassady. Neal was a young juvenile delinquent, just about Ginsberg's age, who had been in plenty of trouble around Denver. Neal boasted that by the time he was sixteen he had already stolen more than five hundred cars. He exuded a strong sexual aura and with an IQ of 120, he was as intelligent as he was charming and personable.

Cassady had been born poor. His father was a part-time barber and a full-time alcoholic who stumbled from one flophouse to another in Denver's run-down Larimer Street district. Neal's mother tried to protect her son from his father's bad influence, but she died when the boy was ten, leaving him to grow up at the mercy of his father and an abusive half-brother. By the time he became a teenager, Neal was already having sex with as many girls as he could talk into bed. As an adolescent, Neal dropped out of school, was sent to a reformatory, and ended up educating himself on the streets. He wouldn't have had much going for him if it hadn't been for his astonishing good looks and uninhibited personality. Some described him as looking like the young Paul Newman. Both men and women were attracted by his charisma and sexuality, and Neal was savvy enough to play his charms for all they were worth. Neal had little trouble convincing Brierly that he wanted to pursue formal studies and possibly follow in Hal Chase's footsteps as a Columbia student, even though he never bothered to graduate from high school.

To this end, Neal hopped in a car, stolen of course, with his equally young and sexually active wife, LuAnne Henderson. They proceeded to New York City on the first of many cross-country jaunts. After ditching the car in the Midwest, the newlyweds landed in Times Square by bus. Like two children arriving in Disneyland for the first time, they found themselves looking out on the bright lights of Broadway as they sat amid the displays of revolving desserts in an all-night cafeteria. Excited and overwhelmed, they were intimidated by everything the big city promised.

Wasting no time, Neal immediately set out to find Hal Chase, whom he knew would help him make essential contacts in the metropolis of eight million. Soon after hooking up with Hal, Neal met Ginsberg and Kerouac in the West End Bar. As had happened so many times before, Allen fell in love immediately with a man he saw as a western Adonis. As for Neal, the consummate con man knew instantly that sex would be the key to their relationship.

The more reserved and less passionate Kerouac saw Cassady as a manifestation of unrepressed freedom and masculine sexuality, a man completely devoid of inhibition. Cassady calculated that by appealing to Kerouac the writer, he could get anything he wanted from him. By then, Jack was already hard at work on the novel that would become his first published book, *The Town and the City*. It was a rambling epic based on his own family life in Lowell and his move to New York. Not initially aware that Neal would become such a large part of his own life, Jack was nevertheless fascinated by Cassady as a potential character.

Burroughs was already on his Texas farm at the time of Cassady's first visit, but when the two met later that year, it was a different matter entirely. Bill could see through Neal's clever scams as the others could not, and because there was nothing that Bill wanted from Neal, he remained cool and aloof toward him. In fact, Bill was to become more than a little jealous of Neal's easy entry into Allen's bed and Jack's confidence.

For a few weeks, Neal and his bride boarded in a rooming house in New Jersey until LuAnne tired of working to pay all the bills and went back to Denver alone. With no one to pay his rent and no intention of finding a job, Neal moved in with a more than willing Ginsberg. To Allen's joy and delight, Neal also became an enthusiastic and experienced sexual partner in bed. Allen described his few days of erotic bliss in his journal, saying that after "a wild weekend in sexual drama with Cassady, I am left washed up on the shore of my 'despair' again." After his short period of sexual fulfillment, he wrote love sonnets and lyrics like never before.

After inviting both Jack and Allen to visit him in Denver, footloose Neal was back on the road himself by March 1947 looking for new kicks. While laying over in Kansas City en route to Colorado, Neal sat in a tavern and wrote his first letter to Kerouac, which would become known as his "Great Sex Letter." In it he described meeting a woman on the bus from New York, how he tried to have sex with her, and when that failed, how he successfully seduced the very next girl he happened to meet. When Kerouac read the letter, it wasn't the content that so impressed him as much as the effortless way in which Neal was able to tell the story using exactly the same words as he would if he were speaking to Jack in person. It was a revelation to Jack to see that it was possible to write in precisely the same manner as people spoke. Up until then, he had consciously used a writer's voice for his literary efforts and a completely different voice when he was engaged in a conversation. From then on, he tried to make his written work sound as unaffected and natural as his spoken words. It was only the first of several major creative breakthroughs that Kerouac discovered through his association with Neal Cassady.

Within a few weeks of Cassady's return to Denver, he met the woman who was to have a profound and long-lasting influence on his life. At the time they met, Carolyn Robinson was a graduate student in art and theater design at the University of Denver. She was a strikingly beautiful blonde who many would say was way out of Neal's league. A bit older than Neal, she radiated a mature and sophisticated glamour, although Carolyn grew up in a straitlaced middle-class family in Tennessee. In one of Neal's earliest letters to Jack and Allen he wrote, "I have met a wonderful girl." Carolyn was beautiful and perfect in every way. Neal mentioned that her only flaw was that she had been a Bennington girl, a flip reference to her education at one of the best liberal-arts colleges in the country. This comment underscored just how different their two worlds were. In the same letter, Neal restated his hope that both Allen and Jack would visit him in Denver, and they both began to make plans to do just that.

Once Burroughs moved to Texas, the daily sessions of "psychotherapy" for Jack and Allen ended. Ginsberg felt that the therapy had been helping him, so he decided to try to find a professional therapist and continue his treatment. He was still bothered by his myriad problems and neuroses, and the intense affair he had begun with Neal had him questioning his own sanity again.

As soon as his classes were over, Allen decided that he would visit Neal for the summer. The trip would also afford him a chance to stop along the way to visit Bill, Joan, and Herbert on their farm in Texas. Kerouac was making his own separate arrangements to drop in on Henri Cru, who was working as a watchman in Marin County, just north of San Francisco. He and Henri planned to pick up merchant marine jobs and work their way back to New York by sea. Carefully Jack mapped out his trip straight across country along Route 6 to the

West Coast. On paper it looked like an ideal way to hitchhike, keeping to the same road the entire time and stopping to visit Neal once he got to Colorado.

His trip began with a minor setback just north of New York City along the Hudson River near Bear Mountain. When Jack arrived at Route 6, the rain was pelting down so hard that he was drenched, and no one passed to give him a lift. Soaking wet, he gave up and made his way back to the city, where he bought a bus ticket for the first leg of his journey. Going west from Chicago he had better luck catching rides. Then he headed for Denver to visit Neal and some of his Columbia friends, such as Hal Chase, Ed White, and Alan Temko.

Those journeys would be the first major road trips for both Allen and Jack. Even with the inauspicious start in the rain, it looked like everything would turn out idyllic once he got to Denver. However, the Denver reunion was far from perfect for Jack. White and Temko couldn't stand Cassady, and since Jack was staying with them, he felt it was wrong to leave them to spend time with Neal.

On Allen's stopover in New Waverly to see Burroughs's place, it didn't take him long to realize that Bill's farm was nothing more than a broken-down cabin in an overgrown clearing in the woods with a few dilapidated buildings scattered about the property. Allen had planned to go on to Denver, pick up Neal, and return for a romantic tryst on the farm, but the condition of the place did not qualify it as a lovers' paradise. Still hoping to make the best of a bad situation, Ginsberg commissioned Huncke to build a large bed, to be ready upon his return with Neal later that summer. Allen dreamed of reenacting the days of eros he had spent in Neal's arms during the previous winter in New York.

When Allen finally arrived in Denver, he quickly realized that bliss would not be so easily attained. Neal was too busy with his many women to spend much time with Allen. Even though he had promised to host Allen during his visit, Neal didn't even have a room of his own to share. Allen was left alone in an unfamiliar city with no money and no place to stay. After spending a few nights on the floor of some nurse friends of Neal's, Allen found his own basement apartment and a temporary job as a night custodian for a department store. For a month and a half Allen stayed in Denver, waiting longingly for a few minutes of Neal's time, a hope that went mostly unfulfilled. Neal was busy juggling his time between the demands of his first wife, LuAnne, and his new girlfriend, Carolyn. In between, he managed to string along a few others, all the while trying to make certain than none of them realized he was seeing anyone else. Carolyn wanted more from her relationship with Neal than just sex and succeeded in fooling herself that Neal was devoted to her alone. She never realized that while she was attending class, Neal was having sex with other women and occasionally with Allen as well.

Since Ginsberg worshiped Neal and had an inferiority complex when it came to his sexual relationship with him, he was only too willing to wait for scraps of Neal's attention. He felt guilty about his own homosexuality, and it was easy for him to blame himself. As the summer wore on, even Allen began to think that he was wasting his time, but to his surprise, Neal agreed to go with him to Burroughs's farm at the end of August. While he was waiting in Denver, Allen received the news that on July 21, Joan had given birth to a son in a local hospital. They named him Billy after his father.

By the time Allen and Neal hit the road for Texas, Kerouac had already left Denver and was in California with Henri Cru. Because of the rift between Cassady and the others, Jack hadn't seen either Neal or Allen for more than a few minutes in Denver that summer, and their friendship was slightly bruised. Once in Marin, he found that the shipping job that Cru had promised fell through. Jack was stranded and penniless. Luckily, Henri was able to fix Jack up with a job as a night watchman at the same construction company where he worked.

Guarding empty buildings and trying to keep hard-drinking construction workers in line wasn't the kind of work that Kerouac was suited for, and by October he was drifting around California's San Joaquin Valley looking for jobs in the fields picking crops. There he fell in love with Bea Franco, a pretty, dark-haired migrant worker with a young son, and for a few short weeks he felt that he had found utopia. Once again his romantic adventure was short-lived. Migrant work sounded fine and noble, but in reality it was backbreaking drudgery for little money. Leaving Bea with a vague promise that he would return someday, he headed back to the one woman he could always depend on to take care of him, his mother. In the end, Jack never saw Bea again.

In the meantime, Allen and Neal hitched a ride out of Denver and headed across the open plains of Colorado toward Texas. In the late August heat, somewhere in Oklahoma, they became stranded and couldn't catch a ride. It gave them a lot of time to talk intimately about their feelings, and Allen again expressed his love for Neal. In the middle of the deserted gravel road outside a crossroads diner, Ginsberg somehow persuaded Cassady to kneel and exchange vows of eternal fidelity to one another. It was one of the most important moments in Allen's life, his first formal declaration of love for another man, but it meant far less to Neal. He would have been willing to do anything to get Allen to stop pestering him about love. Later, Allen called attention to it. "I gather that it meant then (and now) so much less significant to you than me."

It took them two days to reach Burroughs's marijuana farm, where they found everything in a sad state of affairs. The shack was unfit for habitation. There were rats, reptiles, and armadillos everywhere, and neither Burroughs, Adams, nor Huncke was much good at housekeeping. They were all strung out from heavy drug use even though there was a month-old baby to care for. The two children, Julie and Billy, were being left more or less on their own, with the shiftless Huncke commandeered to do much of the babysitting. What irritated Allen most was that Herbert had not been able to make the large double bed that he had asked him to construct. Allen impatiently tried to nail two old cots together, but the structure collapsed as soon as he and Neal sat down on it. This amused Neal, but to Allen it was a disaster. The sexual union he had awaited all summer was thwarted before it could begin. It wasn't long before he was quarreling with Neal and the others and so, less than a week after their arrival, Allen asked that they drive him to Houston. Leaving Neal and company behind to tend the marijuana crop, he found a ship and worked his way back to New York via West Africa.

While Ginsberg was sailing to Dakar, Burroughs, Cassady, and Huncke harvested the marijuana crop and stuffed it into Mason jars. Then they loaded up the car and headed for New York City, but their planned sale of the "tea" never materialized. The leaves, which hadn't been dried correctly, rotted in the tightly sealed jars and were of no use to anyone. Back in New York, Burroughs connected with his pusher, Bill Garver, and in no time he was back on junk again. When Neal had no luck finding a job parking cars, he headed for San Francisco. Carolyn had recently moved there from Denver to pursue her career. From California Cassady wrote to Kerouac to apologize for not waiting in New York to see him, but he blamed it on Carolyn. He declared that she was the only woman he ever wanted. "My conviction that Carolyn was enough is, I find, correct—so don't worry about your boy Neal, he's found what he wants and in her is attaining greater satisfaction than he'd ever known," he wrote. In no time at all Carolyn became pregnant, and Neal started working in a local service station. No matter how much Neal loved Carolyn, he was not cut out for a monogamous relationship. In December LuAnne showed up in San Francisco, and although Neal persuaded her to get an annulment, they continued to sleep together behind Carolyn's back.

Like Kerouac, Allen Ginsberg had also arrived in New York a few short days after Neal departed for San Francisco. With the money he had earned on the Dakar voyage, he was able to rent a small apartment in upper Manhattan and resume classes at Columbia. In the evenings, he wrote long letters to his friends filled with gossip to keep everyone in touch. He even wrote to Kerouac, who was busy retyping the finished manuscript for *The Town and the City* in Ozone Park, where his mother was only too happy to cook and keep house for him.

Unfortunately, Allen was about to be forced into a decision about his own mother that would haunt him forever. Shortly after his return, the doctors at Pilgrim State Hospital, where his mother was being treated, wrote to him about her condition. Naomi had been suffering a series of unsettling and violent seizures brought on by her worsening case of schizophrenic paranoia. In the opinion of the medical staff, her only chance for recovery lay in a risky and unpredictable operation. "It was decided that her mental condition is serious enough to warrant a prefrontal lobotomy," Dr. Harry Worthing wrote. That procedure was becoming the panacea for all the patients at Pilgrim State, and some on the staff reported good results. In order to perform the surgery, they needed the permission of a responsible party, and since Allen's parents had divorced, the decision fell to him.

Reluctantly Allen signed the form, hoping that it would alleviate her suffering. After the operation, when Allen realized that Naomi's personality had been erased along with her violent behavior, he came to see that the surgery had been a terrible mistake. Like many who underwent the operation, Naomi became a virtual walking corpse, and after the surgery, she failed even to recognize Allen. For the rest of his life, he never forgave himself for his complicity.

In California, Neal's marriage to LuAnne was annulled, and he was free to marry the four-months'-pregnant Carolyn. Emotionally it was a tough time for Neal. He became depressed and one night sat in the backseat of a car with a revolver, seriously considering taking his own life. On April 1, 1948, Neal and Carolyn were married in a civil ceremony at San Francisco's city hall. Neal was so broke at the time that Carolyn had to foot the bill for her ring and marriage license. She even found a new apartment on Alpine Terrace at the top of a very steep hill, a decision that she lived to regret as the birth of the baby neared and walking up the hill became exhausting.

In Texas the New Waverly fiasco pretty much ended Burroughs's farming days. He was unschooled in agriculture and unsuited for hard labor. He had pictured himself more as a gentleman farmer with workers tending the crops for him. In addition to the pot failure, his repeated forays into town looking for drugs for himself, Joan, and Herbert had aroused suspicion among his neighbors. He had even been arrested for public indecency when a Texas lawman discovered him and Joan having sex in the backseat of their car.

Burroughs was eager to leave the Texas experience behind him, so he put the farm up for sale and headed to New Orleans, where he hoped to find a more dependable drug supply. Homosexuality was tolerated to some extent in the Big Easy and that was important to him, too. From his boardinghouse in New York, Ginsberg wrote frequently to Burroughs, often exchanging drug information with him. At first the Burroughs family stayed in a small place on Route 61 near New Orleans, but by June 1948, they had located the perfect house across the Mississippi River in the more secluded suburb of Algiers. From there it was a short ferry ride to the city's drug dealers who kept both Bill and Joan well stocked. For the next year they were to call Algiers home.

Chapter 4

Insanity

Ginsberg's father, a high school teacher, had been encouraging Allen to finish his degree. Then, after graduation, he assured Allen there would be time enough to follow his own impulses. In a pinch Allen could find employment as a teacher himself anywhere he wanted. "If you had taken my advice in my letter of a few years ago (instead of . . . laughing at it with Burroughs), you would have been graduated already," Louis wrote to him. Allen agreed with his father, since he still could not yet envision being a full-time poet. Even if he could, he knew from his own father's example that poetry wouldn't pay the bills.

Other factors were weighing on Allen's mind at the time as well. In addition to the usual class assignments, he was engrossed in his own independent study of the poetry of William Blake. One day during the summer of 1948, he sat on his bed in East Harlem masturbating as he read Blake's "Ah! Sun-Flower" over and over again, trying to crack Blake's code of hidden meaning. Without warning, he experienced a flash of blindingly clear epiphany. Ginsberg later told friends that he heard the eternal voice of William Blake speaking directly to him, reciting the poem, and unlocking all the secrets hidden within.

He became increasingly aware of his own consciousness and felt that he would never be more in touch with the spirit that controlled the universe than he was at that moment. His vision proved transitory, and within a few minutes it had faded away. It was followed in the next week by similar moments of brief illumination, but try as he might he was unable to maintain those moments of heightened awareness for long. As dramatic and uplifting as the visions were, they also made Allen fear for his sanity. His mother's dementia was still very much on his mind, and he dreaded following in her footsteps. He tried to describe these visions to others until he realized that he was not convincing them that he had heard Blake, but instead he was proving to them that he had finally gone crazy.

During that summer, he played host to marathon parties at his apartment and invited friends and strangers alike. At one three-day party in July, Ginsberg and Kerouac met a young would-be writer by the name of John Clellon Holmes. Ginsberg liked Holmes, but it was Kerouac who really hit it off with him. The pair quickly became the closest of friends, and since they weren't tied down to academic work as Allen was, they spent a good deal of their time together in wide-ranging literary debates, fueled by alcohol and cigarettes. Holmes, like Kerouac, was a natural-born writer and had read as widely as Jack had.

Holmes had enlisted in the navy during the war and had used his GI benefits to pay for his degree from Columbia. His apartment on Lexington Avenue soon became a salon for literary intellectuals, just as Joan Adams's apartments had been earlier. Many of their activities from the first days of his friendship with Kerouac and Ginsberg ended up in Holmes's first published novel, *Go*. Kerouac covered some of the same ground in his own *On the Road*, where Holmes appeared under the name of Tom Saybrook, punning on the name of Old Saybrook, the town in Connecticut where Holmes's mother lived.

Typical of many writers of their era, Jack and John drank socially and often to excess. They were joined by Allen, but he much preferred the effects of marijuana and drugs, which came without the terrible nausea and hangovers. Sometimes those substances took Allen's mind to places reminiscent of his Blake vision. Even as his friends became addicted to alcohol and drugs, Allen learned to pace himself and never indulged in anything to the point of addiction, except cigarettes. The future benefit was that Allen never had to undergo long periods of sacrifice and deprivation to break those habits as others in the group did.

A case in point was William Burroughs. Just before moving to New Orleans, Burroughs had become so dependent on drugs that he had committed himself to two weeks in the federal detox hospital in Lexington, Kentucky. That terrible experience didn't deter him much, and soon he was hooked again. Later when asked why he had become an addict, he stated flatly that a person didn't need a reason to become an addict; he needed a reason to not become an addict. Burroughs said that he simply felt that he didn't have any reason not to.

On September 7, 1948, a healthy baby girl named Cathy was born to Carolyn and Neal Cassady in a San Francisco hospital. What might have encouraged other men to settle down seemed to provide Neal with the incentive to abandon Carolyn again. He did everything within his power to escape from commitment to his new family. Within a few months of Cathy's birth, Neal had organized a road trip back east to see his friends. He offered to drive an old pool hall buddy of his from Denver, Al Hinkle, and his new wife, Helen, across the country on their honeymoon.

Once on the East Coast, Neal planned to stay only long enough to retrieve Kerouac, who wanted to try his luck looking for work in San Francisco. Neal's itinerary was sketchy, but he wanted to visit Burroughs in New Orleans, Kerouac in Rocky Mount, North Carolina, and Ginsberg in New York. With a newborn baby to care for,

Carolyn couldn't go along, so Neal took advantage of the opportunity and swung through Denver to pick up his first wife, LuAnne, taking her along for sexual kicks.

While waiting in New York for Neal's arrival, Ginsberg was pursuing his own social life. In November he finally consummated his relationship with Lucien after five years of unrequited desire on Allen's part. Lucien was not eager to have sex with Allen, but one night, willing or unwilling, a drunken Lucien Carr wound up in bed with Allen. Characteristically, Allen wrote to some of his friends to tell them that he had finally had sex with Lucien. Now that it had happened, he remarked that it would be the end of it. Once that final barrier had been broken, his curiosity was satisfied, and Allen had no further interest in sexual encounters with Carr. This would become a pattern often repeated by Ginsberg. In the future, he would become infatuated with countless straight men and usually after achieving his goal, his libido would be satiated. It was extremely important to Allen that a straight man would "love" him enough to give in to his sexual desires once. After that, a repeat performance wasn't necessary.

During this period, Kerouac hung out with John Holmes a good deal of the time and they spent many nights discussing their craft over quarts of beer. Together they enrolled in Elbert Lenrow's classes in literature at the New School for Social Research in Greenwich Village. One evening after class they had a philosophical conversation about their own generation. They compared it to Hemingway's "lost generation" but felt that the word *lost* didn't sum up their times. In the course of their discussion Holmes urged Kerouac to characterize the current situation, and Jack responded by saying that he felt their minds and attitude were furtive, chock-full of hidden motives, and that as a result it was a "beat" generation. After some reflection Holmes agreed that it was the best name for the young people who had come through World War II. They were weary, they had been beaten down by society, the war, the need to conform to the times, behind which lurked some sort of spiritual longing.

Beat was a word in common usage at the time and familiar to most jazz musicians and hipsters around the seedier fringe of Times Square. They had frequently heard people like Huncke using the word to refer to themselves and others who were tired of the status quo, maybe even tired of life in general and the continual frustration and despair that came with living, but Jack was the first person to apply it to the whole era.

In December 1948, Ginsberg left his East Harlem sublet where he had experienced his Blake visions and moved to another apartment on York Avenue near Seventy-second Street. He was able to pay the modest rent with the pittance he was earning as a copyboy for the Associated Press in Rockefeller Center. He was working the night shift so that he could continue classes at Columbia during the day. Lucien Carr had worked in a similar capacity for the United Press before being promoted, and it was a common occupation for aspiring writers. Some, like Carr, would go on to become newspaper writers and editors, but for Allen being a copyboy was merely a temporary job.

As Ginsberg was settling into his new rooms on York, Neal, LuAnne, and Al Hinkle pulled into town in Neal's new 1949 gray and maroon Hudson. Neal had placed a down payment on the car with the last of his savings from the railroad, leaving Carolyn back in San Francisco nearly penniless. They had already stopped off in Rocky Mount to pick up Kerouac and his mother, who had been there visiting Jack's sister, Nin, and her husband, Paul Blake. With Neal at the wheel, they had made two quick nonstop trips back and forth from Rocky Mount to New York in order to transport Jack's mother and some of her furniture. As soon as they had her settled back in New York, they went to see Allen.

The group took over Ginsberg's apartment and proceeded to party continually while Allen worked and studied. Kerouac took part in much of the merrymaking, waiting for news about his novel, *The Town and the City*, which he had submitted to a few publishers.

When the time came for them to leave after New Year's, Allen wished that he had the freedom to go along, but he wanted to finish school first. He vowed that later there would be time for trips of his own.

On the initial leg of their trip east from California, Helen Hinkle had been sent ahead to wait for them in New Orleans after she complained about riding in the cramped car. It wasn't a very auspicious start to her marriage. Helen had known Al Hinkle only a short time and must have wondered what she had gotten herself into. In New Orleans, she stayed with Bill and Joan in their tiny Algiers house, an arrangement that didn't thrill either Helen or Burroughs. Bill resented having the new bride dumped in his lap without any warning, and it only increased the ill will he felt for Neal. Impatiently he wrote several letters to Ginsberg asking when the group expected to come down and collect her.

Both Bill and Joan were so deeply involved with drugs that they could do little but take care of their own habits. Bill was actually trying to kick heroin at the time, but Joan's use of amphetamines had reached an alarming rate. She never seemed to sleep and habitually obsessed over everything. Even in the middle of the night, she could be found performing odd duties such as raking the lizards out of the trees in the yard.

After one last party at Ginsberg's pad to welcome in 1949, the group piled into Neal's car and headed south to retrieve Helen. By the time Neal, Jack, Al, and LuAnne reached Burroughs's house, Bill was fed up with the situation and urged their speedy departure. He had already taken a dislike for Cassady, whom he saw as just another of Allen's self-absorbed, con-man acquaintances. "[He is] ready to sacrifice family, friends, even his very car itself to the necessity of moving from one place to another," Burroughs wrote to Ginsberg. Neal had even made the mistake of asking Bill for money in order to continue their trip, and being asked for money was one thing that Burroughs hated. He was not inclined to give a penny to the freeloader and was glad to see the back of him.

One snowy night shortly after they left New York, Herbert Huncke showed up on Ginsberg's doorstep. He was in terrible shape, his feet were bleeding, and he was ragged and tired. He begged Allen to take him in and care for him. Common sense should have warned Allen to tread carefully. Huncke had stolen many items from Allen's last apartment, things that didn't even belong to Allen. Forgiving and generous to a fault, Allen had paid for the stolen items. Seeing his friend in such bad shape now, he allowed him in and gave up his own bed, moving himself to the sofa for the next few weeks.

As Herbert gradually regained his strength, he grew more sociable. He began to help Allen with some of the chores and eventually brought two of his friends back to the apartment. Little Jack Melody and Vickie Russell were small-time crooks like Herbert. They lived by their wits and made money through burglary and stealing things from parked cars. Occasionally Vickie would resort to prostitution in order to earn money for drugs and other necessities. Since burglary was one of Little Jack's specialties, before long he began to store the stolen goods in Allen's apartment. Allen didn't object, and the house filled with more and more plunder.

By spring even Allen realized that things would come to a breaking point if he didn't put his foot down. Since he had just finished his final course at Columbia, he was now at liberty to travel. He thought the best thing to do was to leave his apartment to Herbert for the summer and get away to visit Bill and Joan in New Orleans.

As the day for his departure neared, Ginsberg decided to store his manuscripts and correspondence at his brother's place for safe-keeping during his absence. To repay Allen for his hospitality, Little Jack offered to help. They loaded a car, stolen of course, with several boxes filled with Allen's papers and headed for Eugene's apartment. Along the way, Melody made an illegal turn and wound up driving the wrong way down a one-way street, right in front of a policeman. A chase ensued and the car flipped over, spilling Allen, Little Jack, Vickie, and everything else onto the street. No one was hurt, and

Allen and Vickie escaped into a nearby subway, but Little Jack was caught. The police soon knocked on the door of Allen's apartment and arrested him and Huncke for the possession of stolen goods.

The story made all the New York City newspapers. The case of a bright Columbia student becoming mixed up with drugs, theft, and prostitution made for interesting reading. The reporters even said that Allen became involved with the criminals in order to get firsthand material for a novel he was going to write. Allen's father couldn't figure out how anyone as intelligent as Allen could allow himself to be used by these lowlife crooks. It was all much more complicated than that, though. Allen's need to be loved, his generosity, his growing belief in his own insanity, his lack of self-confidence, and his low self-esteem were all at work.

Louis went to Allen's most famous professor, Lionel Trilling, the most influential man he knew, and asked him to take pity on his wayward son. With Trilling's help, a deal was worked out with the prosecutor. Allen was to be remanded to the New York State Psychiatric Institute for therapy in lieu of prison. Huncke, Melody, and Russell, on the other hand, all had substantial arrest records and were treated as the criminals they were.

Secretly, Ginsberg was somewhat relieved to be going to a mental hospital. He had heard William Blake's voice, he had seen visions, he was homosexual, he was the son of a crazy woman, and so it seemed all too likely that he was mad as well. If hospital treatments could possibly help him, he was eager to cooperate and follow the doctors' advice. In fact, it seemed like it was the answer to his prayers. Ever since Burroughs had stopped his amateur psychoanalysis, Ginsberg had been trying to find psychiatric counseling on his own, but most of the doctors were too expensive for him, and he hadn't been successful in finding treatment at any free clinic.

Throughout these most recent difficulties with the law, Allen worried about what might be happening to Burroughs. Many of the letters that the police found in the car mentioned not only homosexuality, but also ideas for drug deals and descriptions of Bill's use of a variety of illegal narcotics. Allen wrote to Bill immediately to tell him that he had better lay low for a while and destroy all his letters from Allen, but that letter arrived in New Orleans too late, because Burroughs had already been arrested on drug charges unrelated to Ginsberg's incident. Once again Bill's parents were willing to bail him out of his difficulties.

For the first time in years, Kerouac had been ecstatic. Harcourt, Brace and Company had just accepted his novel, *The Town and the City*, but he worried that the police might find incriminating evidence in Allen's letters and journals about him, too. He did his best to distance himself from the group. Jack, who should have been able to celebrate the acceptance of his first novel, could not fully bask in his achievement and enjoy the moment. These were needless concerns, because the police didn't bother to examine the manuscripts, but at the time, Jack and Allen didn't know that.

Holmes tried to cheer Jack up by throwing a large party in his honor. At this early date Kerouac and Holmes were the only two in the group who considered themselves serious writers. Burroughs had not written anything since he and Jack had traded chapters back and forth on the *Hippos* manuscript, and that had been more Jack's idea than Bill's anyway. Allen hadn't written much except for his daily journal. Now and then he would write an occasional poem in a style reminiscent of eighteenth-century verse, modeled after someone like Christopher Smart, but he still hadn't found his own voice.

Kerouac, who had ridden to the West Coast expecting to find a job and immerse himself in "joys, kicks, and darkness" with Cassady, quickly found himself alone and penniless when Neal dumped him on the San Francisco streets the minute they arrived in town. Having nowhere else to turn, Jack wired his mother for bus fare and boarded a Greyhound heading back east via Portland and the great northern route. Since it was the dead of winter, that trip proved to be an adventure in itself. Little realizing that his trip would become an important part of his next book, *On the Road,* Jack felt that Neal had forced him to waste an entire month. Sitting at his mother's kitchen table in Ozone Park, he got back to work on a new novel, which he structured as a continuation of the narrative begun in *The Town and the City.*

Kerouac had been growing tired and bored by his life around New York, so he decided to move himself, his mother, and his sister's family west to Colorado. There he naïvely planned to buy a ranch and live the life of a cowboy, although he had no idea what that entailed. He had received an advance of one thousand dollars from his publisher for *The Town and the City*, and he thought that it would be the first of many checks to follow. With financial security seemingly on the horizon, he could now entertain long-range plans. He even set some of his personal goals down on paper: within two years, he would be married and own "a big wheat farm," he wrote in his journal.

On May 15, 1949, Jack arrived in Denver, certain that once settled, his mother would like the area as much as he did. He was counting on the Columbia contingent in Denver to help him find a place to live. When he couldn't reach Ed White or Hal Chase, he called on Justin Brierly, the man who had once tried to mentor Cassady, who helped him find a temporary room. Then, without much trouble, Jack rented an affordable house on West Center Street in Westwood, a Denver suburb. The first thing he did was to rent a typewriter and begin to work while he waited for his family and their furniture. Jack's mother, Gabrielle, arrived with his sister, Nin, and her husband in June, but they soon came to realize that Jack wouldn't be of much help around their new home. He had always been shy, but now his main ambition was nothing short of complete isolation. He told his friends that once they were settled, he planned to buy a horse and saddle and ride off into the mountains to live the life of Thoreau. Although Jack's mother had initially agreed to the move and was glad Jack was getting away from the baleful influence of people like Ginsberg in New York City, she realized that Denver was too far away from everything that was familiar to her. By the time Jack decided to go to San Francisco to visit Neal in August, she had already packed up her belongings and moved back to an apartment in Richmond Hill, Brooklyn.

It had taken a few months, but Kerouac had finally forgiven Cassady for the way he had treated him on his last visit to San Francisco. He was ready to forgive and forget if it meant new adventures with Neal. Upon his arrival in San Francisco Jack found that Neal's thumb had never quite healed after hitting LuAnne on the head, and the doctors finally had to amputate part of it. That gave Neal some time off from his tire-recapping job to recuperate and to entertain Jack. That was what made Kerouac agree to the trip in the first place. Encouraged by the example of Kerouac and Ginsberg, Cassady had been trying to write the story of his own life. He had made a few aborted attempts to sit down and write, but all he came up with were some letters to Jack describing the events of his youth. Neal begged Jack to give him advice as to how to proceed with an autobiography. Since Kerouac was about to be published, he was certain that he could help his friends write and find publishers, so he was eager to help Neal write his own book.

Chapter 5

The Subterraneans

When Burroughs was arrested in New Orleans, the police searched his house and found heroin, pot, and unlicensed firearms. They hadn't bothered to get a search warrant, though, so with the help of an experienced lawyer provided by his family, Bill was released temporarily. Once freed, he immediately checked into a private sanitarium for a week to kick his heroin habit. After the cure, Bill decided that getting out of town was a better solution than going to jail, and his lawyer agreed.

In May 1949, Bill and Joan took the two children back to a house they rented near Kells Elvins's place in Pharr, Texas. Even with a good lawyer, things were not looking favorable for the outcome of his trial in New Orleans. Since Bill had been in trouble before, he was facing certain prison time on the drug charges. Hoping to avoid jail, Burroughs decided to relocate to Mexico City. That September he headed south of the border looking for a place for the family. He was exasperated with what he deemed to be the puritanical laws and regulations in America. He wanted to be left alone to do whatever he felt like doing without the interference of the police and petty bureaucrats. If he stayed out of the country for at least five years, the statute of limitations would expire on the New Orleans case, and it would be safe for him to return. It would be nearly twenty-five years before Burroughs came back to the United States permanently. Not knowing what the future held for them, Joan and the children moved to their new home on a dead-end street in the Mexican capital. It was there that Burroughs began to write a book about the perilous life of a junkie in America, later to be published as *Junkie*.

During the summer of 1949, while Burroughs was trying to preserve his own freedom, Ginsberg entered the New York State Psychiatric Institute, a division of Columbia Presbyterian Hospital. There he began to spend time with a host of people who were truly insane. It made him aware that his problems were not so insurmountable when compared to those of the people around him. "The rest of the people here see more visions in one day than I do in a year," he reported to Kerouac.

One person that Allen met during his first days in the "bughouse," as he called it, was a young Jewish man named Carl Solomon. When Allen bumped into him in the hall of his ward, Carl was just coming out of shock treatment. With nothing but free time on their hands, the two men struck up a conversation. Allen told Jack that Carl "speaks in a sinister tone to me of how the doctors are driving him sane by shock therapy." The two found that they shared a love of literature and immediately compared themselves to the heroes of their favorite Russian novels. They identified easily with those poor souls who were most helpless to defend themselves against a cruel and callous society.

Solomon was born and raised in the Bronx and, like Kerouac, lived with his mother for much of his life. He had a brilliant, if somewhat fragile, mind. He loved French Dadaists, surrealists, and existentialists, and patterned many of his actions on theirs. In fact, in 1947 he had been in Paris and met the great French surrealist playwright Antonin Artaud one night. Once, during a college lecture on the Symbolist poet Stéphane Mallarmé, Carl began to hurl potato salad at the speaker. Only Carl saw the Dadaist inspiration for his action. Not long after, he stole a peanut butter sandwich from the cafeteria at Brooklyn College and then showed it to the guard. While being questioned about it, Solomon demanded a lobotomy, saying that he wanted to be suicided by society just like Artaud. That had led him to the psychiatric hospital where he met Allen.

At first Ginsberg hoped that his doctors would take an active interest in him and his case, but he soon realized that all they wanted was a patient who would blend in to hospital routine and not make any trouble. His faith in psychotherapy as the solution to his problems was quickly dashed. Still, he decided that he would follow the doctors' recommendations as best he could and hope for improvement. He readily agreed with them that homosexuality was an illness. To cure himself, he promised to reform and to begin dating women. The doctors even convinced him briefly that he had not experienced actual visions of Blake, but was merely the victim of hallucinations.

Each day he recorded anecdotes about Solomon and the other patients in the pages of his diary, little realizing that one day they would end up in his most famous poem, *Howl for Carl Solomon*. During his stay in the hospital Allen came to realize that modern society demanded one not necessarily be normal, but act normal. At the end of February 1950, his doctors felt that they had done all they could for their patient, and Allen was discharged.

In August 1949, while Ginsberg was still getting accustomed to life in the mental ward, Kerouac turned up in San Francisco in the middle of the night and went directly to Russell Street to see Cassady. He knocked on the door of the little bungalow and was taken aback when Neal opened the door stark naked. Once again he marveled at Neal's total lack of inhibition. "He received the world in the raw," Jack famously wrote in *On the Road*. At first he and Neal began to outline Cassady's autobiography, but the lure of the city's many diversions was too great for both men, and soon they were spending much of their time chasing women in the bars and jazz joints around town. While they caroused, Carolyn worked, kept house, and took care of Neal's daughter. That arrangement didn't last long, as Carolyn began to resent being the only "adult" in the house. She was fed up with the whole situation and since she was pregnant again, she could not play the mother role for two grown men as well.

The domestic arguments spawned by his adolescent behavior gave Neal the excuse that he had been looking for to say good-bye. He left Carolyn a farewell note that began melodramatically, "Am leaving today—won't ever bother you again." Then he and Jack made a mad dash for New York City via Denver, Chicago, and Detroit, where Jack hoped to see his ex-wife, Edie Parker, once more. This journey became one of the cross-country jaunts described in the original scroll version of Jack's *On the Road,* but an editor deleted much of his prose about the trip before the final publication.

In New York, Neal stayed with Jack and his mother in Richmond Hill for a few days, but soon he met a woman named Diana Hansen and moved into her apartment on the Upper East Side. Diana was a sultry, dark-haired fashion model from North Tarrytown, New York. She was well-educated and from a middle-class family. Hansen was just beginning her career in the city when she met Neal at a party, and he immediately charmed her. After Neal moved in, it wasn't long before Diana became pregnant, too. She and Neal discussed the pros and cons of marriage, and Neal began to formulate a crazy plan in his mind whereby he could keep both families, spending six months a year with each one.

In San Francisco, Carolyn gave birth to their second daughter, Jamie, on January 26, 1950. Only her new friend Helen Hinkle was there to give her moral support. The next month, Diana informed Carolyn that she was pregnant, and Carolyn agreed to give Neal a divorce so that he could marry her before her baby was born. By the moral standards of the fifties, it was the "proper" thing to do so that the baby would not be born out of wedlock. Maybe Carolyn was finally beginning to see that Neal would never be able to commit to her and her children as she had originally hoped. In June, Carolyn petitioned the court for a divorce. Even though Neal's life was becoming very complicated, he seemed to take no responsibility for any of it, and the women in his life always had to straighten things out for themselves.

Bill and Joan Burroughs settled into their lives in Mexico City, and Ginsberg was about to be released from the hospital, when Kerouac's *The Town and the City* was finally published. It received tepid reviews, with many unflattering comparisons to the works of Thomas Wolfe. Even Kerouac agreed that there were similarities between his writing and Wolfe's, but he didn't see that as a negative quality. He felt that a writer could build on the foundation set by another without diminishing the power of the second. Although disappointed by the critics, he continued to make notes of his experiences on the road and to search for a unique way in which to tell his story. He was beginning to envision his life's work as the creation of a great Duluoz saga based on his own personal history. Duluoz was the fictional name Kerouac commonly used for his own alter ego. His books would be neither fiction nor nonfiction, but an amalgam of the two.

By March 1950, Ginsberg was living in Paterson with his father and new stepmother, Edith. Three times a week he met with his psychiatrists at the hospital, still hoping for a cure. On one of his frequent trips into Manhattan, Ginsberg went to hear William Carlos Williams speak at the Guggenheim Museum. A few days later he wrote to the older poet, who lived near Paterson in Rutherford, New Jersey, and asked if he could visit him to discuss poetics. There was something in his work that struck Ginsberg as important to his own development as a poet. Williams wrote in the vernacular in which people spoke, not in the ivory-tower vocabulary and meter that Allen had been imitating in his own poetry. Williams's more down-to-earth and gutsy language appealed to Ginsberg in much the same way that Neal's letters had appealed to Kerouac.

Williams actually knew Allen's father through Louis's poetry, which had appeared occasionally in the local newspapers. Louis Ginsberg, who liked to call himself "Paterson's principal poet," was well known in northern New Jersey. Williams was inclined to be generous with his time and so he invited Allen to bring some of his manuscripts with him. After looking them over, Williams told Allen that if he continued to use established forms of poetry, then strict adherence to the rules was crucial. He informed Allen of his own mantra, "no ideas but in things," hinting that he shouldn't begin with meaningless abstractions in his poetry, but start with the things themselves and build upon concrete observations. Williams said that you could deal with your feelings, but you should treat them as observed things and not get lost in intangibles.

Ginsberg had put together a collection of his poetry that he titled *The Gates of Wrath* and had been sending it out, hoping that someone would find the poems publishable. Although he received several replies, no publishing house was eager to take on an unknown poet who had just been released from a mental asylum. They suggested that Allen begin by submitting poems to smaller literary magazines and work his way up. Williams agreed with that approach and told Allen that with persistence he would eventually find an outlet for his work.

After returning to New York from San Francisco, Kerouac resumed the life that he found most comfortable. He spent weekends in the city socializing and drinking with friends like Holmes, Carr, and Ginsberg, and then during the week he retreated to his mother's house—now in Brooklyn—to write. In May he convinced Harcourt, Brace to send him to Denver to publicize *The Town and the City*, and at the book signing there, he reunited with some of his Denver buddies.

He also visited with Neal Cassady, who had just arrived in Denver from New York in an old Ford he had picked up somewhere. They decided to visit Burroughs in Mexico, each with a different purpose in mind. Kerouac was still disappointed by the mediocre reception his book had received in New York, and a trip south of the border promised to cheer him up. Having a summer with nothing to do but write, frequent prostitutes, and smoke marijuana was just the therapy he felt he needed. Neal intended to get a quick and cheap Mexican divorce from Carolyn so that he could marry Diana before the baby was born. He came back with a pile of official-looking papers all signed and sealed by the Mexican courts, but later Carolyn suggested that they might not have had any legal bearing. Whatever his marital status, he and Diana were married on July 10, 1950, in New Jersey with Holmes and Ginsberg acting as witnesses.

Neal and Jack had both left Mexico City by the time Lucien Carr visited Burroughs in August 1950. Carr was on a short vacation from his job at United Press, and he and a girlfriend sped south in his car to pay their respects to Bill and Joan. Lucien found that the family was happy in exile. Burroughs had signed up for a few classes at the local school and had located a good source for his morphine supply. Joan had trouble getting her hands on amphetamine, but she had replaced that habit with alcohol, which she drank in quantities that impressed even a hard drinker like Carr.

Burroughs had talked Kells Elvins into coming down and attending school, too, and it was Kells who encouraged Bill to continue working on a story loosely based on his life as an addict. Burroughs seemed to lack the self-confidence needed to begin a big project, but once someone convinced him that he had something to say, he worked continuously. Ginsberg was usually able to exert the same effect on Burroughs. From time to time in the future Allen would reassure Bill that he was a talented writer and then Bill would begin writing again. This time, with Elvins's help, Burroughs finished the first draft of *Junkie* by the end of 1950.

While visiting Burroughs, Lucien told him about a new friend who lived on the same block in Chelsea as he did. His name was Bill Cannastra, a man just a few years older than Carr and Ginsberg.

Like Burroughs, Cannastra had gone to Harvard, but there he had studied law instead of anthropology. Although Cannastra had passed the bar, his life centered more around parties and taverns than the courtroom. He had proved himself to be the ultimate merrymaker, and everyone could count on wild times whenever he was around. If he wasn't throwing a party at his loft on West Twenty-first Street, he knew who was, and his exploits were already legendary by the time he met Carr and company.

At one of his parties, he challenged Kerouac to strip off his clothes and race him around the block. Kerouac, always shy by nature, stripped to his shorts for the run but would not go all the way in the nude as Cannastra did. When drunk, which was most of the time, Cannastra was game for anything outrageous; often he would walk down the street snapping off car radio antennas just for the hell of it.

Cannastra was a member of a group of intellectual hipsters who gathered each night in unpretentious Village bars like the San Remo or Fugazzi's. These were ideal hangouts for a new class of people that Ginsberg called the "subterraneans," a name that Kerouac would later borrow for his novel about these modern hedonists. This new social group expanded the horizons of the previously uptown, Columbia-oriented gang. At night Ginsberg, Kerouac, Holmes, and Carr mingled with the likes of Bill Cannastra, Chester Kallman, Chandler Brossard, Julian Beck, Judith Malina, Alan Ansen, William Gaddis, Bill Keck, Alene Lee, Anton Rosenberg, Gore Vidal, James Agee, Anatole Broyard, John Cage, and Paul Goodman. When Carl Solomon was not in a mental ward, he was a regular member of the set as well. All of them were interested in literature and philosophy, and some of them had either written books or were about to. Getting together on a regular basis gave them all a sense of bohemian camaraderie possible only in postwar Greenwich Village.

Ginsberg was still living with his father and stepmother in Paterson, but frequently he would stay overnight with his friends in the city. He tried his best to follow his doctor's recommendations, and his first order of business had been to find a regular job. He was not successful at that. He tried working as a laborer in a ribbon factory, but after a month he was fired, for he lacked the basic manual dexterity needed to tie off the loose ends of the ribbon. Then he tried everything from dishwasher to office boy, but they all ended in the same disappointing way. He daydreamed more than he actually concentrated on his jobs, and that he couldn't correct.

He also tried to deny his homosexual feelings and began to date women. This, too, was more difficult than he expected because many of the men he was meeting were gay. He went out with a few of the "subterranean" women from the San Remo, but nothing much came of it until he met a friend of Cannastra's named Helen Parker. She was older than Allen and already had two boys aged five and ten by the time she first met him. Parker had been associated romantically with John Dos Passos and even knew Hemingway from her days in Cuba. When Allen was introduced to her she was about to move to her summerhouse in Provincetown, on the very tip of Cape Cod, and she invited Allen to visit her there. It was on one of those weekend trips that he had his first heterosexual experience.

Initially Ginsberg was jubilant, or at least that's what he said in letters that boasted of his newfound heterosexual prowess. "I have started into a new season, choosing women as my theme. I love Helen Parker, and she loves me, as far as the feeble efforts to understanding of three days spent with her in Provincetown can discover. Many of my fears and imaginations and dun rags fell from me after the first night I slept with her, when we understood that we wanted each other and began a love affair, with all the trimmings of Eros and memory and nearly impossible transportation problems," he wrote to Kerouac a few days later.

Just like his situation in the workplace, his straight life with Helen turned out to be short-lived. Allen had no idea how to maintain a relationship with a woman, especially one who had two young children and lived several hundred miles away. Even though he was resolved to become "normal," his own sexual inclinations were stronger than his desire to be straight. He still longed for the affections of male companions. For him having sex with women was something that he had to force himself to do, not something that he enjoyed doing.

One day in October 1950, the subterranean community was shocked to hear that Bill Cannastra, always verging on the suicidal in his reckless antics, had been killed in a freak accident on the subway. Drunk as usual, Cannastra had boarded a train only to decide after the doors closed that he wanted to return to a bar in the neighborhood. He clambered through the subway's open window just as the train started to pull out of the station. Cannastra hadn't made it completely through the window by the time the subway got to the end of the platform, and he was knocked out of the window and crushed on the tracks below in full view of his friends. It was a gruesome way to die and was nearly as devastating to his friends as the sudden death of David Kammerer had been in 1944.

One of Cannastra's closest friends was a woman named Joan Haverty, who was distraught over the loss. Following the accident, she took over Cannastra's loft with the vague notion that she should preserve it just as Bill had left it. On November 3, 1950, shortly after Cannastra's death, Kerouac stopped by the loft looking for Lucien Carr and met Haverty. Within a matter of days, Jack suggested that Joan marry him. It was almost as if getting married had been on Kerouac's list of things to do and he was intent on getting it over with, even if he didn't know who the bride was to be. Joan seemed to be equally vague about her reasons for accepting Jack's proposal. In her memoir, *Nobody's Wife,* published in 2000, Joan made it clear that love was not the motive for either of them. She painted a rather passionless picture of the circumstances surrounding their marriage, leading one to wonder why they even bothered.

On November 17, 1950, barely a month after Cannastra's death and two weeks after they met, Joan and Jack were married. They were in such a rush to have the wedding over with that Jack had to find a judge who would perform the ceremony after business hours. The marriage seemed like merely another excuse to continue the frenetic round of parties that Cannastra had begun. In short order they realized that Cannastra was just about the only thing they had in common. Even her plan to preserve Bill's apartment fell through because when December's rent came due, neither one of them could afford to pay. The newlyweds moved in with Jack's mother in her tiny Richmond Hill apartment. It didn't take Joan long to realize that there really was not enough room for another woman in Jack's life. He already had his mother, Gabrielle.

Kerouac continued to plug away at this new novel, which he had decided to call simply *On the Road*. It was the story of his friendship with Neal Cassady and the adventures they had shared traveling back and forth across the country. By this time, Jack had been working on it for years, but for some reason it wasn't developing as he had hoped. He was still following Wolfe's narrative style, and that didn't seem to fit this type of anecdotal story. The prose wasn't capturing the true spirit of Neal's rapid-paced, frenzied personality. Luckily, at the end of December 1950, Jack received a letter from Neal Cassady that would change all that. In the mail came a seventeen-page stream-of-consciousness-style letter that would forever be known as the "Joan Anderson Letter." In it Neal wrote of an affair he had had with a woman by that name years before, but he described the minute details of their relationship just as if he were speaking to Jack face-to-face. It had been written rapidly and was spontaneous, breezy, and effective in capturing the unfettered nature of Neal's life. "At first the mother of this frantic fucking filly confided in me and, to get me on her side, asked me to take care of Mary, watch her and so forth. After awhile, as Mary got wilder, the old bitch decided to give me a dressing down . . ." and so on. Jack saw the style of Neal's letter as the inspiration he was looking for, and before long he decided to rewrite his entire novel in the same wild, unrestrained manner.

The "Joan Anderson Letter" was only one of several that Kerouac received from Cassady during 1950, the height of Neal's letter-writing activity. In the years that followed, Neal's ability to create such dynamic letters faded, but based on his letters at the time, both Jack and Allen were convinced that Neal had a promising future as an important writer. They passed the letters back and forth and read them aloud to their friends. Carr and some of the others did not share their enthusiasm for Cassady's style and his use of imagery, but Jack saw it as a pivotal moment in literary history.

When Joan realized that no one could take better care of Jack than his own mother could, she gave up trying to compete with Gabe and moved into her own apartment in Manhattan. Even though Jack must have sensed that his marriage was already over, he followed Joan to her new place. She hadn't invited him, but he showed up on her doorstep with his rolltop desk and his typewriter. Reluctantly she let the movers bring in his stuff.

On April 2, 1951, inspired by his rereading of Neal's dynamic letters, Jack sat down and began to type a completely new version of *On the Road*. Responding to his new wife's question, "What was it like to be on the road with Neal?" he addressed the book to her by way of explanation. "I first met Neal not long after my father died . . . I had just gotten over a serious illness that I won't bother to talk about except that it really had something to do with my father's death and my awful feeling that everything was dead . . ." he wrote in the first draft. Kerouac, a fast typist, decided that he would ignore punctuation, paragraph breaks, and traditional form, and type the story in one long sustained burst of energy. For this book, he would put the words down on paper as fast as they came into his head without stopping to revise. In order to avoid the pauses that are inevitable when the typist stops to change sheets of paper in a typewriter, Jack glued long strips of paper together and fed them into his typewriter as a continuous scroll. That way he never had to interrupt his train of thought or the free flow of words. His athletic background and piping hot cups of coffee gave him the strength and stamina to press on for nearly three weeks, barely stopping to rest.

As Joan tried to sleep in the small apartment, Jack continued writing. Joan maintains that at one point, Jack became so aroused by what he was typing about his steamy relationship with the migrant girl, Bea Franco, that he woke Joan from a sound sleep to have sex. She didn't have time to insert her diaphragm, and Jack fathered their daughter that night. As marital disagreements intruded on his creative effort, Jack left the apartment and finished the manuscript at Lucien Carr's apartment on April 22. By that time, with the help of his notebooks and earlier drafts, Jack had managed to produce a scroll nearly 120 feet long crowded with dense, single-spaced lines of text. The manuscript was unlike anything that anyone had ever seen. When Jack presented it to his editor at Harcourt, Brace, Robert Giroux's eyes bulged. Without reading it, he handed the scroll back to Jack and told him that in that form no publisher on earth would be interested.

When Joan realized that she was pregnant, Jack immediately denied his paternity. He accused Joan of having screwed a Puerto Rican man she worked with at a restaurant. That was the last straw, and it precipitated the couple's final separation. Once again Kerouac had found a way to avoid making a commitment that would tie him down. He was never able to face the responsibilities of being either a husband or a father. For the rest of his life he spent a good deal of energy denying that the child was his and manufactured various excuses to avoid paying alimony and child support. It wasn't an endearing quality, but Kerouac was never able to take care of others. He always needed someone, usually his mother, to fall back on. Being tied down by a family was completely out of the question in his mind.

Chapter 6

Literary Lives

While this domestic drama was being played out in Kerouac's personal life, the literary lives of those in his circle were beginning to take form. Burroughs sent a draft of his new book, tentatively called *Junk,* to Ginsberg for his opinion. Bill was en route from Mexico City to South America in search of yage, a new drug that he had heard about. Just before Kerouac rewrote *On the Road,* John Clellon Holmes had shown him the draft of his own first novel, *Go.* It was a more traditional novel but based on the same people and subjects that Jack was writing about. As it turned out, *Go* was to be published a full five years before *On the Road,* much to Kerouac's displeasure. It would become widely recognized as the first published Beat novel.

Still living with his family, Ginsberg continued to write poetry. Much of it was academic in style, but Neal's letters were beginning to have an effect on him, too. "I read a letter you wrote to Jack describing (at one point) meeting early girlfriend at drugstore counter etc.," he wrote to Neal, "and remembrance of other times meetings. I noticed then what was partly unsaid, the machinery of consciousness of place and time, memory, at work in astonishing solidity of grasp . . ." Allen could see that Neal had the ability to write about anything and make it interesting, no matter how mundane the topic. Allen recognized that literature didn't have to be epic to be good as long as it was from the heart.

Ginsberg's personal life was still in turmoil. Not surprisingly, he continued having difficulties in his relationships with women. It thoroughly irritated Burroughs when Allen wrote to him about his plight. Allen had discovered that he could have passable sex with women if they were interested in him and if they initiated it. He would remain passive. This approach to sex wasn't satisfying to anyone, but Allen believed that he was living up to the expectations of his psychiatrists.

Burroughs felt that Ginsberg was getting terrible advice from his therapists. Bill considered Allen's having sex with a woman a serious case of self-deception and told Allen bluntly that he couldn't turn queerness on and off like a faucet. "Laying a woman, so far as I am concerned is O.K. if I can't score for a boy," Bill wrote. Using himself as an example, he compared sex with women to eating tortillas. "But no matter how many tortillas I eat I still want a steak." That didn't change his sexuality, he told Allen. Bill's wife, Joan, read the letter before Burroughs sent it and added a note of her own, agreeing that what Bill said was true, but adding wryly that "around the 20th of the month, things get a bit tight and he lives on tortillas."

Burroughs also sent sections of his manuscript about the life of a junkie to Lucien, who had offered to show it around to his publishing contacts. From time to time, Bill sent along a new chapter to be inserted into the manuscript, but most publishers felt that a first-hand account of addiction would be of interest only to other junkies. Since Lucien had no luck, Allen continued the work by sending Bill's manuscript to a few contacts of his own.

While in Mexico, Bill had been able to kick his heroin habit. It was an easy process, he once explained to Allen. He had kicked five times in the last two years, he said, unaware of the irony in his statement. He was able to write best during his stints without junk, and his most recent break of six or seven months had been very productive. The new chapters were intended to be added to the end of *Junk,* but since he had come off dope, he found that the writing somehow seemed as if it was from a different hand. Those new sections later became the backbone of his book *Queer.*

In addition to writing, Burroughs also shared Ginsberg's love for the unobtainable lover. Bill had recently become infatuated with a fellow student who was studying in Mexico City on the GI Bill. The young man was named Lewis Marker, and Bill decided to take him on a trip to Panama and Ecuador in search of passion and adventure. Marker wasn't sure that he wanted to be seduced by Bill, though. In the aftermath of their trip, not certain whether he wanted to continue their relationship anymore, Marker went home to Florida and stopped communicating with Bill. Within the year, however, he was back in Mexico, once again willing to travel with Bill.

Joan Burroughs took all this in her stride, for she knew Bill's nature better than anyone did. However, by 1951, her self-abuse with drugs and alcohol was taking its toll. It seems impossible that she was able to care for two small children in her condition, but somehow she managed to do it. Bill was no help whatsoever. He often said that he could easily do without women or children, and he took great pleasure in frightening the kids as often as he could. They kept away from him, and he was just fine with that.

In August 1951, when Lucien took his annual vacation, he and Ginsberg drove from New York City to Mexico City to visit Bill and Joan. It was a spur-of-the-moment trip, so when they arrived they found Bill away on his junket with Marker. Joan was in worse shape than ever, but undeterred by her pitiful condition, they spent a few days engaging her in even heavier drinking and carousing. One day they went for a drive through the Mexican mountains with Allen and the two children cowering in the backseat while a drunken Lucien and Joan took turns steering the car at breakneck speeds around hairpin turns. It was a miracle that they weren't all killed.

On the drive home, Lucien's Chevrolet broke down in the summer heat, and Allen stayed behind in Texas to wait for the repairs while Lucien flew back to his job. He was still in a Galveston hotel when he opened the newspaper to read that Bill had killed Joan in a drunken game of William Tell right after Allen and Lucien had left Mexico City. Bill had taken a gun with him to a party hoping to sell it to someone there. For some unknown reason Joan had placed a whiskey glass on her head and dared Burroughs to shoot it off. Usually Bill's aim was steady even when he was drunk, but on this day his marksmanship was off and the bullet hit her squarely in the middle of her forehead. She died in the hospital a short time later, and Bill was arrested immediately. The children were sent off to their respective grandparents, Julie to Joan's parents in Albany and Billy to Bill's parents in St. Louis.

With the help of a sharp lawyer, Burroughs was released on bail after twenty-one days in jail. He stayed around Mexico City awaiting trial, but he began to sense that the Mexican legal system, as corrupt as it was, might not be as malleable as his lawyer had suggested and that officials might actually send him back to prison. He toyed with the idea of skipping bail and leaving the country. Joan's death was one of the worst in a whole series of tragedies to hit the group. They all loved Joan and remembered her fondly from the early days when they had first gathered in her apartment on Morningside Heights. She had been a great companion and was always willing to provide a safe haven for them whenever they needed one. Joan was also one of only a handful of women they knew who could hold her own in their intellectual discussions, and they all respected her intelligence. In the future, Joan's specter would come back to haunt many of them.

Stunned by Joan's gruesome death, Burroughs returned to his writing. Years later he would tell interviewers that he never would have become a writer if it hadn't been for the shooting. That event "motivated and formulated" his writing, he said. Although he showed little remorse, he said he needed to write in order to escape possession by the evil forces, or "ugly spirits," as he called them, that had overtaken him.

As soon as Kerouac had finished typing the scroll version of *On the Road,* Allen begged to read it. When he did, the book made a profound impact on him. He realized at once that Jack had made the breakthrough he was looking for. It was one of those books that Allen couldn't put down once he began to read it. Kerouac's prose left him wanting more, even though he had to agree with Robert Giroux that in the current form it was not publishable. Kerouac's method pointed Allen in a new direction that he could apply to his own poetry. It reinforced Allen's new belief that he should write down his thoughts without examining them for literary merit. That idea had come to Jack through Neal's example.

It would still take Allen a few more years to turn this technique into a poetic form of his own, but Neal's "Joan Anderson Letter" and Jack's *On the Road* manuscript set him on a quest for what he wanted to achieve through poetry. At the time, literary theory per se was a common topic of conversation, and during this period, Kerouac worked on a formal explanation for his new writing style—which he called the "Essentials of Spontaneous Prose." Eventually he was able to give friends a written outline of the techniques he used, a "how-to" manual of writing. Allen treasured it and looked for ways to apply Jack's principles to his own poetry.

Ginsberg was spending more of his time in New York again and found work as a temporary employee with market-research firms. Whenever the companies needed extra manpower to tabulate public opinion polls, Allen and friends like John Clellon Holmes and Carl Solomon were called in on an hourly basis. They enjoyed the money and the flexible hours that this kind of work offered. During the early fifties Ginsberg's career goals were still highly fluid. Occasionally he considered going back to college to follow his early dream to become a labor lawyer. At the moment, though, his goal was simply to save enough money so that he could travel.

He still thought that his poetry was sterile, and he couldn't see it going anywhere, but he continued to document his life almost daily in the pages of his diary. Following his therapist's advice had made his life dreary, and he compared himself to Melville's insipid character, Bartleby the scrivener. His friends were his only source of pleasure, but many of them had drifted apart. Death, tragedy, marriage, ambition, and simple distance had all been contributing factors to their diaspora, and correspondence became a crucial means for keeping in touch.

Occasionally Ginsberg broke his heterosexual resolve and had one-night stands with male partners, but usually he tried to play his "straight" role and continued to date women. Some of them became close friends after the initial romance faded. Dusty Moreland was one of those young women. She was an artist who had come to New York from Wyoming to seek her destiny. Dusty, or Dustbin, as Allen sometimes called her, was an attractive, dark-haired woman who reminded Allen somewhat of his mother. Maybe that was her appeal.

One day as Ginsberg was having a drink at the Pony Stable, a popular lesbian bar in the Village, he noticed a very handsome, talkative young man sitting nearby. Ginsberg had gotten over his shyness, and he struck up a conversation. The other man was also a poet, and his name was Gregory Corso. Corso had just been released from an upstate prison where he had spent the past three years for the theft of a topcoat, only the most recent in a long string of juvenile crimes. Gregory was a dynamo—curious, animated, and on the hustle for whatever he could find. Under his arm he carried a sheaf of poems that Ginsberg read with interest. Barely into his twenties, Corso told Allen that he had dropped out of school long ago and grew up by his wits on the New York streets. In jail he had taken the advice of older inmates and educated himself by reading everything in the prison library. He had a special appreciation for the romantic poets Keats and Shelley and talked about them as if he knew them personally.

Ginsberg was attracted to Corso for several reasons, not the least of which was sexual. When the subject got around to women, Allen quickly found out that Gregory was straight. In the course of their conversation Gregory told Allen a story. He said that an attractive neighbor frequently undressed in front of the window, and Corso often watched her. He dreamed of meeting her, he said. The more they talked, the more Allen realized that the woman Corso was talking about was his own girlfriend, Dusty Moreland. Not being the least bit jealous and not wanting to miss a chance to befriend the handsome young man, Allen told him that he had secret powers. He told Corso that he would prove his magic if Gregory came to a certain address that night where Allen promised to conjure up the mysterious woman. Gregory followed Allen's directions and before long he was sleeping with Dusty himself.

Gregory wasn't interested in Allen sexually, but that didn't interfere with them becoming good friends. Like Huncke and Cassady, Corso was a natural con man who had the kind of street smarts that never failed to impress Ginsberg. As was Allen's habit, he introduced Gregory to his friends and even took him to meet his old professor Mark Van Doren in the Village. There Allen praised Corso's poetry to one of the few academics that he truly respected.

One night after a bout of heavy drinking, Corso was beaten outside a bar. He found his way to Ginsberg's apartment. Ginsberg, in his Jewish motherly fashion, bandaged Gregory's cuts and made him a bowl of hot chicken soup. One thing led to another and before he knew what was happening, Corso found himself in bed with Allen. According to Gregory, it was the one and only time that he and Allen ever went to bed together, but for Allen once was usually enough.

Corso felt he had been taken advantage of, but he knew the ropes and did not let the matter rest. He turned the situation to his advantage, milking Allen's aggressive behavior and the guilt he felt afterward for all it was worth. He demanded that Allen make it up to him repeatedly through acts of kindness and generosity. That one night of indiscretion set the tone for their fifty-year relationship. Not long after the beating, Corso, still trying to decide what to do in life, left for Los Angeles hoping to break into the newspaper business. There he went to work in the obituary department at the *Los Angeles Examiner*. But Gregory wasn't cut out for any nine-to-five job, and so he stayed in California only a few months before returning to New York.

In the meantime, Jack Kerouac decided once more to visit the Cassadys in San Francisco, where Neal promised to find him work on the Southern Pacific Railroad. Originally, Jack had been planning to visit Burroughs in Mexico City, but Joan's murder put an end to that idea for the time being. No matter the destination, Jack needed to escape New York. Joan Haverty wanted her support money from him, and to underline her demand, she had Jack hauled off to jail. Jack's mother was also getting tired of New York and wanted to live closer to her daughter in North Carolina. Jack was highly motivated to pack up and travel.

That fall Kerouac had begun to develop a method of sketching with words. Earlier his Denver friend Ed White had suggested to Jack, "Why don't you just sketch in the streets like a painter but with words?" It sounded like a good idea, and Jack began to write quick descriptive passages wherever he was. Every day Jack practiced by writing a fast, dense paragraph or two about someone or something. He tried to pour all his creative energy into that one precise piece. Then, the following day, he would read it again and decide whether it stood up or not. Jack saw it as not only sketching, but also as a variation on what bebop jazz musicians were doing in clubs in those days. His method was akin to the short jazz riff solos that each member of a band was encouraged to take during a performance. This concept helped Jack move toward an even freer prose that he applied to *On the Road* as he retyped it yet again, this time onto traditional sheets of paper instead of one giant scroll. Working with a tape-recorder, Jack spontaneously improvised sketches later to be transcribed onto paper. That worked so well that he suggested the tape-recorder method to Cassady, who was still suffering from writer's block with his memoirs.

After spending years in and out of mental hospitals, Carl Solomon, Allen's friend, had been deemed sane enough to work for his uncle in publishing. Carl's uncle, A. A. Wyn, owned Ace Books, and he hired his high-strung but well-read nephew to edit manuscripts for the firm. The position was ideal for Carl in several ways, for he loved everything about books. He read voraciously and was a good critic. For Carl, the difficult part of the job would be dealing with temperamental authors.

Allen and Lucien realized that Carl's new job provided an opportunity for everyone. Finally, they knew someone on the inside who could recommend books by Kerouac and Burroughs for publication. Allen even thought that Ace might eventually publish his own poetry. With Solomon's help, Rae Everitt, Kerouac's new agent, landed a contract with Ace for *On the Road*. Ace agreed to pay Jack an advance of one thousand dollars on the book, which wasn't a fortune, but it was enough money to allow Kerouac to travel again. A month later, at Ginsberg's insistence, Solomon was also able to produce a contract for Burroughs's book, *Junk*, which they later decided to call *Junkie*. Around that time, Kerouac tried to interest Ace in Cassady's memoir, *The First Third*, but Neal's book was still little more than an idea, and nothing ever came of that proposal.

Flush with $250 in his pocket, his signing fee from Ace, Kerouac set out for California on October 25, 1951. He was happy to leave New York and decided that he would hide his future whereabouts from Joan Haverty, hoping she wouldn't be able to track him down again. Two weeks later, after stopping at his sister's house in North Carolina, he knocked on the door of Neal and Carolyn's Russell Street house once again. They had already prepared a room for him in the peaceful attic, away from the noise of the children, an arrangement that suited him perfectly. Awaiting him in his new room were a typewriter, a tape recorder, and an assortment of drugs that Neal had reserved for Jack's exclusive use. Relaxed and content for once, Jack began working on his current manuscripts, which included what would become *Doctor Sax, Visions of Cody,* and additional tweaking of the road novel.

Living in Neal's attic turned out to be an idyllic situation for Jack. As promised, Neal did help him get a job on the Southern Pacific, so he was able to support himself and still send some money back to his mother. While Jack was living in San Francisco that winter, Joan Haverty gave birth to a daughter, whom she named Janet Michelle Kerouac. She looked to Jack for child support in addition to alimony. Kerouac was more convinced than ever that he was not Jan's father, a claim that he continued to make, even when Jan turned out to look very much like him. For the short term, his life was governed by his need to evade Joan, and he developed elaborate schemes to disguise his whereabouts.

Kerouac always envied other couples, but he could never commit to a lasting relationship of his own. Living with Neal and Carolyn further complicated his attitude toward love and marriage. Neal continued to sleep with other women without Carolyn's knowledge. In order to divert the attention from his infidelity, he led Carolyn and Jack to believe that he wouldn't be jealous if they had their own affair. For a brief time this turned out to be an ideal solution for all three of them. Jack was always shy when it came to women, so he didn't have to seduce anyone, and Carolyn wasn't left at home alone wondering what Neal was up to. Neal didn't have to account for his time away, so it was easier for him to pursue some of his other relationships. For Jack, it meant that he didn't have to make a commitment, since Carolyn wasn't looking for another husband anyway. She would always be Neal's wife, and Jack could enjoy the benefits of married life without any of the responsibilities.

These idyllic days were not to last. Guilt and jealousy were inevitable, and the puerile antics of Neal and Jack were bound to get them into trouble with Carolyn sooner or later anyway. On Neal's twenty-fifth birthday, Jack coaxed Neal out of the house to celebrate with an all-night binge with two prostitutes. In the morning, Carolyn caught them as they were trying to sneak one of the girls up the stairs into Jack's attic. An argument ensued and realizing that their ménage à trois had ended, Neal drove Jack to the Arizona-Mexico border. There Jack boarded the next bus for the long ride to Mexico City, and Neal returned to Carolyn.

During those days of frequent travel, the group exchanged letters and remained in close contact. In New York, Ginsberg served as their anchor and circulated letters from Bill, Jack, Neal, Gregory, and the rest to one another. Kerouac and Holmes kept in touch with one another directly and spent much of their time discussing books and the craft of writing. They were truly interested in literary theories, something that held only a passing interest for the others in the group, and by then Jack had come to value John Clellon Holmes's critical opinions.

In a letter to Carl Solomon, Kerouac tried to pin Carl down on a publication date for *On the Road,* but he learned that Ace was having second thoughts about his book. Carl's uncle, who published mostly pulp fiction, believed the book was too radical and avant-garde for his readership, so he decided not to move forward on it in spite of their contract.

When Ace canceled their plans to publish Jack's book, Allen was afraid that they would renege on their contract with Burroughs, too. At first he gently tried to exert pressure on Solomon, but Carl was extremely sensitive to any criticism, and pressing him was counterproductive. At the time, Ace was Allen's only solid publishing connection, and that depended entirely on Carl's employment there. Unfortunately, Allen didn't see any reason why Carl shouldn't push harder to get all his friends published and paid no attention to Carl's fragile mental condition.

As time passed and none of the members of the small group had any publishing success, Ginsberg took it upon himself to visit the offices of New York publishers personally. He hoped that he could build interest in the works of Kerouac, Burroughs, Cassady, and himself. He showed manuscripts to anyone who would look and contacted his old English professors Trilling, Weaver, and Van Doren for their advice.

During this time, Ginsberg also continued to visit William Carlos Williams in New Jersey. Williams liked Allen's poetry and was willing to help him in any way he could. One day Dr. Williams suggested that Allen look in his old journals for bits of prose that could be converted into poetry. Responding to that idea, Allen sent several pages of short prose fragments, reformatted to look like poetry on the page. Williams wrote back enthusiastically, declaring that Allen had made a major breakthrough and inviting him to come over to his house to discuss the new work. More important, he offered to write an introduction for Allen's poetry and promised to recommend it to his own publisher, James Laughlin at New Directions.

Buoyed by this good news, Ginsberg attended the wedding of his oldest friend, Lucien Carr, who had decided to marry the daughter of a *New York Times* executive. At the reception Allen and Lucien put their heads together and sang a chorus of "Wedding Bells (Are Breaking Up That Old Gang of Mine)," finding some melancholy truth in the lyrics. Although Carr remained a close social friend of Allen's, the regularity of his job and the responsibilities of family life ushered in an inevitable change in their relationship. Over time, as Carr slid deeper into an alcoholic haze that also made him abusive to his family, he ceased to play much of a role in the literary lives of his friends.

Had Burroughs and Kerouac been in New York they would have attended Carr's wedding, too, but they were together in Mexico City.

Burroughs was there awaiting trial for Joan's shooting and worrying about the possibility of a long prison sentence, but Kerouac was finding Mexico to be the perfect retreat. It was an exotic and inexpensive place to live, with drugs, liquor, and women readily available. With Burroughs and some of Bill's friends nearby, Jack wasn't lonely, and he could still head back to his own room for peace and quiet whenever he wanted to write. Even Cassady was close enough to pop in from time to time from California for visits and kicks.

Mexico City afforded a pleasant break for Kerouac, secure in knowing that he could always return to his mother's house if he had to get away from the many evil influences there. Depressed by his rejection at Ace Books, Kerouac actually needed some time to be alone, and he plunged into the writing of *Doctor Sax,* one of his most experimental and masterful books. His methods of sketching and spontaneous prose had now matured into what he believed was a significant new style that would establish him as a writer on a par with Joyce and Proust.

Burroughs continued to plug away at his continuation of *Junkie,* writing chapters that would later be published separately as *Queer.* In addition to writing every day, both he and Jack were indulging in all the many vices that Mexico City had to offer, and it soon took its toll on both of them. Jack was losing weight, had run out of money, and continued to be depressed. To ease his conscience about everything that had transpired the previous winter in San Francisco, Jack wrote a long, apologetic letter to the Cassadys. "I don't think Neal was jealous, he just didn't know what we expected him to do, and we didn't either, I personally felt quite calm about the whole thing and still do except for qualms about how you feel, both of you," he wrote. As the months rolled by, Jack's melancholy became something of a burden to Bill. In order to speed things along, Burroughs uncharacteristically lent Jack the bus fare to return to his family in North Carolina, underscoring just how tiresome and homesick Jack had become.

As one problem for Burroughs departed, another one arrived, this time in the form of William Garver. Garver had flown to Mexico from New York in search of cheap heroin and decided to settle in with Burroughs. He used his contacts to establish a lucrative drug business, and, with the profits, he helped Burroughs pay the bills, which was a welcome change, as it was usually Bill's money that supported his freeloading friends. Garver was even able to loan money to Bill when it was needed, but he always demanded prompt repayment plus interest.

Bill's young traveling companion, Lewis Marker, had been estranged from Bill for months, but he came back to visit and they began to plan their second trip to South America. By that time Bill was certain that his court case would not go in his favor if he stayed to see it through. Late that November, Burroughs learned that his own lawyer, Bernabé Jurado, had killed someone himself and had skipped the country. Officially labeled a "pernicious foreigner," Burroughs decided to follow Jurado's example and get out while he still could. For a few weeks he stopped to see his parents, who were raising Bill's son, Billy, in Palm Beach. They had just moved there from St. Louis, but Bill was noncommittal about Florida. He didn't like it, he said, but he didn't dislike it either. It was a short stay, and by January 1953 he had set off again for Panama, intending to forge on to the jungles of South America. He hoped that Marker would meet him there for company while he continued his search for the elusive hallucinogenic vine known as yage.

Chapter 7

The Name of a Generation

Still restless, Jack Kerouac stayed with his family in North Carolina just long enough to finish the first draft of *Doctor Sax*. Then he headed west by bus to live with the Cassadys once more, this time in their new home in San Jose. When Neal and Carolyn had received Jack's sweet letter of apology, they wrote back encouraging him to return to California and help Neal write his book. "I'm completely stuck with my book and unless you come out and stab me in the ass with just enuf to get me over this hump I'll be still stuck until D. Day," Neal wrote. No sooner had he arrived than he and Carolyn took up where they had left off sexually, once again with Neal's blessing. Kerouac was called back to the railroad as a brakeman, and for a while everything appeared to have the makings of a trouble-free visit.

But this time, as Jack began to settle into the joys of family life, Neal became irritated by Jack and Carolyn's happiness. It was an odd turn of events, because instead of being angry about losing his wife, Neal was jealous that Carolyn was taking away his old pal. Seeing that his relationship with Neal was in jeopardy, Jack moved to a flophouse hotel that was near the San Francisco train station. Sitting in a rocking chair at the Cameo Hotel, looking out at the winos and hookers who lined the street below, he wrote his short story masterpiece of spontaneous prose, "October in the Railroad Earth." In it, he described the satisfaction he found in his life as a railroad worker. But for Jack railroad jobs were temporary and when he was laid off again, Neal drove him to the Mexican border as before. For the second time in less than a year, Jack wound up in Mexico City.

Without Burroughs's companionship this time, Jack was alone and lonely. Only Bill Garver was left in the old apartment on Orizaba Street, and Garver was happy to supply Jack with far too much benzedrine. Garver was so busy pushing that he had little time to socialize with Jack. High on "Benny," Kerouac stayed in his room for days at a time writing a story about his high school sweetheart that was eventually published under the title of *Maggie Cassidy*. Even though Jack was able to live well on little money in Mexico City, he was lonely and homesick. In spite of his continuing fear that Joan's lawyers would find him, he returned to pass the Christmas holidays with his mother, who was back in her Richmond Hill apartment.

In New York Kerouac reconnected with many of his old friends. By then Ginsberg had found his own place on East Seventh Street in what was still known as the Lower East Side, where he continued his open-house policy. When he wasn't working, Lucien Carr could usually be found either at Allen's or at one of the dive bars in the neighborhood. Other friends, like Ed White, Alan Ansen, and Jerry Newman, regularly dropped in to Allen's apartment, too. Even Corso, who had returned to New York from job hunting on the West Coast and Florida, was staying with Allen. With Jack's arrival, it left only Burroughs and Cassady out of the circle. Kerouac quickly returned to his usual pattern of drinking in the city and writing at his mother's house. Throughout the winter he continued to work at her kitchen table on the manuscripts of *Doctor Sax* and *Maggie Cassidy*.

In 1952 one member of the group did manage some success, but it did not cheer everyone in the circle. Scribner's offered John

Clellon Holmes a contract for his first book, which he planned to title simply *Go*. In it, he chronicled the period from 1948 to 1949 when the whole group of friends and subterraneans were hanging out together around his apartment in New York. On the very day when Holmes got word that *Go* had been accepted, he was working alongside Ginsberg tabulating market-research statistics. It was one of the high points of Holmes's life and since it looked as if his dreams of becoming an author were about to be realized, he quit his temp job on the spot.

At first Allen was happy for his friend, but Kerouac soon tainted Allen's feelings against *Go*. Jack believed that Holmes had poached subject matter that was rightfully his, and in no uncertain terms, Jack wrote to Allen about Holmes. "The smell of his work is the smell of death. . . . Everybody knows he has no talent [. . .] His book stinks." Even though the subject matter of *Go* is similar to Kerouac's, the style of the book is much more traditional in composition. It was difficult for Allen, but he managed to maintain his allegiance to Jack and kept his friendship with John, too.

Now flush with enough money to provide liquor for anyone who stopped by, Holmes held court on Lexington Avenue. With the publication of *Go*, Holmes considered himself a young writer on the verge of "making it." Jack was simply jealous and irritated that his friend was having such easy success, and it took Jack nearly a year to get over it, but eventually he and John resumed their friendship.

Meanwhile, Burroughs sent news of his Latin American adventures to Allen every few days. Letters arrived from Panama, Colombia, and eventually from the jungles of Peru. In addition to travel news Burroughs sent stories he came to call "routines." These were wild, macabre short stories dredged mainly from the darkest recesses of Bill's drug-addled imagination. Like Scheherazade's stories, these tales were meant to keep Allen's interest in Burroughs alive from one letter to the next. Ever since they had first met nearly ten years earlier, Bill had quietly maintained a sexual interest in Ginsberg. He was well aware that Allen's preference was for strong, handsome, heterosexual young men like Kerouac, Cassady, Carr, and Corso, but he still held out hope.

For his part, Allen was not interested in Bill as anything but a friend. Still, without encouragement, Bill remained convinced that their romance stood a chance. When Ginsberg placed Bill's book with Ace, Bill dreamed that maybe being a published author would induce Allen to fall in love with him, but Allen remained unaware of his friend's secret feelings.

In the meantime, still acting as Bill's agent in New York, Allen had asked Jack to provide a blurb for Bill's book *Junkie*. Surprisingly, Jack refused. He feared that praising a book by and about a drug addict might attract unwanted attention. Jack was concerned not only about his own reputation, but he also feared that Joan might be able to track him down through Bill's publisher. Ginsberg was dumbfounded by Jack's selfishness and sent him a sarcastic business letter, distancing himself from Kerouac. "Dear Sir," it began. Their spat was short-lived, but it was a harbinger of disagreements to come as Jack became more selfish and self-centered in the years ahead.

Then in November 1952, the *New York Times* commissioned John Clellon Holmes to write an article about the young writers of his generation. In that article, Holmes recalled the conversation he and Jack had had about it being a "beat generation." Holmes titled the piece "This Is the Beat Generation," and although he credited Jack for coining the term, his became the first article to use that phrase in print.

Jack sulked and pouted and at one point even refused to speak to Holmes. He wrote to John, "I have ask'd that my name be withdrawn from all yr. councils—I have my own new ideas about the generation, this isn't 1948, there's nothing beat about these sleek beasts & middleclass subterraneans."

In spite of Ginsberg's continuing efforts to find a publisher for Jack's books, Kerouac was mad at Allen, too. He was beginning to consider him part of a giant Jewish conspiracy that kept his books from being published while books he considered mediocre, like *Go,* found audiences. "I shall certainly never find peace till I wash my hands completely of the dirty brush and stain of New York and everything that you and the city stand for," Jack bitterly wrote to Allen. It is interesting to note that at the very moment the public first heard about the Beat Generation, Kerouac, the man who coined the phrase and would become synonymous with it, was beginning to distance himself from the group.

Ginsberg sensed correctly that he would not be able to keep his friendship with Jack and represent him in business, too, so when Sterling Lord agreed to become Kerouac's agent, Allen was happy to step aside. A major problem that Lord inherited was that *On the Road* was not only nontraditional in terms of style and subject, but Jack's use of real people as characters opened up questions of liability and privacy. Even for a professional agent like Lord, it would be a difficult book to place.

Throughout the spring of 1953, Burroughs's letters continued to arrive from South America, and each one brought a new, even more outlandish routine. Allen could see a book taking shape in all these stories, but it would be a book without an outline and in a form unlike any other. Finally, on one of his expeditions in April, Bill stumbled upon a source for yage. Upon ingesting it, he experienced what he called absolute "sheer horror," reporting that it wasn't called the death vine for nothing. To Burroughs the ghastly visions that the drug induced were worth all the horror, and he recorded his terror and sent the descriptions on to Allen. Missing Burroughs's friendship, Allen reminded Bill that when he was ready to return to the United States after his trip, his door would always be open.

During the same month that Burroughs was battling the monsters conjured up by yage, Neal Cassady was lying in a hospital bed. He had been injured in a fall from a freight car, breaking several bones in his foot. Out of work, on crutches, and bored, he invited his East Coast friends to come to San Jose to visit while he convalesced. Jack was already heading for California to resume work on the railroad when he heard the news. Out of respect for Neal's relationship with Carolyn, Jack didn't even consider living with them this time. Instead, he found a cheap hotel room in San Luis Obispo, far to the south of San Jose. Since Jack's mother was getting older, she didn't want to live alone anymore, so Jack began to look for a house there for him and his mother to share. He made good money on the railroad, so he could afford the rent, at least until he was laid off again.

Ginsberg received his own invitation from Neal and saw it as his opportunity to get away and explore the country. He had managed to save a little money from his various jobs and had finished his court-mandated (and therefore free) psychotherapy. Everyone else had been free to travel while Allen took care of his personal problems, and now he wanted to hit the road himself. But until he left the city, Allen continued to frequent the publishing houses, still trying to place his friends' books.

Allen took great pleasure in planning his trip. He borrowed books and maps from the public library and began to lay out his itinerary. He was still engaged in that phase when Burroughs returned to New York from South America carrying a package of yage to share with his friends. For the next few months he stayed with Allen, telling him stories about the jungle and the "medicine men" he found there. Burroughs's accounts made Allen all the more eager to begin his own adventures.

Once in New York, Burroughs ardently pressed his love for Allen. He frightened Allen with all his talk about loving someone so much that their two bodies would literally merge in one giant "slurp." At that point, Burroughs had been away for six years, and Allen was put off by the changes he saw in his old mentor. No matter how many stories he told, Bill began to realize that Allen was not going to go to bed with him.

As Burroughs began to speak about their future life together, Allen felt forced to be blunt. "I don't want your ugly old cock," he callously told his old friend without stopping to think how much it would hurt him. As soon as the words were out of his mouth, he regretted it. To soothe matters, he spent long hours having heart-to-heart conversations with Bill. In the weeks that followed he even slept with Bill a few times to compensate, but the emotional pain that his comment caused his friend haunted Ginsberg forever.

Allen was still deeply in love with Neal. In fact, he had accepted Neal's invitation to visit him in California in order to rekindle their love affair. In New York Allen was still halfheartedly sleeping around with a number of women as his doctors had suggested. As a lover, Dusty had nearly faded from the scene, but she was still a close friend and even kept her clothes at Allen's apartment, much to Burroughs's consternation. So Allen still had other affairs to tend to before he left town.

Kerouac, too, had been using Allen's apartment whenever he came into Manhattan from Brooklyn for his long weekend binges. Just before Bill's arrival, Jack had met a beautiful black woman by the name of Alene Lee, who lived only a few blocks from Allen's place. Their love affair was brief, due mainly to Jack's old fear of commitment. During the summer, when Jack seemed to lose interest in Alene, she slept with Corso, and that conflict created some tension between the two men. Gregory somewhat innocently thought that she was fair game, since Kerouac didn't seem to know what he wanted.

Since Alene was an expert typist, she was able to be of practical help assembling the letters and "routines" that Burroughs had sent from South America. The result was a book of correspondence that they came to call *The Yage Letters*. Kerouac described that whole summer of romance and betrayal in his short novel *The Subterraneans,* describing Alene as Mardou Fox in the book. It was another of the phenomenal books that he wrote in a single burst of energy at his typewriter.

As 1953 progressed, John Clellon Holmes was readmitted to the circle of friends on East Seventh Street, and he continued to observe these fascinating characters as possible fodder for future stories. Herbert Huncke was paramount among them, having recently been released from prison. Jail hadn't changed him, and he began to use his old underworld skills to find drug connections for all of them, but this time Allen tried to keep the illegal activity away from his apartment.

Another friend they had gotten to know well at the San Remo bar on Bleecker Street became a central part of their group that fall. Alan Ansen was a superb intellect and in years previous had acted as W. H. Auden's private secretary. He was a poet himself and a skilled editor who gave them practical advice on the organization of *The Yage Letters*. Like Burroughs, he was a Harvard graduate who read voraciously and had an encyclopedic memory. Ansen lived with his spinster aunt in Woodmere, Long Island, and commuted to the city whenever he wanted excitement.

When Ansen's aunt died that autumn, he rented her house to another San Remo regular, the writer William Gaddis. With his modest inheritance in a trust fund, he decided that he would travel extensively for the first time in his life. By then Ansen and Burroughs had become close friends, and they decided that Ansen would use his editorial skills to help Bill assemble all his routines into a book. Over time these stories would metamorphose into books such as Burroughs's *The Naked Lunch*, which was published years later.

Even though they had been to bed together a few times, the hoped-for romance with Ginsberg was not going to materialize, and Burroughs sensed that it was time to move on. His income from his own trust fund was limited, only a few hundred dollars per month, but he speculated that in Europe or Northern Africa it would be enough to live on comfortably.

Ginsberg had remained sedentary long enough and intended to tour extensively through Cuba and Mexico on his way to California.

It was to be his first extended trip out of the country at leisure, and he was determined to take his time and enjoy everything along the way. Once out west he planned to settle down in the Bay Area and get a job. Maybe he would even work for the Southern Pacific like Neal and Jack, despite his lack of manual dexterity.

His first stop was in Washington, DC, where he hoped to visit Ezra Pound. Nearly ten years earlier, Pound had been sent to St. Elizabeth's Mental Hospital in lieu of prison for his treasonous activity during World War II. When Allen arrived at the asylum door unannounced, Pound refused to see the young poet, and Allen continued on his way, disappointed but resolved to meet Pound someday.

As he passed through Florida, he stopped to visit Lewis Marker and spent Christmas with Burroughs's parents before taking a cheap ferry to Cuba. He was disappointed when he found nothing of interest to keep him in pre-Castro Havana for more than a few days. He found the false gaiety of the casino world out of place in such a poverty-stricken country. Without further delay Allen took his first airplane, flying over the Caribbean from Cuba to Mexico's Yucatán Peninsula. He had studied pre-Columbian cultures in preparation for his trip and wanted to explore all the Mayan ruins along his route. Slowly he made his way west to Chiapas, the heart of the ancient Mayan civilization. It was in the jungle near the massive ruins of Palenque that he ran out of money.

Chapter 8

To the West Coast

While sharing Ginsberg's apartment in New York, Gregory Corso had turned on the charm and made friends with Violet (Bunny) Lang, a literary force and one of the founders of the influential Poets' Theatre in Cambridge, Massachusetts. As Allen made his way around Mexico, Gregory was being introduced to some of Harvard's brightest students that year. John Ashbery, Frank O'Hara, and Edward Gorey were all active in Lang's Poets' Theatre. No one knew that Bunny's life would be cut short by cancer; she died two years later at the age of thirty-two. When Gregory arrived, Bunny was involved in the production of several theatricals, and while Corso was hanging out with her in Cambridge, he decided to write his own play. He called it *In This Hung-Up Age,* and some drama students staged it that year. Although the play was not memorable, Gregory liked to tell people that he introduced the first "Beat" characters to the theatrical world. While he was in Cambridge, Corso also dropped in to audit an occasional class or two at Harvard and studied the Romantic poets in the Houghton Library. From that experience came his poem "I Held a Shelley Manuscript" demonstrating again the high regard he had for those poets.

Corso found the academic life so appealing that when he made friends with the Pulitzer Prize–winning poet Archibald MacLeish, he began to toy with the idea of becoming a professor himself. After growing up as a street tough in New York's Little Italy, it must have pleased him to picture himself as a tenured professor in a leather chair surrounded by a bevy of brainy young coeds hanging on his every word. Gregory lacked the self-discipline necessary for serious academic study, but while at Harvard, he did write enough great poetry to fill his first book. Friends in Cambridge contributed money to fund that publication, *The Vestal Lady on Brattle and Other Poems.*

When he left Ginsberg's New York apartment, Burroughs stopped off in Florida long enough to say hello to his parents and son, Billy. From there he went to Rome to look in on Alan Ansen, who had arrived there ahead of him. After a few weeks, Bill realized that he didn't care for either Rome or Italy very much, and when Ansen left for Venice, Burroughs headed to Tangier. In Morocco he thought he'd find an environment that was more to his liking, and he did. People in the internationally diverse city of Tangier left him alone to do as he pleased, and the local police were not interested in looking over his shoulder as they had been in the United States and Mexico.

For the next twenty years Burroughs divided his time between Tangier, Paris, and London. He became addicted to drugs repeatedly and sought cures just as often. Through it all, he continued writing and somehow managed to produce a substantial body of work. Even if the "ugly spirits," as he called the possessive forces, could not be exorcised, they could be kept under control, he discovered, through the process of writing about them.

On the other side of the world, Kerouac had landed a job as a parking lot attendant in California after being laid off by the railroad. It didn't seem to matter to his employers that he wasn't a competent driver. It is interesting to note that Jack never drove on his cross-country jaunts for the simple reason that he never had a driver's license. He wasn't alone in that; Ginsberg couldn't drive either. So they both relied on others to take them around. Also like Ginsberg, Kerouac had long since discovered that he wasn't suited for manual labor and preferred to write and drink instead. Although he saw Neal occasionally, they began to drift apart. Cassady's immobility due to his broken leg had brought Neal and Carolyn closer together, and they were focused on their family to the point of excluding old friends.

Early in 1954 Neal discovered a book called *Many Mansions,* which was to influence him greatly. It told the story of the popular American psychic Edgar Cayce. Until his death in 1945, Cayce was famous for channeling answers to myriad questions from the spirit world. Following Cayce's death, many of his disciples continued the method he had pioneered of diagnosing spiritual, physical, and personal problems through psychic readings. Cayce's belief in reincarnation and the individual's ability to change his life appealed to the Cassadys, and they began to spend a good deal of time studying his ideas.

According to Allen, Neal fixated on Cayce as the solution to every problem and became something of a bore on the topic. On the one hand, Allen was glad that Neal had found a spiritual center for his life, but a nucleus that was based on Christianity, dream interpretation, and clairvoyance did not ring true for the rational Ginsberg. Kerouac agreed with Allen's assessment, and the more Cayce occupied Neal's time and thoughts, the more Jack found himself isolated from him.

Even though Burroughs was now settled in Morocco, he tried to remain in close contact with Ginsberg. When Allen ran out of money and was stranded in Chiapas, Bill began to worry and wrote to Kerouac and Cassady that he believed something terrible had happened to Allen. He visualized all sorts of catastrophes that could have befallen him, and his concern was infectious. No one realized that Allen was only broke and hung up in a remote part of Mexico so that he had no way to communicate. Allen had spent all his money, but he was safe and staying with someone he had met there. He had decided the best thing to do was wait in the jungle until he got some money so that he could continue his journey. After a few months word finally arrived that Allen was safe, and his father sent him enough money to finish his trip. In the meantime, Bill had managed to instill anxiety in everyone of their circle.

As a result of Burroughs's infectious fear, Allen was greeted as the prodigal son when he finally arrived in San Jose that June. Neal and Carolyn both insisted that he stay with them for as long as he wanted. No sooner had Allen unpacked than Neal drove him up the freeway to San Francisco for his first visit to the city that would change his life. Allen wrote to his brother enthusiastically saying "California is the only state outside of New York that seems like home." The public would consider San Francisco the capital of the Beat Generation within a few years.

Although Ginsberg loved the Mediterranean feel of San Francisco, initially he preferred the quiet surroundings of Cassady's home where he could recoup his strength after his long trip. Regrettably, by the time Allen turned up in San Jose, Kerouac had grown disgusted with Neal and his Cayce obsession and had returned east to his mother's house. Jack's absence was a disappointment for Ginsberg, who was looking forward to seeing Jack again. While Jack had been in California, he had discovered Eastern spiritualism and spent much of his time in the public library researching the life of the Buddha. Over the next few months via their correspondence, Jack repeatedly urged Allen to explore Buddhism for himself.

Jack's studies were to have a major influence on his personal philosophy, and his writings reflected this new fascination. The notes that Jack made in the San Jose library eventually found their way into his book *Some of the Dharma*. Back in New York Kerouac continued his research and sent long reading lists of Buddhist texts to Allen. Allen borrowed some of them from the public library and did his best to catch up, but in spite of Kerouac's encouragement, Ginsberg was not ready for the discipline of Buddhist practice yet, and although he tried to understand it through the literature, without a meditation teacher it was too abstract for him to grasp.

Ginsberg was glad to see that both Kerouac and Cassady had become more interested in spirituality. Unfortunately, neither Buddhism nor the New Age spirituality of Cayce appealed to Allen. He did believe that Buddhism had some substance, but he considered Cayce to be a quack, with nothing worthwhile to offer. Allen was still on his own spiritual quest that had begun years earlier with his Blake visions.

Neal's talk of channeling and reincarnation didn't mean much to Allen at the time. His immediate desire was to enjoy the pleasures of gay sex once again with Neal as his mentor, just as he had when they first met in 1947. Now that Neal was hobbled by his injury, it seemed like they might have a good deal of time to play around while Carolyn was out of the house. In San Jose that summer, Allen and Neal did renew their sexual relationship, but it wasn't the long-awaited erotic reunion that Allen had hoped for. Although Neal engaged in sex with Allen, his heart didn't seem to be in it anymore. For Allen it was another emotional letdown.

The occasional moments of sexual passion were not very satisfying for Allen, and to top it off, one day as Allen was having sex with Neal, Carolyn walked in on them. Neal did not bother to make excuses for his actions but simply put on his clothes and left the house. Allen took the full brunt of Carolyn's anger in large part because she had already convinced herself that Allen was an evil person bent on leading her innocent husband astray. Her bitter words ended only when she dropped him off in the North Beach section of San Francisco, in front of the run-down Marconi Hotel. Once more Ginsberg found himself alone and penniless in a strange town. He took a cheap room in the hotel and began to take stock of himself yet again.

Allen believed that his psychiatrists had been right when they told him that his homosexuality would only lead to unhappiness. He resolved once more to force himself to change. Because he knew no one in San Francisco, he considered leaving town altogether. Burroughs had been urging Allen to fly to Tangier to live with him. It would have been an easy way out for Ginsberg, but Burroughs's needy state of mind would have smothered Allen. At least he realized that until he could take care of himself, he could never satisfy Bill's needs.

Desperately broke, Ginsberg's first priority was to find a job. After being turned down by the local newspapers, he went back to the only real occupation he knew, market research. Within days he landed a good job with the firm of Towne-Oller Associates in the city's financial district. They immediately put him to work researching the reasons behind people's purchasing of certain brands of toothpaste. Following Kerouac's advice, Allen looked up Al Sublette, a merchant marine friend, who turned out to be a dependable drug connection. He even found a girlfriend. From that moment on, things evolved rapidly for Ginsberg, things that would utterly change the course of his life and eventually have a profound impact on the entire group.

Allen's new girl, Sheila Williams, held down odd jobs as she pursued a career as a jazz singer in some of the local clubs. Although she was younger than Allen, who had just turned twenty-eight, she already had a child. Before long, she invited Allen to live with them in her modest Nob Hill apartment. It took little coaxing to get him to move out of his North Beach flophouse. His new job paid well, and he even had his own office and secretary. He could have afforded his own apartment, but he preferred to live frugally with Sheila, saving his money for future travel. The dilemma of his new way of life was the same as always. Having a full-time job, there was no time left to write, but without a job, Allen couldn't afford to live. He had witnessed it with his father who taught school all day and then tried to squeeze in a few minutes to write poetry in the evenings. It wasn't very conducive to creating great art, but it was a fact of life unless you were independently wealthy.

For the time being, the steady income and "normal" lifestyle seemed to be just what Allen needed to restore the stability that had been shattered by the recent Cassady misadventure. He believed that he was nearing the brink of madness again after that upheaval. The emotional roller-coaster ride continued when, only a few days after Carolyn discovered Allen and Neal in bed together, Neal began to visit him in San Francisco to renew sexual contact.

Burroughs, who had flown to Florida to visit his parents, asked if he could come out to see Allen in San Francisco. Since Allen knew Bill wanted to stake his claim on him, it worked to Allen's advantage to be able to tell Bill that he was living with Sheila and once more intent upon pursuing a heterosexual life. Although Bill still believed that it was futile to forsake one's sexual orientation, it did turn Bill off, much to Allen's relief. He decided to head back for Morocco without venturing to the West Coast.

Even though Ginsberg's days were occupied with a nine-to-five job, a girlfriend with a young son, and an apartment, Allen was still interested in sampling new drugs for experimentation. When one of Sheila's friends showed up at the apartment with peyote, Allen was eager to try it. He wondered what new visions this psychoactive cactus would conjure up. That evening, October 17, 1954, he ingested several of the peyote buttons. As the drug took effect, Allen looked out the window and was transfixed by the nearby Sir Francis Drake Hotel. In the San Francisco fog that shrouded the building, he saw the hotel begin to glow with the monstrous face of Moloch, the Phoenician god that was described in the Old Testament as a child-eating demon. It was a horrible, terrifying vision, but one that gave Ginsberg a new insight into the greed of man, and the vision lingered in Allen's brain long enough for him to write down a detailed description. Those notes would become the basis for *Howl*, the major poem that Allen was to write the following year. However, in his current busy life, it was just a fleeting, albeit disturbing, revelation.

Flush with money from his new job, Allen decided to see a therapist for an hour or so each week. Over the course of his sessions,
he began to feel at ease with the young psychologist. He seemed
much more in tune with Allen's feelings than the overworked shrinks
had been in the New York Psychiatric Institute. Allen and Dr. Hicks
talked mainly about Allen's love life during the sessions. Sex with
Sheila was not proving to be the panacea that Allen had hoped for.
Within a few months, he was cruising the gay bars around Polk
Street, making new friends, and looking for sex. He felt he was slipping back into his old ways.

One evening the painter Robert LaVigne came over to Allen's
table in one of the bars and struck up a conversation. LaVigne was
personable, friendly, and easy to talk to. He had been in the city
working on his art for only a few years, but he already knew many
people. The two hit it off and Allen, now financially comfortable,
mentioned that he might be able to buy some of LaVigne's work. For
that reason, Robert invited Allen to visit his studio on Gough Street
to look at his larger paintings.

In the entryway to LaVigne's studio, Allen saw a painting of a
stunningly attractive nude young man. Allen later recalled that he
was the most handsome man he had ever seen. The picture was entitled *Nude with Onions,* but it wasn't the onions that caught Allen's
attention. Within a few minutes the model himself, Peter Orlovsky,
casually walked into the studio. As had happened before in Allen's
life, it was love at first sight. Orlovsky did not have the same initial
reaction to Allen, but he greeted him cordially.

Peter had recently been discharged from the army for psychologi-
cal reasons when he refused to carry a weapon; he was not cut out
for military service. Peter came from a family with a long history of
severe mental problems, and several of his siblings had been institutionalized. Although Peter was sweet and sincere and the sanest
of the family, he had problems that the army was not equipped to
handle. For Allen, Peter's mental illness only added to the attraction,

for he loved the wacky things that Peter said and did. The key problem in their relationship was that Peter was not interested in men sexually. To be sure, he had been sleeping with LaVigne, but that was more out of a feeling of obligation to Robert for taking care of him after the military had kicked him out. When Robert told Allen that he was thinking of going to Mexico and leaving Peter behind, Allen wondered if he might have a chance with the young man after all.

Sheila did not demand that Allen be monogamous, but she couldn't understand why Allen would prefer a reluctant man's sexual favors to her own. She enjoyed Allen's company and wanted to maintain their relationship if she could, so she begged him to stay with her. Allen's heart was already set on Peter, but he didn't want to hurt Sheila either, so he didn't know what to do. Essentially he still believed that homosexuality was an illness that could be treated through proper psychotherapy; at least that's what he hoped.

Carolyn Cassady was unaware that Neal was slipping off to San Francisco at every opportunity. He was not only visiting Allen for sex, but he was sleeping with a number of women as well. One of the young women that he began to see was Natalie Jackson, a model for Robert LaVigne. Soon she became Neal's most frequent lover. Carolyn and Neal had managed to gloss over that summer's dalliance with Ginsberg, both willing to blame it on Allen. It was easier for Carolyn to treat it as an isolated event than to see it as a symptom of Neal's truly deceitful nature. But Neal was out of control sexually, having sex with anyone from the youngest girls to elderly women, and on occasion with other men.

Finally, when Neal's settlement money came through from the railroad for the injury case, the couple was able to make a down payment on a suburban house in Los Gatos. There in the hills south of San Jose, Carolyn hoped the family could establish permanent roots and live a peaceful, middle-class life. It would take a few more years for Carolyn to realize that life, and then it would only be without Neal.

Allen continued to receive letters from Gregory Corso, who was now dividing his time between Greenwich Village and Cambridge. It was in Cambridge that Gregory met the girl who turned out to be the love of his life, Hope Savage. She was only seventeen years old, the daughter of a wealthy, prominent family in Camden, South Carolina. Hope, who preferred to be called Sura, became Gregory's muse just as Peter Orlovsky was to become Allen's. Worried about his rebellious daughter, Sura's father once had her committed to a mental hospital for shock treatments, but her spirit remained unbroken. It was obvious that living a bourgeois life was not going to be in her future. She dreamed of escaping, and the more remote and exotic the destination the better.

Eventually, Sura decided to settle in India and tried to convince Corso to go along with her. Gregory loved her, but he was not ready to make such an extreme move just when he was beginning to have some success with his own poetry. He did agree to live in South Carolina with Sura and her family, but her father was unhappy with both his daughter and her choice of boyfriends, and so that arrangement did not last long. As time went by, Sura took off for Paris on the first leg of her trip to Asia, and Gregory promised to follow her as soon as he could afford it.

Chapter 9

Nightmare of Moloch

Kerouac kept busy in New York with his studies in Buddhist philosophy and doctrine. Without a meditation teacher, he learned as much as he could from the books he read independently. Self-educated in Buddhism, he developed a unique, personal form of meditation practice. Usually a practitioner adopted a teacher, or guru, and learned from his example, but Kerouac did it on his own.

Occasionally, Jack would go into the city for weekend binges, but he was always cautious lest Haverty's lawyers find out where he was and serve him with court papers. When Malcolm Cowley placed a short story of Jack's called "Jazz of the Beat Generation" in *New World Writing*, Jack asked that it appear under the pseudonym of Jean-Louis. In spite of his attempts to hide his whereabouts, Joan took him to court in absentia for child support. Early in 1955 Jack asked Allen's brother, Eugene Brooks, who was practicing law, to represent him. Brooks told the court that Jack was suffering from a debilitating form of phlebitis that was not only painful but rendered him unable to work. Joan sympathized with Jack and said that she hadn't realized how serious his condition was. She agreed to postpone the case for one year. Both Jack and Eugene were pleasantly surprised by her honest concern and generosity, but aside from that good news and the publication of his story in *New World Writing*, things were still not going well for Kerouac. He was carrying around the completed manuscripts of five major books and he was still unable to find a publisher for any one of them.

While Kerouac agonized over his lack of success on the East Coast, Ginsberg struggled with his emotional problems on the West Coast. Allen had come to have confidence in his new therapist, Philip Hicks, believing that he was the best shrink he ever had. One day he asked the doctor what he thought he should do about the major conflicts in his life. Everything that Allen desired appeared to be improper in the eyes of society. Instead of telling Ginsberg what he should do, Hicks used a bit of common sense and asked Allen to tell him what he'd like to do. Without much hesitation Allen replied that he'd like to quit his job and become a poet. He also wanted to be open and honest about his love of men instead of forcing himself to sleep with women. Allen was surprised when the doctor asked him point-blank, why he didn't do those things. "Well, what if I find that I'm unable to support myself, et cetera?" Allen replied. "Oh, I wouldn't worry about that if I were you," said Dr. Hicks. He told Allen that he had a winning personality and that his friends would always be around to help him if he got into trouble. Allen then had an epiphany and realized that if he was not true to himself, life really was not worth living. He resolved to change in the ways that he wanted to change and not alter his feelings just because others thought he should. It was a turning point in his life and in the course of American literature.

It was the perfect timing for such a suggestion, especially because Allen was just getting to know Peter Orlovsky. Within a few months, he packed up and left a disappointed Sheila, rented a large apartment at 1010 Montgomery Street in North Beach, and asked Peter to move in with him. Their romance was rocky from the very start, but they decided to give it a try. Peter always preferred the company of women, and he wasn't certain that he should get involved with another man after his experiences with LaVigne. Possibly he chose to stay with Allen simply because he didn't think that he had many other options. In truth, he was as frightened by Allen's possessiveness as Allen had been by the same quality in Burroughs. Still, Peter was impressed with Allen's intellect and enjoyed most of the time they spent together. He resigned himself to tolerate the occasional sex if that was what was required to be a part of Allen's life.

Allen's next decision was to leave his market-research job. His resignation upset his employers and they even offered Allen a promotion with a transfer to their New York office if only he would stay with the firm. That offer wasn't tempting to Allen because now that he had met Peter he didn't want to leave San Francisco. Things were just beginning to improve, and to move back closer to his family might make him abandon his new resolve to be the person he wanted to be, instead of the person they wanted him to be. It would be much easier for him to remain true to himself if he was three thousand miles away. He even looked forward to living on his meager unemployment checks for the next six months.

At first Allen didn't reveal his decision to William Burroughs, being aware that Bill might jump on the next plane to be with him. At the same time, unknown to Allen, Burroughs was going through his own drug-induced hells and was seeking a cure for his current heroin addiction. He discovered a competent doctor in Tangier named Appfel who cured addicts with a two-week sleep remedy, and that occupied Bill for a while until he realized that he was a bit of a quack. "He come near killing me with his fucking cold turkey sleep cure," Bill wrote to Jack and Allen. So while Jack was suffering over nonpublication and court battles, and Bill was suffering through withdrawal, Allen was inventing a new life for himself in San Francisco.

Just down the street from his apartment, Allen discovered the perfect independent bookstore. It was the first in the country to sell nothing but paperbacks. Until that time, cheap paperback books were not sold in "real" bookstores, but instead were relegated to spinning racks in drugstores and bus stations. They were usually stocked without any regard for the quality of the literature, and finding a good book was hit or miss. This particular bookstore had been founded in 1953 by Peter Martin, the publisher of a little magazine christened *City Lights* in honor of the Charlie Chaplin film of the same name. Martin had decided to open a store to subsidize the magazine, and while he was putting the sign over the door, a thirty-four-year-old man passed by and struck up a conversation.

Lawrence Ferling (it was to be a few years before he restored the name to his family's original Ferlinghetti), thought that the idea of an all-paperback bookshop was a great one. For a small investment, he became a partner in the store and in no time the two men were selling interesting, well-selected books that appealed to the new group of literary bohemians who were moving into the cheap apartments of the city's old Italian neighborhood of North Beach.

By the time Ginsberg happened on the store, Martin had grown tired of the business, sold out to Ferlinghetti, and gone back to his native New York City. That suited Lawrence, because he had his own ideas about how he wanted to run the business. After serving in the navy for the duration of World War II, he had gone to Paris as a student on the GI Bill. There he had noticed that many of the best French bookstores also published books, and it was his idea to do the same in San Francisco. The first City Lights imprint was to be a small collection of Ferlinghetti's own poetry, which he called *Pictures of the Gone World*. Lawrence already had arranged to follow that book with new books by two of the older San Francisco literary giants, Kenneth Patchen and Kenneth Rexroth. It was the beginning of a bookstore and publishing company that has continued ever since in the same location, expanding continually.

Even for someone as charming as Neal Cassady, his double life was difficult to keep secret. Before long Carolyn realized he was yet again involved with at least one other woman, and the couple separated. She was left alone in her new house in Los Gatos to support and raise the family, which now included two girls and a boy. Neal moved up to San Francisco to be with Natalie Jackson, both living for a while in Ginsberg's apartment on Montgomery Street. From there Natalie found her own apartment in an old building on Franklin, and Neal moved with her. Peter didn't mind sharing the house with Neal and Natalie, especially since Peter loved women nearly as much as Neal did. Neal wasn't the least bit monogamous, so he wasn't jealous when Natalie spent time with Peter. They even wrote to Kerouac and tried to entice him to come out and live with them all communally. Jack considered the offer.

Back on Long Island, Peter Orlovsky's family was having difficulties of their own. Peter's father had abandoned his family years earlier, and the children grew up in extreme poverty. For years Peter's disabled mother and siblings lived in what was little more than a converted chicken coop in Northport, about an hour out of the city. That July his mother decided that it would be better for his brother Lafcadio if he went to live with Peter in San Francisco. Otherwise, she threatened to have the fifteen-year-old boy, who suffered from schizophrenia, committed to a mental hospital. Peter did not want Lafcadio to end up withdrawn and silent like his older brother Julius, who had been in an institution for the past six years, so he agreed to fetch him.

After a weekend camping trip in the Sierras, Peter and Allen parted in Reno where Peter stuck out his thumb to begin hitchhiking back east. He was determined to rescue Lafcadio and keep him out of the clutches of the bughouse. From Reno, Allen returned to Montgomery Street to make his own plans for the fall. Before Peter left, he and Allen had agreed that it would be best if Peter and Lafcadio lived on their own. In their few short months together, Allen and Peter's relationship had gone from bad to worse, so it seemed like a good time to take a break from each other. They were uncertain about what the future held for them as a couple or whether there would even be a future.

Ginsberg had been toying with the idea of going to graduate school at the University of California, Berkeley. If he earned a master's degree, he felt he could always fall back on teaching to earn a living. Then he wouldn't ever have to return to market-research work, which he considered a waste of time. In the interim, until Peter returned and Allen's classes began in September, he had a chance to work undisturbed on some new ideas for poems.

One of the poems he wanted to work on had been inspired by his peyote-induced vision of Moloch the previous fall. Alone in the apartment he worked uninterruptedly on his idea. He constructed the poem as an open letter to Carl Solomon, who Allen had just learned was once again back in a mental hospital. Originally, the working title for the poem had been simply "Strophes." Kerouac, always able to come up with pithy titles, later suggested that he call it *Howl,* and that appealed to Allen, so he called it *Howl for Carl Solomon.*

Alone at his Montgomery Street desk, Allen began to write, "I saw the best minds of my generation destroyed by madness . . ." It all spilled out of his head onto the paper as he typed, all the pent-up anguish and sorrow for the broken souls of the people he had known destroyed by the insensitive, money-hungry world of Moloch. "They broke their backs lifting Moloch to Heaven!" he wrote. Allen wasn't thinking only of Carl Solomon at the time, but all those poor souls from David Kammerer to Joan Adams to Bill Cannastra, who had been unable to find a place in a society dominated by postwar conformity. "What sphinx of cement and aluminum bashed open their skulls and ate up their brains and imagination?" he questioned.

It was an act of purging for Allen, who was able to spew it all out before Peter returned at the end of August. He was proud of his new work, but initially he felt that the poem was far too personal to ever be of interest to any but his closest friends. He sent samples of it to Kerouac, his brother, Eugene, and a few other friends, but he thought of it more as an exercise in emotional expression than as a piece for publication. "Most of my time is actually occupied with this type thought and activity, writing a lot and therefore beginning to change style, get hot, invent and go on interesting kicks," he wrote to his brother. He continued to feel that his best poetry continued to be those poems that he extracted from his old notebooks as William Carlos Williams had suggested. He had been concentrating on prose converted into poetry. It would take time for him to realize that this new long-line creation was indeed the first manifestation of that unique voice he had been searching for since college.

On September 1, 1955, a day or two after Peter and Lafcadio got back to Montgomery Street, Allen moved into a small cottage he had leased in Berkeley, a few blocks from the campus. He was now in the midst of a fertile period when poems seemed to come to mind one right after another. In the course of the next month he wrote some his best-known poems, "A Strange New Cottage in Berkeley," "A Supermarket in California," "Four Haiku," "Sunflower Sutra," "Transcription of Organ Music," and "Sather Gate Illumination." His new friend Lawrence Ferlinghetti looked over some of these poems and hinted that he might consider them for publication by City Lights.

By the time Allen moved the rest of his clothing to Berkeley, Kenneth Rexroth, the great literary gadfly of San Francisco, had already been in touch with him about organizing a reading of new writers. At first Allen thought that maybe he, Kerouac, and Cassady could read together, but Jack was terribly shy, and Neal didn't have much written down yet, so that concept didn't go very far. Allen didn't really know the other writers in the Bay Area that Rexroth had suggested to him. He hadn't met many poets in his short time in the city. He had been introduced to Robert Duncan already, but wasn't enthusiastic about Duncan's poems. In truth, he felt that San Francisco was much too provincial to tender any great poetry.

Rexroth knew more people than Ginsberg and suggested that

Allen get in touch with Michael McClure, whose early poetry was extremely powerful and infused with an uncommon awareness of nature. McClure had come from the Midwest, hoping to study painting with Mark Rothko and Clyfford Still, but they had left town before he arrived. He loved the feel of San Francisco, though, so he stayed and took a few classes in poetry from Robert Duncan. McClure's words were to grow into a new voice that coupled ecological and environmental concerns with a respect for the sacred spirit of all living creatures. Since he was also new to the city, he was interested in meeting new people like Allen, and the idea of a poetry reading appealed to him.

Another poet suggested by Rexroth was Gary Snyder. Snyder shared Rexroth's interest in both Buddhism and Asian culture. He combined those concerns with an enthusiasm for nature similar to McClure's in intensity. Allen had once met McClure earlier at a party, but he didn't know Snyder at all, so one day Allen decided to go over to the other side of Berkeley to meet Gary. Snyder remembers their first meeting vividly. Gary was in the yard of his little cottage on Hillegass working on his bicycle when Ginsberg dropped in. He was impressed most of all by Ginsberg's curiosity about everything. They talked about some other young poets who were in the area, and Gary recommended one in particular. Philip Whalen, a classmate of his from Reed College in Portland, Oregon, was living in the Bay Area at the time. Philip shared Gary's interests in Eastern religions, especially Zen Buddhism, the outdoors, and poetry that was rooted in America's western landscape. After Ginsberg met Whalen, he was impressed. "Whalen I think the most interesting of new 'S.F.' poets. He is sincere and open and learned and calm and non hysterical and good company," he wrote. These were new influences for Allen to consider. Previously he had always looked toward European-oriented literature for his models.

In addition to Phil Whalen, Rexroth also suggested Philip Lamantia as a possible reader. Allen knew Lamantia from the San Remo bar

scene in New York, and even remembered that he had seen his poetry in some surrealist magazines a decade earlier, but he wasn't aware
that he was on the West Coast. Like many of the other young writers
gathering in San Francisco at that time, Lamantia was in the midst
of a nomadic period and had been traveling extensively. Ginsberg
had heard that Lamantia had been having visions of his own, not unlike Allen's Blake visions, so he was eager to renew his acquaintance
and compare notes. Lamantia's visions had been brought on after he
suffered a nearly fatal scorpion bite in Mexico. After his visions, he
was converted to a mystical form of Catholicism that intrigued both
Ginsberg and Kerouac.

In those days the Six Gallery was a small storefront space in San
Francisco's less-than-posh Marina district. The directors of that gallery had offered to host Rexroth's evening of new poets on October 7,
1955. At the time, no one could have guessed that the reading would
become the seminal event that would ignite the literary community
of San Francisco and reverberate through literary society for the next
decade. The small audience in attendance witnessed the birth of both
the San Francisco Renaissance and the Beat Generation as forces to
be reckoned with.

By coincidence, while Ginsberg and Snyder were getting to know
each other, Jack Kerouac arrived in Berkeley. In fact, he was waiting at Allen's little cottage on Milvia Street when Ginsberg returned
from Snyder's place. Allen was thrilled to see Jack and tried to coax
him into participating in the reading, but public readings were in-
timidating to Kerouac, and he declined. He promised he would be
there to give the poets moral support, but he was too self-conscious
to perform in front of an audience.

Kerouac had been at his sister's house in Rocky Mount with his
mother while Allen was writing *Howl*. Since all their efforts to find
a publisher for *On the Road* had repeatedly failed, Jack was nearly
broke. During the summer, he had decided to retrieve his unpublished manuscripts from various publishers and work quietly on a

book he was planning to call *Visions of Bill*. Similar to his *Visions of Neal*, this book would be about Burroughs, an even more interesting subject for a book than Cassady. At the time Bill was still living in Tangier and working on *Interzone* while he tried to kick yet another junk habit. The "Interzone" was Bill's term for the International Zone of Tangier where nothing was taboo and everything was permitted. The stories he wrote there were some of his most macabre and disturbing, as well as some of his best. These featured some characters who would become synonymous with his work, creations like the diabolical Doctor Benway and Spare Ass Annie. To do research for his book, Kerouac needed to spend time with Bill in Morocco, but at the moment, he didn't even have a dime to spend on getting there. In fact, Jack had been forced to borrow money from his mother just to get to California.

In July he set out from Rocky Mount for San Francisco, but on the spur of the moment decided to swing south through Mexico City to pick up some cheap penicillin to treat his phlebitis, which had become aggravated again. Once in Mexico he remembered how much he really liked the carefree life there and stayed for more than a month before moving on. During Jack's visit he had a fling with a prostitute who he said reminded him of the Virgin Mary. He began to write *Tristessa*, the story of his relationship with her. His layover in the Mexican capital was a productive period for Kerouac, and he filled notebook after notebook with poems that became his *Mexico City Blues*. It was a book that Ginsberg was to consider the best poetry ever written.

Chapter 10

The Six Gallery

As the date for the Six Gallery reading neared, Ginsberg tried out a few of his poems at the San Francisco Art Festival being held in Aquatic Park near Fisherman's Wharf. It was Ginsberg's first public reading, and he felt it went well. He read some of his breezy, funnier poems to that audience, "amid much laughter and applause," he wrote to Robert LaVigne, but for the Six Gallery he decided that he'd read his new long poem, *Howl*. He wasn't certain how people would react to the uncompromisingly serious subject matter or the sexual content of the poem, but since it was to be read in such a small venue, he felt that it didn't matter. Of the five young poets on the platform, only Lamantia had read in public before, so the night was a bit of an experiment. Snyder and Ginsberg collaborated on a postcard announcing the event and sent it to as many of their friends as they could think of; about a hundred people showed up, none of them expecting anything out of the ordinary.

First to speak was the venerable Kenneth Rexroth, who acted as the event's master of ceremony since he was the only person who actually knew all of the poets slated to read. After a few introductory remarks to an audience that included Kerouac, Ferlinghetti, and

Cassady, Rexroth handed the stage over to Lamantia. Many people were expecting Philip to read his own surrealist poetry, so they were surprised when he pulled out a packet of John Hoffman's poems typed on fragile onionskin paper.

Hoffman had been a friend of Lamantia's and had died three years earlier in Mexico. In the aftermath of his recent visionary experience and subsequent conversion to Catholicism, Lamantia had decided that his own poetry was not worthy. He considered his work trite and maybe even blasphemous. His choice of Hoffman's poems was perfect, and they helped set the tone for the evening. Kerouac said that they had him "crying inside with laughter." They were laconic and surreal, unlike anything the listeners had heard at a poetry reading before.

The second poet to read was Michael McClure, the youngest at twenty-three and physically the most striking of the group. He began his set by reading a poem by Robert Duncan. McClure had grown to respect the clarity of perception in Robert's work, and since Duncan was out of town, Michael represented him well. Following Duncan's poem, Michael read his own powerful "For the Death of 100 Whales." It was a sobering poem that detailed a horrifying example of man's cruelty to other creatures. McClure had just read that the military had used a pod of whales off the coast of Iceland for target practice. The story had broken his heart. Protecting the environment was not yet an issue of public interest during the 1950s. Through his poetry, McClure would guide readers to a new respect for the planet.

Philip Whalen, Snyder's shy classmate from Reed, was the next poet to take the stage. The poems he read were distinguished by their "very personal relaxed, learned mystical-anarchic" nature, as Ginsberg would later describe them. Whalen was the nearest person anyone had ever seen to an American Buddhist Bodhisattva, and his poetry had an air of dry humor to it. His poem "If You're So Smart, Why Ain't You Rich?" closed the first set on just the right note of whimsical insight, and the house erupted in applause.

After the intermission, during which Kerouac passed around some gallon jugs of cheap wine, Ginsberg got up to read. Jack encouraged Allen with shouts and whoops in the manner of a raucous bebop jazz performance. Allen was slightly drunk from the wine himself, which probably helped give him the courage to read *Howl,* and at times he nearly broke down into tears. At the time of the reading, Allen had only completed one part of what would become a longer, four-part poem, but the section that he read was powerful enough to shock and electrify the audience. In the short time he read he managed to combine the long lines associated with Walt Whitman with rhythms derived from Bach and bebop. He tied the composition together with strong words that condemned the dehumanizing nature of America's corporate culture. Many in the audience were aware that Ginsberg was making poetry out of his innermost thoughts in a way that had never been done before. Nothing was hidden behind a veil of poetic rhetoric. All his feelings were laid bare, undiluted and direct, exposing society's raw nerve to a group of attentive listeners.

As Gary Snyder, the evening's final poet, rose to read, it seemed that he would never be able to follow Ginsberg's transcendent performance. Fortunately, Snyder did not try to compete with Ginsberg's emotional buildup in his work. He exhibited his own slow, deliberate, intellectual style that focused on every word in his poems instead of the sum of the parts. Emphasizing their different personalities, Gary stood on the stage in his hiking boots, a sharp contrast to Allen, who had read in a jacket and tie. More important, Gary's poetry was strong enough to hold its own. He read parts of his epic *Myths and Texts* and ended with "A Berry Feast," a mixture of Native American lore with a wisdom that came from his Buddhist meditation practice.

Much of Gary's work echoed McClure's concerns about the environment and reinforced the idea that the earth was indeed in peril. That night, all of the readers proved to be relevant to an audience eager for something fresh and original. All the poets who took the stage seemed to be larger than life, and each in his own way had certainly heeded Ezra Pound's suggestion to "make it new."

At the conclusion of the evening, it was obvious to everyone in attendance that new energy had been infused into the stagnant world of poetry. This impression was not lost on Ferlinghetti, who immediately wrote to Ginsberg paraphrasing Emerson to Whitman: "I greet you at the beginning of a great career. When do I get the manuscript?" Even though Ginsberg and Ferlinghetti had been discussing the possibility of a book of Allen's poems for months, the reading at the Six Gallery fired Lawrence's enthusiasm. He wanted the new poem to be the centerpiece of Allen's book, which would be *Howl and Other Poems,* the fourth in the City Lights Pocket Poets series.

That night the Beat Generation was made whole. This extended family would grow over the next few years to accommodate a few other names, but the group's original nucleus of Kerouac, Ginsberg, and Burroughs was forever united with the San Francisco poets by this reading. In the eyes of the outside world, those links would never be erased. To many who witnessed the event at the Six Gallery, it appeared as if a movement had been born. No matter that every one of the writers had his own individual style and his own unique voice, they were bracketed together forever as the Beat Generation. From that moment on, they would be connected by this pivotal reading and by the magnetic nature of Allen Ginsberg, who had the ability to find common ground among diverse people and bring them together.

While in San Francisco Ginsberg continued to spend a lot of his time reading books in the tiny City Lights shop and got to know Ferlinghetti and the store's manager, Shig Murao, very well. City Lights was one of the first bookstores in the country to encourage readers to linger in the store and read the books. They provided chairs to relax on. As a result, the store became headquarters for the literary community of North Beach, and people would drop in just to see what was new and who else might be there.

When Ferlinghetti put out his own first book a month after the Six Gallery reading, he called it *Pictures of the Gone World*, a hip reference to his love of painting. The critics complained that it wasn't poetry at all, in part because they felt it was too accessible. It was as if they believed that since anyone could pick it up and enjoy it without having a degree in English literature, it must have no intellectual value. Lawrence made it look so effortless that his detractors said that it wasn't worthy of serious consideration. His combination of European sensibilities, allusions to popular culture, and humor made it all too easy to dismiss as lightweight pabulum. In spite of that, his book sold steadily and is still in print today.

At the time of the Six Gallery reading, both Gary Snyder and Philip Whalen had just returned from summer jobs in the mountains. They had spent several summers as fire spotters on the highest peaks of the Cascade Range, enjoying the wilderness solitude that came with their assignments. When Snyder moved to his Berkeley cottage, he began to translate the poetry of Han Shan, a Chinese hermit mountain poet, for his class on East Asian studies at the university, and grew to admire the ancient poet.

The more they got to know one another, the more the young poets found that they had quite a bit in common. Allen was not only interested in Snyder's and Whalen's poetry, and their knowledge of Buddhism, but also in the fact that each had used peyote. Kerouac was attracted to them more because of their common interest in Buddhism and their experience in camping and hiking. He admired the pair for having gone off on Thoreau-style retreats into the pristine mountains, something that he had long dreamed of doing himself. It encouraged him to believe that if Whalen was fit enough to be a fire spotter, he might be able to do it as well. Gary had helped Phil get his first job with the forestry service, and with any luck, Jack could follow his example.

Although born in San Francisco, Gary Snyder had grown up on the western slopes of Washington and Oregon, and at a young age had begun to climb the various volcanic peaks along the Cascade Range in both summer and winter. He was an outdoorsman who loved the quiet beauty of the mountains. It had long been a dream of Jack's to get away from everyone and find a peaceful hermitage; in Gary, he had finally met someone who could give him the practical advice on just how to do it. Together they visited army-navy surplus stores, and Gary taught Jack how to select proper camping equipment. By the time they met, the hiking season was nearing its end, but there was just enough time for Snyder to take Kerouac up into the Sierras near Bridgeport for one trek before the winter snows closed the passes. Jack was thrilled by the experience and described the weekend superbly in *The Dharma Bums*, published in 1958. That book helped inspire a whole generation of younger readers to take to the mountains with their rucksacks, and Japhy Ryder, Jack's name for Snyder in the book, became a role model for young trekkers.

By November, Jack had become brooding and touchy, and, after an argument with Allen, he went back to live in the old flophouse hotels near the train station in San Francisco. Ginsberg and Whalen were asked to read for the Poetry Center at San Francisco State, and Allen even helped teach a class there on poetics. Peter and his brother Lafcadio continued to live apart from Allen in North Beach and had plenty of their own difficulties. Peter's heart was in the right place, but he was ill equipped to take care of a rebellious teenager who was schizophrenic to boot. One bright spot was that after repeated debate, Peter was able to convince Lafcadio not to drop out of high school as he had planned to do.

Even though he was now trying to follow the path of Edgar Cayce, Neal Cassady remained the same old con man he had always been. That November Neal convinced Natalie Jackson to impersonate Carolyn so that they could withdraw ten thousand dollars from Carolyn's bank account. Neal's plan was to bet the money on a sure thing at the racetrack and have Natalie return the ten thousand dollars before Carolyn ever knew that it was missing. Natalie forged

Carolyn's name successfully, but Neal's sure thing at the track turned out to be anything but, and he lost all the money.

Even at her best, Jackson was a fragile creature with plenty of emotional problems, so the anxiety that this turn of events caused was too much for her. She worried continually about going to jail for check forgery and what would happen to her there. Neal was much more blasé about it. Although he could see that it was troubling Natalie, he knew that he could talk his way out of anything with Carolyn. One night, worried that Natalie might hurt herself, Neal asked Kerouac to stay with her while he went to work. Jack turned out to be an unreliable custodian and while he napped, Natalie slashed her wrists. Jack awoke to an apartment drenched in blood and called the police for help. As the sirens drew near in the street below, Natalie became even more hysterical, certain that the police were not coming to help her, but to take her to jail for stealing Carolyn's money. To escape she ran to the roof and threw herself over the parapet to the sidewalk four floors below. Jack and Neal were so afraid of becoming personally involved that they couldn't even bring themselves to identify Natalie's body, and the newspapers initially reported her as "an unidentified blonde woman" who had plunged to her death.

Shaken, Jack retreated with Neal to Carolyn's house in Los Gatos before returning to the calm of his mother's kitchen in North Carolina. By Christmastime he had also settled in Rocky Mount to spend the winter with his sister's family. Over the holidays, when his mother and the rest of the family went to visit relatives, he found himself alone in the little house near a stand of pine trees. He sat at the kitchen table and began to write *Visions of Gerard,* the sad story of the death of his nine-year-old brother thirty years earlier. In addition to *Visions,* Jack worked on a half-dozen other books and ideas in a creative burst of energy stimulated by the recent tragedy of Natalie's suicide.

During the whole of 1955, Burroughs remained in Tangier alternating between shooting junk and trying to kick his habit. That summer he became friendly with Paul Bowles, the author of *The Shel-tering Sky,* who lived outside the medina, and his wife, Jane, herself a prominent writer. The two men shared an interest in both drugs and boys and they spent a good deal of time swapping tales. Bowles's stories always were about the inhabitants and customs of Morocco, but Bill never had much interest in local color. He seemed to live in his own world, isolating himself from his immediate surroundings as best he could. It was through Bowles that Burroughs met an artist by the name of Brion Gysin that summer. Initially, they didn't seem to have much in common, but years later they would become best of friends.

Even during his worst bouts of addiction and the even worse cures that followed, Bill was able to write. In a letter to Ginsberg, he tried to explain: "I am trying to create something that will have a life of its own, that can put me in real danger." He was referring to his prose style, but it might as well have been a reference to his personal life.

Unfortunately, the treatments Bill underwent to kick his habit never seemed to have a lasting effect. In 1956 he learned of a doctor in London named John Yerbury Dent, who was reporting fabulous results with addicts. Dr. Dent had discovered a cure using apomor-phine, a derivative of morphine but nonaddictive, that seemed to have real promise. Burroughs asked his parents for five hundred dol-lars for the two-week cure and headed off to England for treatment.

He had been following the adventures of his friends in California through letters from Ginsberg and Kerouac, but Bill had become too strung out on junk to do anything more than wish that they would visit. Although he continued to write routines each day, the stories seemed disconnected, and he couldn't summon up the energy needed to shape them into anything marketable. Page after page was strewn about his room, waiting for someone to come edit them.

On January 1, 1956, the lease on the Montgomery Street apart-ment expired, and Peter Orlovsky and his brother moved to a low-income housing project called Turner Terrace, south of downtown

San Francisco. As often as was possible, Ginsberg visited them there, leaving the cottage in Berkeley more and more to Phil Whalen, who had moved in when Kerouac had moved out. He liked the area and found a job nearby at the university.

Late in January, Snyder and Ginsberg took off for the Pacific Northwest for a winter outing into the mountains. Allen had heard so much about Snyder's skills as a woodsman from Kerouac that he wanted to experience the great outdoors with Gary for himself. After exploring the city of Seattle and then hiking into the evergreen forests, they returned to Portland where they gave a reading at Gary's alma mater, Reed College. The pair visited with Lloyd Reynolds, a well-known professor who had taught not only Whalen and Snyder, but also another poet and friend of Gary's named Lew Welch. Snyder was happy to show Ginsberg around the natural world that he loved so much, and although Allen wasn't much of an outdoorsman, he loved the camaraderie of this type of fellowship. He even developed a bit of a crush on Snyder in the process.

Soon after they returned to Berkeley, Gary packed his things and moved to a small cabin in Mill Valley in preparation for his move to Japan. The cabin was on the property of Locke McCorkle, one of Snyder's fellow Buddhist practitioners at the American Academy of Asian Studies. He lived with his family in the house below the cabin in a manner that presaged the next decade's hippie movement. From Marin-An, as Gary came to call his little cabin, he corresponded with Kerouac in North Carolina and invited him to visit once again and stay with him. Jack had already filled out the paperwork that would lead to a job that summer as a fire spotter on Desolation Peak. Spending time in the Bay Area seemed like a good stepping-stone, and he took Gary up on the offer.

Word of the momentous success of the Six Gallery reading was widespread; the literary community clamored for an encore performance. The Town Hall Theater in Berkeley offered to host a reenactment of the event on the night of March 18, 1956. All of the original participants were there with the exception of Philip Lamantia, who had already returned to Mexico to immerse himself in his study of the Cora Indians. The Berkeley event was well organized and much better publicized than the original, and a larger crowd attended. The producers put Robert LaVigne's artwork on display in the lobby and since it was a theater, the lighting and sound systems were professional. This time they remembered to record the reading, something the organizers had forgotten the first time, and excerpts from this second performance were made into a record album. News had been spreading throughout the Bay Area about a renaissance in poetry that was under way, and the second reading helped cement the reputations of those poets as leaders of that new movement.

Chapter 11

Desolation and Loneliness

In the meantime, Allen Ginsberg had been drifting from job to job, washing dishes and handling baggage, while he continued to work on his manuscript for publication. By the time Ferlinghetti was ready to publish, Allen had finished three more parts of *Howl* to go with a dozen other shorter poems. While working on his own poetry, Allen tried to interest some publishers in Snyder's book, *Myths and Texts*. Gary had read from the manuscript at the Six Gallery and put the finishing touches on it at his Mill Valley cabin. No matter how hard he persisted, Allen could still not get editors interested in his friend's writings and made little progress on behalf of Gary with either City Lights or New York publishers. It did not dampen Allen's enthusiasm, as is revealed when he wrote to introduce him to poet Charles Olson. He boasted that Snyder "took a lot of peyote and knows Chinese and Japanese, and is a great cocksman and ex hitchhiker and logger and is very learned and digs Wobblies, the Zen shot is like the wobblies and he wants a rucksack revolution of Dharma bum poets."

For the time being, Gary was not concerned about publication. He was working on a new project. While attending a series of lectures in San Francisco by the Japanese painter Saburo Hasegawa, Snyder had hit upon the idea of writing a long poem that would transmit through words the same spiritual effect that Japanese landscapes did with paint. His new epic work would take forty years to complete and eventually be published as *Mountains and Rivers Without End.*

At the end of March, Jack Kerouac returned once more to the Bay Area. His intention was to make notes about Snyder for a new book that he envisioned as a *Visions of Gary,* modeled along the lines of his recent book-length studies of Neal and Gerard, and the aborted one on Burroughs. Living with Gary in his tiny cabin on the mountainside turned out to be perfect for Jack. With the hero of his story nearby for reference, he was able to study his subject as much as he liked. When he needed a break from writing, he could hike through the redwood forest or talk with Gary late into the night about Buddhism. Every weekend Marin-An became the center for giant parties around a campfire that burned all night. Their new friends made the trip over from San Francisco bringing wine, marijuana, and phonograph records. Their idyll together lasted little more than a month, because on May 6, 1956, on the heels of one last monumental three-day party, Gary boarded the freighter that would take him to Japan. There his immediate plans were to study under Miura Isshu Roshi at Shokoku-ji, an ancient Buddhist Temple in Kyoto.

By the time Snyder left the country, Gregory Corso was making plans to visit California himself. After Harvard, he had gone to visit his girlfriend, Sura, in South Carolina. There, under her parents' watchful eyes, he had tried unsuccessfully to write a novel. Gregory found that he lacked Kerouac's physical stamina and wasn't able to sit and work creatively for long periods. His genius was for the quick flashes of inspiration that imaginatively brought together unlikely words and phrases that made his poetry so remarkable. Sura was eager to get away from home, so when she left for Europe, Gregory took Ginsberg up on his open invitation to come west. Allen had told him about all the new poets and the great times they were sharing together in San Francisco. Without writing to tell Allen that he was on his way, Gregory caught the next bus out of town. Late that spring, he made one more trip to Cambridge, picked up additional copies of *The Vestal Lady on Brattle,* and then headed west to find out what Allen and Jack were up to.

Corso was hungry for success and longed to be recognized as a talented writer. At the time, he had plenty of energy, even if writing a prolonged project like a novel was more than he could accomplish. Since his creativity seemed to come in spurts, practice and discipline could not help him. Anyway, he was having too much fun enjoying life to hide in a room and write for weeks at a time.

As Snyder was boarding his ship for Japan, Ginsberg was down at the waterfront himself. By the spring of 1956, Allen had come to the end of his student days and had all but given up the idea of getting a graduate degree. Now that Ferlinghetti was about to publish his book, he thought he would wait and see what developed after publication. In the meantime, he needed to make some real money so that he could live through the summer without financial worries. The only way that he knew to make quick money without returning to the daily grind of market research was in the merchant marine. In May he signed on to the USNS *Sgt. Jack J. Pendelton* as a yeoman-storekeeper. The ship was in the harbor being fitted to supply the bases on the DEW Line in the Arctic Circle just as soon as the ice broke up that summer.

A few days before Allen's ship was to weigh anchor, he received a letter from his father. Louis told him that his mother, Naomi, had just passed away in Pilgrim State Mental Hospital on Long Island. "As I saw her coffin lowered into the hospitable earth, I thought that now she would at last have peace and rest," his father wrote. Allen was stunned. No other person in his life had ever meant as much to him as his mother, and even though he had witnessed her protracted withdrawal from human contact, he never anticipated that death could come to her so soon. He wept inconsolably.

Following his father's advice, Allen had decided not to return for the funeral for financial reasons. The trip would have been expensive and also would have disrupted his planned working voyage. Louis felt that the trip was unnecessary, but Allen's inability to say good-bye to her would haunt him for years. He made a mental note to himself then that he would write a poem to memorialize her passing.

At least Naomi would no longer suffer her mental torture, and for that he was grateful. In addition to the sudden shock of losing his mother, Allen was surprised to learn that she had left him one thousand dollars in her will. That windfall, along with the money he would earn on the summer's voyage to the Arctic, would be more than enough to pay for his passage to Europe and northern Africa. There he hoped to stay for an extended visit with Burroughs and Ansen. Two years earlier, when he visited the Mayan ruins in Mexico, he had promised himself that he would compare them to all the ancient monuments of Europe. His small inheritance now assured him of the necessary means to travel.

Louis Ginsberg had been divorced from Naomi for nearly a decade at the time of her death, and since she had no close family or friends left besides Allen and Eugene, she was buried in a cemetery on the grounds of the hospital. The hospital officials had not performed a Jewish ceremony, and the Mourner's Kaddish, a fundamental Hebrew prayer, was never recited for her. To the gravediggers, she was just another sad, lonely case buried in a potter's field.

As Snyder and Ginsberg were preparing to ship out, Robert Creeley, a poet and friend of Robert Duncan and Kenneth Rexroth, happened to arrive in San Francisco. Creeley was teaching in Albuquerque after having spent a year at Black Mountain College, an experimental liberal arts school in the mountains of North Carolina. He had gone to Black Mountain to study poetics under Charles Olson, the Melville scholar and author of *The Maximus Poems*. Olson was the inventor of projective verse, a type of free-form poetry that ignores formal structure and relies on a poet's pattern of breathing to determine line breaks and pauses. At Black Mountain, Bob had taken on the duties of editor of the *Black Mountain Review*. In that capacity, he had already corresponded with many of the San Francisco poets, although this was to be the first time that he would meet some of them face-to-face. Their letters had made him curious about what was happening in the city, and he had come to find out for himself. Rexroth had told him all about the renaissance under way there, and another friend, poet Ed Dorn, had offered to put him up at his apartment.

Creeley's reputation as a heavy drinker and a womanizer had preceded him. He liked to have a good time but was known to have a bad temper when drunk. That often led to fights and brawls, even among friends. He spent a total of two months in the city, a period of one unruly party after another. On the day of his arrival, Rexroth threw a dinner party for him, to which Bob arrived already drunk. Later that same night he met Ginsberg for the first time in a North Beach bar. Allen told him about his friends Burroughs, Corso, and Kerouac, and they discussed the merits of Charles Olson's highly influential projective verse until dawn. The next day Creeley visited Michael McClure who was editing a magazine of his own called *Ark II Moby I*. The two editors traded suggestions for new, unknown poets worthy of publication.

Ginsberg soon decided to introduce Creeley to Kerouac and arranged for them to meet at a local bar. They were both pretty drunk, and Bob was confused because he thought that Jack was the person who had shot his wife in Mexico City. A day or two later, after learning that Kerouac was not Burroughs, their friendship really took off. Since both men were from New England, they felt that they shared much in common. Creeley also liked Snyder and Whalen when he met them later that same week. After a fistfight with his friend Dorn, Bob decided to move to Kerouac's place in Mill Valley. There the two continued their literary discussions fortified with a good deal of booze.

Although they were both well on their way to becoming alcoholics, the difference between Jack and Bob was that Creeley was a violent drunk. Jack liked to argue and debate, but he was a gentle man. Even though he was a well-built athlete, he made it a point never to hurt anyone physically. Creeley's brawling was his way of testing a person, to find out what they were really made of. During their parties at the cabin, both Jack and Bob loved to pound percussion on pots and pans and neither of them minded when Allen and Peter danced around the campfire naked. Although Bob was straight and nearly as shy as Jack was, it didn't keep him from enjoying the antics of those who were less inhibited.

In the wake of Snyder's farewell party, Jack and Bob escorted him to his ship. Not wanting to end the good times, they dropped into the Cellar bar while they were in the city to listen to jazz. As usual, Bob became rowdy, and the two were thrown out. In the course of events, the bouncer knocked a tooth through Creeley's lip. The police were called, and Creeley wound up in jail for the night when he threatened more violence. Jack walked all the way back across the Golden Gate Bridge to Mill Valley alone, but at least that sobered him up. After Creeley left town, Kerouac stayed on in Snyder's cabin until it was time for him to go into the mountains to begin his lookout job that summer.

During that spring, the parties continued every weekend and at one of these fests, they all met Bob Kaufman, a young black poet who hailed from New Orleans. They liked him at once, not the least because he brought along peyote and jazz records for the whole group to enjoy. Like many of them, Kaufman was a veteran of merchant marine duty and had worked on freighters from time to time. He displayed his unique literary talents through improvisation, and he usually created his poetry spontaneously, at the time of delivery. The disadvantage of his impromptu verse was that he didn't bother to write it down before or after performing it. Because it was completely oral, not many of his earliest poems survive. His poetry has been compared to scat singing or jazz riffs, and is recalled as having remarkable strength and beauty. His use of rhythm and sound was infectious and part of a growing movement in the city that combined poetry with jazz in one form or another.

Even though he enjoyed himself and made many friends, Creeley was not comfortable living in an urban environment. He much preferred life in the country, so he didn't stay long in San Francisco. When he headed back to New Mexico, he made the mistake of taking Kenneth Rexroth's wife, Marthe, with him. It wasn't the first time that he had become sexually involved with the wife of a friend, and he lived to regret it. Marthe had been thinking about leaving Kenneth, and Bob provided her with the perfect opportunity. Their affair had begun when they were both working at the San Francisco Poetry Center doing temporary office work.

Rexroth was distraught when he realized that Marthe had abandoned him, and since Creeley had been living with Kerouac in the cabin, Rexroth placed much of the blame on Jack for aiding Creeley in the seduction of his wife. For once, Jack was completely innocent, but that didn't stop Kenneth from changing his opinion about the entire group of younger poets. Formerly he had championed Kerouac and the Beat Generation, but after this event he wrote several scathing attacks against them. For some unknown reason, when Rexroth's wife later returned to him, he was able to forgive Creeley, but he never got over his hatred for Kerouac.

By the time Marthe returned to San Francisco, Jack had already left the Bay Area. He headed for the Skagit Valley in Washington state on his way to his fire-spotter job on Desolation Ridge. In the cool days of June, he hiked up to his isolated watchtower, looking forward to a nice, quiet break after the antics of spring. He planned to spend his time in contemplation, meditation, and writing. It was debilitating to maintain the wild pace he often craved, and he always needed time away from the distractions of friends and taverns. This job provided a good opportunity to earn some money until his books were published, although his hopes for publication had been fading over the past five years. With one rejection after another, he was beginning to think that none of the manuscripts he carried around with him would ever make it into print.

Jack's desire to escape to remote locations was never far from his mind, and he continually looked for someplace out of the way where he could hide from his ex-wife, Joan Haverty. She was still threatening to take him to court for the nonsupport of their daughter, Jan. That summer Jack also wanted to get his drinking under control, but the total abstinence that the mountaintop demanded worried him. It was physically impossible to carry in enough liquor to keep him going for the summer, so withdrawal was something he knew he would have to face if he took the job. It appeared that a few months in retreat might do him good, so he pushed on up the steep trail. Little did he realize that Desolation Peak not only would give him the break from society that he needed, but would also shake his innermost beliefs. Once he got to his lookout station, he had a clear view of the rugged Mount Hozomeen on the horizon. It reminded him of an evil fortress and became the subject of nightmares that would haunt him for years.

Just as everyone was leaving San Francisco, Corso arrived intending to stay on Ginsberg's floor for a few months. Since he hadn't bothered to write ahead to announce his arrival, he didn't have the right to be upset, but he was. He felt abandoned and contacted Allen on his ship to tell him that he was disgusted and that he was planning to pack up and go back east. Allen encouraged him to stay and reminded him that, since everyone was employed only for the summer, he should stay put until Allen and Jack returned. In the meantime, he suggested that Corso make the best of the beautiful city and meet some of their new friends. Gregory wrote back, "Don't like San Francisco. Reminds me of hip mid-western town," but he waited nonetheless.

Gregory had brought along twenty copies of his *Vestal Lady* to sell, so Lawrence Ferlinghetti was the first person he looked up. Corso's books were placed in the window of City Lights, and they sold out fast. The interest in his book encouraged Ferlinghetti to consider publishing Gregory's poetry in his new series along with Allen, but first Corso would have to write enough new poems to fill the book. Making the rounds to visit Allen's contacts, Gregory went out to Potrero Hill to meet the Orlovsky brothers and they quickly hit it off. Not everyone shared Allen's high opinion of Gregory, and by all accounts, he was not an easy person to get along with. Before long he had managed to antagonize both McClure and Cassady. Via letters to the Arctic, he informed Ginsberg that he didn't care much for Neal Cassady, Robert LaVigne, or even Henry Miller. He even questioned Allen, "Why hasn't my name ever appeared in any of your poems? You goofed," once more playing the guilt card. As usual, Gregory was able to find a woman to support him while he stayed in her Masonic Avenue home and waited for Allen's return from Alaska.

Over the course of the summer, Ferlinghetti and Ginsberg communicated back and forth, working on the proofs for *Howl and Other Poems*, and by September the first copies had arrived from Lawrence's printer in England. The book wasn't the only good news to come from England that summer. They were delighted to hear that Dr. Dent's apomorphine cure been successful for Burroughs. He was clean and intended to stay that way. He also reported that he didn't care much for London's overregulated life, so he was intending to move on to stay with Ansen in Venice. At least from Ansen's report, life in Italy appeared to be much more relaxed.

Not caring much about the great art and fabulous architecture of Venice, Burroughs moved on. By end of the summer, he had sailed back to Tangier, where he began working in earnest on the stories that would soon be gathered into *The Naked Lunch*. He established a pattern for working that suited him perfectly. He would get up around noon each day and begin to write after breakfast, often typing well into the night, throwing the completed sheets onto the floor as he pulled them from the typewriter. Encouraged by the report that Burroughs had finally broken his drug dependency, Allen suggested that he, Corso, and Kerouac might visit Bill in Morocco and help him organize his manuscript, which littered the floor of his small room.

During that same summer, while Kerouac was roughing it in the mountains of the Pacific Northwest and Ginsberg was sailing along the Alaskan coast, Snyder was adapting to his austere, new life in a Kyoto monastery. He wrote to Allen that he had found the "Japan of old arty temples and a few stern monks" that he had been looking for. He claimed that he enjoyed the sacrifices required for monastic life. He and his fellow monks had little to eat, slept only a few hours each night, and put in long, hard days of work. It made him more aware that the whole point of Buddhism was not to avoid suffering, but to learn to accept it as an inescapable part of life. When he had time off, he went mountain climbing in the northern hills, so Gary wrote to them, delighted to discover that Japan was everything he hoped it would be.

Ginsberg spent long hours under the Arctic's midnight sun working on the proofs for his City Lights book. As his freighter eased its way through the foggy Bering Strait just a few miles from the coast of Russia, his mother's native land, he threw a few coins into the sea in her memory. He reflected that he had promised to write a poem to commemorate her life, but the idea was still incubating in his mind. In his journal he noted that he would write an "Elegy for Mama" as soon as he had the time and the inspiration.

Although Jack had been looking forward to his summer on the mountaintop, it had not turned out to be a rewarding experience. With so much time to kill sitting on his isolated perch, he did manage to write quite a bit and worked on several old ideas. He developed the beginnings of a new book, *Desolation Angels,* which was well under way by the time he hiked back down the trail to civilization. But what he remembered most about that summer was the lack of alcohol, the endless boredom, and the sleepless nights, interrupted by horrible dreams whenever he did happen to nod off. After two months, Kerouac collected his pay from the forest service headquarters and headed straight for the bars in North Beach. He had gone too long without liquor and its absence weighed on him. As soon as he hit town, he made up for abstinence quickly.

Only two weeks later, he left San Francisco for Mexico City, still wondering whether *On the Road* would ever be published. Malcolm Cowley, who was a member of the Lost Generation and a friend of Hemingway and Fitzgerald, had tried to edit Jack's book so that Viking Press would accept it, but a letter waited for Kerouac in which Cowley suggested that Jack should combine *On the Road* with *Doctor Sax* and *Maggie Cassidy* to form one large book. Jack was furious and rejected this new suggestion. It helped lower his opinion of all editors and publishers even more.

As the Arctic Sea began to freeze again, Ginsberg's ship headed back to San Francisco and once more most of the old group assembled in North Beach. With Allen back to play the role of impresario, he signed Corso up for a few readings around the Bay Area. At one of the many parties they were invited to, Gregory made a positive impression on the guest of honor, Randall Jarrell. Jarrell was touring in his capacity as poetry consultant for the Library of Congress and was looking for new talent. His position was the closest thing America had at the time to a poet laureate. Jarrell was fascinated by Corso's biography. He saw him as a young man with no roots, self-educated in prison, and the creator of marvelous poetry. By the end of his visit, Jarrell had invited Gregory to stop and visit him at his home in Washington, should he ever find himself in the nation's capital. Jarrell wanted to record Corso reading his poetry for the Library of Congress's archive project. Since his days in Cambridge where he had associated with key writers like Archibald MacLeish, Gregory had wanted to break into the academy and Jarrell seemed to be offering a golden opportunity to do just that.

Chapter 12

Censorship and Vindication

Before seeing what Washington had to offer, though, Gregory and Allen had a few commitments to meet on the West Coast. Allen had scheduled them both to read in Los Angeles at a benefit for a literary magazine. The whole group planned to leave San Francisco one by one that fall and reconvene in Mexico City a few weeks later. Kerouac hopped a freight train and was soon followed by the Orlovsky brothers, who took a bus. Allen and Gregory set out on the road, hitchhiking, arranging to meet up with Peter and Lafcadio at the Mexican border. Together they'd cross the mountains into Mexico City.

The reading in LA turned out to be an especially memorable event. While Corso was speaking, a drunk in the audience got up and challenged him to a fight. Allen stood up and tried to defend Gregory, but the belligerent drunk asked him what he was trying to prove. Allen replied that "nakedness" was his goal. That confused the surly drunk who asked him what he meant, giving Allen the chance to strip naked on stage. That was the poet's job, Allen said, to appear naked before his audience. It stopped the drunk in his tracks and gave Allen the opportunity to disrobe, something he had wanted to do ever since he had heard that Robert Duncan had done the same thing during a theatrical performance in San Francisco. This story about Allen circulated and grew with each retelling. After he became famous, the media routinely reported that Ginsberg always stripped naked at his public readings, when in fact this was the only time he ever did so.

Allen was elated when City Lights released *Howl and Other Poems*. Holding the new book in his hands, Allen wanted to believe that all of his dreams were about to be realized at last. He imagined it as the first publication in a series of books that would include all of Kerouac's novels and the poetry of Corso, Snyder, Whalen, and the rest. He even hoped that with their collective help William Burroughs might be able to get his manuscripts together to create another book of his own.

It was November when they all rejoined Kerouac on Mexico City's Orizaba Street. Neal Cassady was missing, but Allen hoped that soon even he might jump in his car and drive down to be with them. With Neal, the old circle would be nearly complete, lacking only Burroughs. (It was impossible for Bill to risk returning to Mexico, since he was still wanted by the authorities for the death of Joan.) Never wanting to miss an opportunity to meet other poets, they all went to visit Denise Levertov at her home in Guadalajara for an overnight visit. Impressed by her hospitality, they all agreed that she was a great woman and that her poetry was worth taking notice of.

For Corso the Mexican leg of the trip proved to be one of the most productive periods in his career. He wrote all the time, or at least whenever he and Lafcadio weren't vying like children for the seat next to the bus window. Ginsberg reported to Kerouac that Gregory was in the middle of a "golden inspired period" where great poetry flowed from his fingertips. Together the gang toured the city, visiting the Aztec pyramids and the floating gardens. Gregory even took time to stop in at the Mexico City zoo where he was surprised to find ordinary American cows, and even that became the subject of a short poem.

After spending a month in Mexico, they all agreed it was time to move on. They spotted an ad in a local paper announcing that someone wanted company on the long drive to New York City, so Jack, Allen, Peter, and Lafcadio set out with the driver. Sura's father had promised to send Corso an airline ticket for his return so he stayed behind, expecting the ticket to arrive at any moment. He wanted to fly to Washington, DC, in style, eager to take Jarrell up on his offer to visit him. After a delay of a few weeks, Gregory received his ticket and met Sura in Washington, but she stayed only a day or two before leaving for Europe. They promised that as soon as Gregory could get some money together, he would follow her to Paris.

Randall Jarrell and his wife liked Corso, but when Kerouac stopped to visit on his way from New York to his sister's in Rocky Mount, the quiet life of the Jarrell family was disrupted. Jack and Gregory broke into their best whiskey and drank it all. Then they made paintings for Jarrell, which Gregory insisted on nailing directly to the walls of their house. When Gregory left to party with Allen in New York on New Year's Eve, Jarrell politely asked him not to return. That put an end to Corso's dreams of entering the ivory towers of academe.

After the first day of 1957, Ginsberg, Corso, Kerouac, and Orlovsky took a bus to Rutherford, New Jersey, to visit William Carlos Williams. Allen wanted to introduce his friends to Williams and to thank him for writing an introduction for *Howl*. He gave him a copy of the book, which he inscribed warmly. Allen knew that Williams would enjoy meeting his quirky friends and in spite of Kerouac's drinking a bit too much, they all had a great time. Jack, who was then living with a girlfriend named Helen Weaver, had relapsed into heavy drinking whenever he was away from his mother's house. Helen's therapist told her that Kerouac was going to drag her down with him if she didn't do something. She ended their relationship.

During his January stay in New York with Helen, Kerouac finally received word through his agent, Sterling Lord, that Viking
had agreed to sign a contract for the publication of *On the Road*.
While Jack took care of the publishing details, Corso, Ginsberg, and
Orlovsky made their travel arrangements. Gregory wanted to catch
up with Sura before she left Paris, so he booked passage to France,
while Allen and Peter decided to stop off in Tangier to visit Burroughs first. As soon as Jack's meetings with Viking were wrapped
up, he borrowed his two-hundred-dollar fare from Allen and took a
Yugoslavian freighter to Morocco. With the money he had inherited
from his mother, Allen was able to bankroll the trip for his friends,
and planned to go after them as soon as he and Peter wrapped up
some loose ends.

When Kerouac arrived in Tangier, he put his skills as a speed typist to good use helping Burroughs organize all the routines destined
for *The Naked Lunch*. Over the next few months, the preparation
of that manuscript became a communal project for everyone. Burroughs had been writing continually, but he lacked the focus and
ambition needed to assemble a unified book out of all his stories. In
March, Allen and Peter arrived and checked into a tiny room on the
floor above Burroughs at the Hotel Villa Muniria. By the time they
arrived, Kerouac was already bored with Morocco. It was exotic but
with Bill in one of his reclusive periods, he had not spent much time
with Jack. Even though young male prostitutes were cheap in Tangier, female prostitutes were not. It was the opposite of Mexico and,
as a result, Jack was lonely. By the time Allen arrived, Kerouac was
anxious to move on to Paris, so when Jack left on the ferry for the
Continent, Allen and Peter took over his larger room in the hotel.

With Jack's French Canadian background, he expected to find
Paris to be a friendlier city than Tangier. Since Corso was already
there, Jack naturally thought that he could stay with Gregory for
a few weeks and enjoy Parisian bohemian life cheaply. Corso had
arrived in France just in time to see Sura off on the next leg of her

trip to India and by the time Kerouac came to town, Gregory was involved with yet another woman who was paying his bills. He was reluctant to host Jack, fearing that his patron would object to having another mouth to feed. In fact, none of Kerouac's contacts in Paris was willing to take him in, so he had to use his own money to stay in a hotel. Jack was not at his best during this trip. He admitted in a letter that because of his ragged appearance, people thought he was a drunken bum, and they didn't want him around. Parisians looked down on Jack's attempts to speak to them in his Canuck patois. He did not receive the welcome he had expected and soon he abandoned his idea of a longer stay. He headed for home.

Near the end of March, as Ginsberg and Orlovsky were settling into life in Tangier, dramatic events began to unfold in California that were destined to radically change Allen's life. On March 25, the San Francisco inspector of Customs, Chester McPhee, seized the second printing of *Howl and Other Poems* just as it was arriving from Ferlinghetti's British printer, Villiers. Justifying his embargo on the book, McPhee was quoted in a newspaper as saying, "You wouldn't want your children to come across it." To circumvent this problem, Ferlinghetti arranged for a new printing of *Howl* to be made in the United States. That way Customs would not have jurisdiction over the book. In May, after copies of the American edition of the book went on sale, the United States Attorney decided not to proceed with the Customs department's case against the book. Once the seized copies were returned to City Lights, the matter should have been forgotten.

Throughout this process, only a few articles had appeared in the press about the seizure. A handful of interested people knew about the case locally, but if nothing else had happened, the public's attention might never have been focused on *Howl* or Ginsberg or the Beat Generation. But developments were about to change all that.

With five thousand copies of the book in print, it would have taken Ferlinghetti a long time to sell them all. In fact, Allen feared that Lawrence might never have been able to recover his investment if it had not been for the San Francisco Police Department. Their juvenile bureau agreed with the Customs agent that this book was obscene and would be harmful if it fell into the hands of children. Despite the U.S. Attorney's reluctance to prosecute the book, the police department raided City Lights on June 3, 1957, intent on censoring it themselves. They arrested Lawrence Ferlinghetti and the bookstore's manager, Shig Murao.

Ferlinghetti had anticipated attacks from censors even before he published the book. To be prepared, he had already secured a promise from the American Civil Liberties Union to defend City Lights if the government interfered with the store's right to publish the book. Quickly, the ACLU bailed Lawrence and Shig out of jail and began to build a case in their defense.

From that moment on, the press covered the story in great detail. Not everyone agreed with the police about censorship. Many people did not think that every book published had to be "safe" for children. Others questioned whether it should be the police who determined if something was obscene. Obviously, a small poetry collection like *Howl* was not the type of book a child would pick up and read anyway, and if one did, would he or she even understand it well enough to be adversely affected by it? The courts had recently ruled that not everything had to be written for children, but the district attorney ignored that and pressed on, bringing the case to trial.

The situation was an outrage to the literary community, and the national press took notice of the controversy. Some reporters were already aware of the new spirit of artistic freedom and vitality that was growing in places like North Beach and Greenwich Village, and the *Howl* case provided them with a context in which to discuss not only censorship, but the emerging avant-garde as well.

In San Francisco the case attracted the attention of noted figures like Kenneth Rexroth, Berkeley professor Mark Schorer, and Walter Van Tilberg Clark, the author of the best-selling *Ox-Bow Incident*.

Though still upset with many in the Beat group because of his wife's affair with Creeley, Rexroth put those grudges aside to fight for their First Amendment rights. The country was beginning to recover from the communist witch hunts of Senator Joseph McCarthy that had already destroyed the lives of many writers and artists; a new creative era was under way. In the wake of the artistic stagnation under McCarthyism, many Americans wanted the freedom to exchange ideas freely once again, and it was apparent that a renaissance was coming to all the arts.

The literary community rose in support of Ferlinghetti, and others began to speak up on both sides of the issue, splitting as always into liberal and conservative factions. The trial took place that August before a standing-room-only audience in a San Francisco courtroom a few blocks from the City Lights bookstore. Newspapers reported the proceedings each day and published editorials, mostly in defense of the First Amendment. The government had difficulty finding credible witnesses to speak against the poem, and as a result, its witnesses proved to be weak and somewhat embarrassing to the prosecution. All of this made for entertaining reading.

The defense waived a trial by jury, and Judge Clayton Horn thus heard the case. That seemed a stroke of bad luck for the defendants, who were more than a bit dubious about Judge Horn's impartiality. The judge, a highly religious man, had recently made headlines when he sentenced two teenage shoplifters to attend a screening of the movie *The Ten Commandments*. As their punishment, they were told to write an essay about their sins. Rulings like that made Ferlinghetti wonder whether he stood a chance, but Judge Horn took the *Howl* case seriously. He did a good deal of research and delved into other censorship cases, even taking the time to read James Joyce's once-banned book, *Ulysses*.

On October 3, 1957, the judge found that *Howl* was not obscene because it had "some redeeming social value." Ferlinghetti was exonerated. The *Howl* case set a precedent allowing other important literary works to be published in America without fear of censorship. Within a few years, Grove Press was able to publish books such as D. H. Lawrence's *Lady Chatterley's Lover* and Henry Miller's *Tropic of Cancer* as a direct result of the *Howl* trial. Banned books would soon become a thing of the past in the United States.

In northern Africa in the spring of 1957, Ginsberg had little contact with Ferlinghetti and the legal proceedings taking place in California. When he had first heard about the seizure, he wondered if he should return to San Francisco and help in the fight but decided against it. He had just arrived in Tangier. In addition to wanting to help Burroughs finish the manuscript of *The Naked Lunch*, Allen really couldn't afford to go back and forth across the Atlantic. Ferlinghetti had assured him that the ACLU was doing all that needed to be done. Ferlinghetti also told him that it was City Lights that was on trial, not Ginsberg, and that he would let him know if they needed him to appear.

In April, shortly after Ginsberg and Orlovsky moved into Kerouac's vacated room at the Villa Muniria, Alan Ansen arrived in Tangier to assist in the editing of *The Naked Lunch*. By that time, all the random pages that Burroughs had strewn about the apartment were stacked and sorted, and weeks were spent putting them in order. Most of the routines were well written and complete, but they didn't hang together to form a linear narrative as in a traditional book; it was still an unorthodox and confusing collection of vignettes. For the next few months, the team spent every day working on the manuscript until it was in a form that they believed an avant-garde publisher might consider. Kerouac had already dropped off several chapters with the Olympia Press when he passed through Paris, so they hoped that interest would develop there. If the publisher of that press, Maurice Girodias, liked what he read, they had more to send him now.

From Paris, Corso wrote to tell Ginsberg and the others that his reunion with Sura had not gone well. Although he said that, "Sura is a little too unreal for me," he did suggest that he, Burroughs, and Ginsberg might still follow her to India, an idea they all considered, but only Ginsberg ever realized. After Kerouac passed through Paris, Gregory had a falling-out with his newest patron, Niccole, and so he took a trip to Barcelona and the south of France to get away. Depressed, he bought a gun and toyed with the idea of suicide. He decided, however, to return to Paris to await the arrival of Ginsberg and Orlovsky.

Kerouac sailed home on a fourth-class packet ship and went straight to his mother's place in Orlando, where she had recently relocated. He stayed only long enough to convince his mother that they should both move to California permanently. She readily agreed and after packing their belongings, they hopped the next bus heading west. Joan Haverty was still trying to track Kerouac down for child support, so Jack thought it best to stay peripatetic. In Berkeley, Philip Whalen, still living in Allen's old cottage, helped Jack and his mother find a cheap apartment in the same neighborhood.

While Jack was in California he saw Neal a few times, but their old camaraderie had faded. Even Carolyn, who had once loved Jack nearly as much as she loved Neal, wrote letters accusing Jack of being a bad influence on Neal. In Kerouac's eyes, Neal had changed. He seemed interested only in women, marijuana, and Edgar Cayce. Less than two months after their arrival, the Kerouac's California sojourn ended as quickly as it had begun. Gabrielle became homesick for her daughter and asked that they return to Florida. Jack agreed, putting an end to their short stay in the west. By July they had settled into a small apartment on Clouser Street in Orlando, close to his sister, Nin.

While Jack's wanderlust was playing out in America, Burroughs and his team of amateur editors had done their best on the manuscript of *The Naked Lunch* in Morocco. They were now beginning to split up and go their separate ways in Europe. Ginsberg's reasons for traveling had been not only to help Burroughs, but also to tour the great cities of the Old World. As long as his money held out, he wanted to see everything that Italy, France, and Spain had to offer.

In June 1957, he and Peter crossed the strait to Spain, planning to travel leisurely to Venice and Paris, where they could stay for free with Ansen and Corso. Burroughs decided that he would travel to Denmark to see his old friend Kells Elvins, who was in Copenhagen then. For Allen, Europe was a dream come true. In each town they visited, he investigated as many museums and ancient monuments as he could. He maintained his daily journal and wrote long letters describing his trip but seemed to have little energy left for poetry.

Peter Orlovsky was relieved to be on the move again after what had been for him an unpleasant stay with Burroughs. After hearing so much about Bill, Peter had been looking forward to meeting Allen's mentor, but Burroughs had taken an instant dislike to Peter. Bill could not understand what Allen saw in Peter aside from his good looks. He regarded Peter as a stupid, shallow, and somewhat dim-witted fellow. No doubt jealousy was at the root of much of the hostility, because Burroughs still harbored a crush on Ginsberg and Peter stood in the way. Peter felt liberated when they stepped off the ferry in Algeciras, Spain.

As he sat in a monastery in Japan, Gary Snyder tried to keep in touch with his closest friends, Whalen and Welch, and his newest friends, Kerouac and Ginsberg. A steady stream of letters flowed to and from Kyoto. Having finished his initial training in Buddhist studies successfully, Gary felt that he needed to take a break and earn some money. In August 1957 he boarded the S.S. *Sappa Creek* in Yokohama and worked his way around the world as a seaman for the next eight months. His long-range plans were to return to his studies in Japan and live on the wages he earned at sea.

While Snyder sailed from port to port, others in the group were traveling around Europe and America. Back in Paris in September Corso had located a hotel that was so cheap he could afford it without having to be dependent on wealthy friends to pay his rent. Guy

Harloff, an artist that Ginsberg had met through Alan Ansen, had recommended a hotel on the Left Bank at 9, rue Git-le-Coeur and Gregory confirmed that it was indeed a bargain. They would come to know it as the "Beat Hotel," where nearly every member of their group would stay at one time or another, but it was Gregory who first stayed there. The hotel was close to the Seine, where Gregory loved to comb the bookstalls for tattered copies of his beloved Shelley and Keats. When he moved in, he believed that his stay there would only be temporary, since he still planned to go to India with Allen and Bill before too long.

After his failed attempt to relocate to California, Jack decided that he needed a break from everyone, his mother included. He headed for the one retreat he had always been able to count on in the past, Mexico City. Only there did he feel completely independent and at peace with all his responsibilities left behind. From his mother's place in Florida, he took the bus, hoping to get to Mexico quickly and immerse himself in work on *Doctor Sax*. He had landed a contract for the manuscript from Grove Press, but he had to deliver it to the publisher that autumn. This time his trip turned out to be less idyllic than his previous visits. He discovered that their old friend and drug connection, Bill Garver, was dead and that Esperanza, Jack's old girlfriend, had vanished. He decided to stay in a place that had been converted from a brothel into cheap rooms. There he rented a typewriter and finally got down to work again.

Chapter 13

Fame

One of the first projects that Kerouac needed to tackle was an article that Viking had commissioned him to write explaining the Beat Generation. What resulted was his article, "Aftermath: The Philosophy of the Beat Generation," later published in the March 1958 issue of *Esquire*. While Kerouac had been traveling in Europe and in California, Sterling Lord had urged Viking to stop dragging their feet and to set a publication date for *On the Road*. For more than five years, Jack had replies from a host of publishers promising to bring out his books, but nothing had materialized. Finally, in part because of the coverage of the *Howl* trial in San Francisco, Viking realized that the public was hungry for information and work by this "new" literary phenomenon. Overnight, the Beat Generation had become a topic of national conversation. Before long, it seemed, every magazine wanted to run stories about the trial and the new avant-garde movement that was emerging on the West Coast.

Viking editors had at last come to understand the commercial potential of *On the Road*. That book told the story of a young man, Sal Paradise, coming of age as he ricocheted back and forth across the country, "dreaming of the immensity of it," with his inexhaust-

ible friend, Dean Moriarity. The main characters were easily identified versions of Kerouac and Cassady in search of kicks, atonement,
and redemption. Jack's editors finally realized that the book would
speak to a much broader audience than just the young rebels that
the story celebrated. It was to become the seminal work of the Beat
Generation, whose central theme could be seen as a search, not only
for their individual birthrights, but also for an elusive quality. Sal
summed up the puzzling object of all those trips with the line, "In
God's name and under the stars, what for?"

Kerouac managed to employ the new spontaneous style, which
he had first recognized in Neal's letters, to craft a book original in
both style and substance. The basic story of people leaving their pasts
behind and striking out on their own in search of something was not
new. That is one of the longest traditions in literature from *Ulysses*
to *Huckleberry Finn,* but Kerouac's genius was in writing a story in
which the stated search for Dean Moriarity's father was not actually
the true goal. Through his wanderings, he discovered that everyone
he encountered along the way was a reflection of God. There are no
villains in Jack's stories, only angels. The irony of the story is that Sal
wants to settle down and give up the road that is so appealing to the
very people who read his book. The published novel was to strike a
chord with millions of readers over the next fifty years, all of whom
wanted to hit the road with Sal and Dean and discover their own
place in the universe.

As Viking rushed to get the book out during the fall of 1957, they
asked for Jack's definition of the Beat Generation in order to pave the
way for further publicity and attention. By then, Jack was defining
the movement as a religious one invented by young men on a quest
for a spiritual foundation to their lives. Kerouac was quick to point
out that the movement had already ended by 1950, when many of
them "vanished into jails and madhouse, or were shamed into silent
conformity." Naturally the press ignored the fact that Kerouac said
the Beat period had ended almost a decade earlier and continued to

write about it in the present tense. For Jack, the Beat Generation had ceased to exist, and his *On the Road* documented the final years of that wonderful, youthful period during which he and his friends had come of age. For the American press, *On the Road* stood for something that was not history, but the beginning of what it wanted to call the Beat Generation.

The need to be current won out in the end. In order to sell their product, they needed a movement that was still active and growing, a movement that they could build on in the press for their own purposes. Even though Kerouac invented this term, the press ignored his opinion that it was a phenomenon of the past and applied it to contemporary writers associated mainly with the San Francisco Renaissance. In order to insure future interest and marketability, it was important that people believe the Beats were up and coming.

After finishing his article and sending it off to the publisher, Kerouac lived through a catastrophic earthquake that struck Mexico City on July 28, 1957, and killed more than a hundred people. In the wake of that disaster, the city's water supply and sanitation systems were compromised, and Jack came down with a serious case of the flu. He left for home and arrived at his mother's house in poor health during the hottest part of a Florida August. Within a few weeks Kerouac was feeling well enough to make a trip he had already scheduled to New York City to coincide with the publication of *On the Road*. On that trip Jack stayed with Joyce Glassman (later Johnson), a young woman he had dated the previous winter. On September 5, 1957, they walked to the newsstand to pick up a copy of the early edition of the *New York Times,* which was supposed to include a review of *On the Road*. The review was to change Kerouac's life forever.

For what seemed like the first time in Kerouac's professional life, he managed to have a stroke of good luck. The regular book review editor for the *Times* was a conservative man named Charles Poore, who would probably have panned Jack's book. But Poore was away when the advance copy of *On the Road* came in, and it was assigned to a new reviewer named Gilbert Millstein. Millstein loved the book and declared that Kerouac's was the voice of a new generation. "The fact is that *On the Road* is the most beautifully executed, the clearest and the most important utterance yet made by the generation Kerouac himself named," he wrote. Millstein's glowing praise brought the name of Kerouac to the attention of the reading public. He proclaimed Jack one of the major forces behind the new Beat Generation that they had been reading about for the past six months. Millstein compared *On the Road* to the works of Ernest Hemingway and Thomas Wolfe, but praised Jack's originality as well. Overnight, Jack Kerouac was famous.

Kerouac was relieved when he read the review. More than seven years had passed since the publication of *The Town and the City;* finally it appeared that he was about to receive the recognition and financial success that he had prayed for. The book made it onto the *New York Times*'s bestseller list for several weeks, and publishers began to consider some of Jack's other manuscripts. Excitement for his work even pushed Grove Press to work faster on the release of *Doctor Sax.* Many of the larger New York publishing houses still could not see the potential value in his more experimental writings like *Sax* or *Visions of Cody,* and they wanted him to write something exactly like *On the Road.* To keep those publishers happy, he began to work on a sequel.

Ginsberg was thrilled by Kerouac's success, little realizing that fame was about to put unbearable pressure on the shy Kerouac and eventually help to destroy him. In San Francisco there would have been many poets and writers to share the burden of "Beat Generation" publicity and criticism, but in New York, Jack stood nearly alone. To field the never-ending questions and give interviews freely to reporters, he drank more and more. He needed it to muster up the courage to face both his fans and detractors.

Disregarding the media blitz in America, Ginsberg continued his

Allen Ginsberg, Lucien Carr, and William Burroughs were the first of the Beats to become friends when they met in December 1943. This picture was taken a decade later in 1953 in Lucien's Greenwich Village apartment at 92 Grove Street after he began working for United Press.
Photo Courtesy of Allen Ginsberg Trust

Jack Kerouac and Lucien Carr posing in front of the fountain on the steps of Low Library at the Columbia campus in the summer of 1944.
Photo Courtesy of Allen Ginsberg Trust

Hal Chase, Jack Kerouac, Allen Ginsberg, and William Burroughs mugging
for the camera on Morningside Heights during the winter of 1944–45.
Photo Courtesy of Allen Ginsberg Trust

Hal Chase and Jack
Kerouac arguing in the
snow near Columbia,
winter 1944–45.
*Photo Courtesy of Allen
Ginsberg Trust*

Herbert Huncke in his room in a cheap hotel near Times Square during a brief period of freedom between prison terms, ca. 1953. *Photo Courtesy of Allen Ginsberg Trust*

Jack Kerouac imitating a character from André Gide's novel *The Counterfeiters,* ca. 1944. *Photo Courtesy of Allen Ginsberg Trust*

William Burroughs posing with a sphinx at the Metropolitan Museum of Art during his fall 1953 visit to New York City. *Photo Courtesy of Allen Ginsberg Trust*

Neal Cassady in San Francisco, ca. 1956. He was the handsome and sexy muse of both Kerouac and Ginsberg. *Photo Courtesy of Allen Ginsberg Trust*

John Clellon Holmes, the author of *Go* and the first person to use the term "The Beat Generation" in print. *Photo Courtesy of Allen Ginsberg Trust*

Jack Kerouac, Al Hinkle, and Carolyn Cassady with children Jamie, Cathy, and Mark. *Photo Courtesy of Carolyn Cassady*

Jack Kerouac, Allen
Ginsberg, Peter Orlovsky
(above), Gregory Corso,
and Lafcadio Orlovsky
(kneeling) have their photo
taken as a souvenir by a
street photographer in
Mexico City's Alameda
Park in November 1956.
*Photo Courtesy of Allen
Ginsberg Trust*

Gregory Corso and
Ray Bremser having a
conversation before their
poetry reading at the Seven
Arts Coffee Gallery at 596
Ninth Avenue in New
York, 1959.
*Photo Courtesy of Allen
Ginsberg Trust*

LeRoi Jones and Allen Ginsberg discussing poetry, ca. 1960.
Photo Courtesy of Allen Ginsberg Trust

Peter Orlovsky, Allen Ginsberg, Denise Mercedes (with pig), Bonnie Bremser and daughter Georgia, Ray Bremser, Julius Orlovsky (standing), Allen Deloach, and Gregory Corso in the yard at Ginsberg's farm, summer 1969.
Photo by Gordon Ball. Copyright Gordon Ball

Gary Snyder taking a nap after hiking in the hills near the Sea of Japan, early July 1963. *Photo Courtesy of Allen Ginsberg Trust*

Paul Bowles, Gregory Corso, Allen Ginsberg, and William Burroughs outside Burroughs's room at the Villa Muniria, Tangier, Morocco, summer 1961. *Photo Courtesy of Allen Ginsberg Trust*

Peter Orlovsky, Gregory Corso, and an unidentified woman at a party for Man Ray in a jazz club in Paris, June 15, 1958. *Photo Courtesy of Allen Ginsberg Trust*

One-eyed poet Robert Creeley in his room at the Vancouver Poetry Conference, late July 1963. *Photo Courtesy of Allen Ginsberg Trust*

Ray Bremser pausing for
a Ginsberg portrait in the
1960s. *Photo Courtesy of
Allen Ginsberg Trust*

Allen Ginsberg posing for Peter Orlovsky in front of a carved stone Hindu mandala near the
Parasuramesvara Temple in Bhubaneswar, India, 1962.
Photo Courtesy of Allen Ginsberg Trust

Joanne Kyger smiling at her husband, Gary Snyder, in their home in Kyoto, Japan, summer 1963.
Photo Courtesy of Allen Ginsberg Trust

Timothy Leary and Neal Cassady talking on board Ken Kesey's bus *Furthur* while it was parked at Kesey's Castalia Foundation in Millbrook, New York, during the fall of 1964. Cassady had just driven the bus filled with the Merry Pranksters all the way from California in less than a week.
Photo Courtesy of Allen Ginsberg Trust

Neal Cassady as he appeared in New York during the summer of 1964. On this visit, Neal and Jack Kerouac saw each other for the last time at the end of the cross-country bus trip described by Tom Wolfe in his book *The Electric Kool-Aid Acid Test. Photo Courtesy of Allen Ginsberg Trust*

The last photo that Ginsberg took of Jack Kerouac, when Jack came to visit Allen in his 704 East Fifth Street apartment on the Lower East Side in the fall of 1964. Jack had just sampled some DMT that Ginsberg had been given by Timothy Leary. *Photo Courtesy of Allen Ginsberg Trust*

Alan Ansen and William Burroughs touring the ruins of a temple in Greece, ca. 1970. *Photo Courtesy of Allen Ginsberg Trust*

Michael McClure performing on the autoharp with Allen Ginsberg on the harmonium in the late 1960s. *Photo Courtesy of Allen Ginsberg Trust*

Bob Dylan and Allen Ginsberg in the alleyway behind the City Lights bookstore in San Francisco, December 1965. The alley was later renamed Jack Kerouac Street.
Photo Courtesy of Larry Keenan

Allen Ginsberg, Herbert Huncke, and Peter Orlovsky exploring the countryside near Ginsberg's Cherry Valley farm in the 1970s. *Photo Courtesy of Allen Ginsberg Trust*

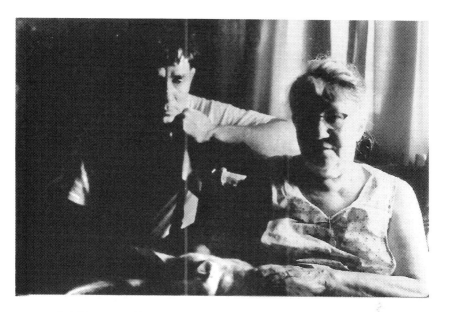

Jack Kerouac and his mother, Gabrielle, in their home in Hyannis, Massachusetts, August 1966. *Photo by Ann Charters*

Carl Solomon fishing from the dock at City Island, New York, in the late 1980s. *Photo Courtesy of Allen Ginsberg Trust*

Lawrence Ferlinghetti and
his dog in the editorial
offices of City Lights
Books, San Francisco, in
the mid-1980s.
*Photo Courtesy of Allen
Ginsberg Trust*

William Burroughs visiting
New York City from Kansas in
the mid-1980s. *Photo Courtesy
of Allen Ginsberg Trust*

European holiday and used Ansen's apartment in Venice as a home base for several months. Occasionally, the press would track him down, but it wasn't much of a distraction. In September he and Peter pressed on to Paris only to find that Corso had been forced to flee to Amsterdam after passing some bad checks. Their first night in the French capital, Allen and Peter managed to find the cheap hotel that Gregory had recommended on the rue Git-le-Coeur, but Corso wasn't there, and there were no vacancies. The two were too excited to sleep anyway and spent the night wandering the streets. They made a future reservation at the hotel and set out to find Corso in Holland, where they would stay until the room was available in Paris.

It was while he was bouncing around northern Europe that Allen received news of the verdict from the San Francisco trial. Since Judge Horn ruled that *Howl* was not obscene, Ferlinghetti was now free to publish and distribute the poem. All the news outlets ran stories on the trial, and the coverage from magazines like *Time, Life,* and *Look* boosted *Howl'*s sales nationwide.

Even though the press in general had sided with Ferlinghetti and made fun of the local San Francisco politicos in their feeble attempt to censor *Howl,* that didn't mean the critics embraced the Beats. Many, like Robert Brustein in his *Horizon* magazine article, "The Cult of Unthink," believed the typical Beat writer was "a man belligerently exalting his own inarticulateness." Reporters were dispatched from their European offices, hoping to track down Ginsberg, Corso, and Burroughs for interviews. In no time at all, many of the writers in the group were being solicited by publishers around the world. In Amsterdam, Corso had already met a group of Dutch poets who were very interested in what was happening back in the States. They even paid him to write an article on the revolution in American literature for their magazine.

What little positive attention the Beat writers received was short-lived. City Lights's victory in court and the publication of *On the Road* represented the high-water mark of the Beat period. After a flurry of postpublication activity in New York, Kerouac retreated to his mother's place in Florida. From there he wrote urging his agent to find publishers for more of his manuscripts, seven of which had been gathering dust on his shelves. Although the initial *Times* review had been remarkably favorable, other reviewers were not as kind to Kerouac. Even before another book came out, he had fallen under critical attack from more conservative members of the literary establishment. He was labeled the "King of the Beats," and articles came out denouncing Jack's spontaneous prose as nothing more than a gimmick. "It isn't writing," Truman Capote quipped on a talk show, "it's typing." All the subsequent negative criticism stung the extremely sensitive Kerouac, yet he clipped out and read every word of abuse.

When Allen, Peter, and Gregory finally got back to Paris that fall, they found that the notoriety of the trial had preceded them. There was a growing interest in the Beat Generation in Europe just as in the United States. At least the publicity on the Beats in the French newspapers made it easier for Ginsberg to convince Girodias to accept *The Naked Lunch* for publication. It had not been an easy battle because Girodias himself did not like the book. Olympia had made a name for itself by publishing what they liked to call DBs (dirty books), and Maurice felt that it would not sell many copies of Burroughs's book since it had little sex in it. Americans often bought Olympia's books to smuggle home in their luggage. Occasionally, Girodias happened to publish a masterpiece by accident, like *Lolita* and *The Ginger Man*, but DBs were his real bread and butter.

Burroughs had his supporters at Olympia. One, Mason Hoffenberg, who was an advisor for Girodias and had written deliberately debauched DBs himself, most famously *Candy,* had told Maurice that *The Naked Lunch* was the "greatest greatest book." Reluctantly, Girodias agreed to go ahead with the publication and hoped it would sell.

Unfortunately for Bill, Girodias's terms for *The Naked Lunch* were unfavorable, but Allen advised Burroughs to sign the contract anyway. He expected there to be more income from future books after Bill's reputation was established. The most important step was to publish the book while interest in the Beats was still high; profits would certainly follow. For Ginsberg especially, the publication of a work was the only thing that really mattered. It wasn't important to him if a book brought in little or no money as long as it was out in the world for everyone to read. This was advice Allen followed with his own poetry, but his example was difficult for many of his fellow writers to follow.

In the case of *The Naked Lunch*, Burroughs agreed to Olympia's terms in order to get the book out quickly, but later Bill regretted his decision when the book began to sell widely. Try as he might, he wasn't able to get out of the one-sided contract that made money for Girodias but paid Bill almost nothing. Once the contract was signed, it took Girodias quite a while to get around to publishing *The Naked Lunch*, and that happened only after excerpts from it had created another censorship stir back in the United States.

Now that the Beat Generation was a marketable commodity, Ginsberg encouraged all his friends to continue writing. Orlovsky, who hadn't thought of himself as a poet at all, gave in to Allen's coaxing and wrote his first poem. The slightly dyslexic author titled it "Frist Poem" and the title stood. Even though Peter continued to be a reluctant poet, he eventually created enough material to be collected into a single volume twenty years later, *Clean Asshole Poems and Smiling Vegetable Songs*. Ginsberg also continued to chide Cassady in California for not working hard enough on his own memoir. Other friends like Herbert Huncke and Carl Solomon also put pen to paper at Allen's insistence.

Following the publication of *On the Road*, interest in the Beats swelled. In December 1957 Kerouac was offered a considerable amount of money to give a weeklong series of readings at the Village Vanguard with the J. J. Johnson Jazz Quartet. It was the last thing in the world that the bashful Kerouac wanted to do, but the promise of good money was a proposition he couldn't turn down. By most accounts, the readings were terrible, and his engagement was cut short before the week was over. Before, during, and after each performance Kerouac found himself resorting to alcohol, his habitual crutch. The critics who saw him at the Vanguard were not sympathetic to him and ridiculed not only his drunken presentation and disheveled appearance, but also the material he chose to read. Except for his closest friends, the only personality who believed in the value of Jack's prose seemed to be television host and composer Steve Allen, who caught a few of the performances at the Vanguard. He recognized Kerouac's talent and asked him to collaborate on a record album that would pair Steve Allen's music with Kerouac's words.

After four months in Paris with Ginsberg, Orlovsky set sail for home. Once again his family had reached a point of crisis, and his mother and siblings were all dangerously close to being institutionalized. Peter wanted to get back and see what he could do before everyone wound up in mental wards. His older brother Julius had become catatonic in a mental hospital and he didn't want it to happen to anyone else in his family.

Being involved with Peter and his family's mental illnesses reminded Ginsberg of his own mother's sad death alone in the asylum. He had never followed up on his promise to write something about her, and Peter's departure spurred him to do just that. One afternoon while sitting at a tiny table in the Café Sélect in Paris, Allen began the poem that would eventually become *Kaddish,* widely regarded to be his finest work. His mother, crazy as she was, had shaped his life more than anyone else had, and he needed to pay homage to her.

Even though the Orlovsky family problems were the main reason for his hasty return to America, Peter needed to take another break from his relationship with Allen. As they said good-bye, Allen feared that they might be separating permanently. He realized that things were not going well between them and perhaps that was the reason that he chose to stay behind in Europe.

The same day that Orlovsky set sail from France, Burroughs checked into the Beat Hotel in Paris. It was no coincidence. Bill wanted nothing to do with Peter and hated to see Allen fawn over this young man whom Bill considered beneath them intellectually.

As soon as Burroughs arrived, drugs began to play an even more prominent role in the lives of the group at the Beat Hotel. Bill was surprised to discover that the heroin in Paris was purer and much cheaper than it had been in Mexico and Tangier. Even with his modest monthly trust fund check, he was able to afford a habit. Initially Allen limited his own use of drugs to avoid addiction. He even made elaborate charts to regulate his use of specific narcotics, but during this period in Paris, Ginsberg came as close to addiction as he would ever get. Although his intellect told him that he had to refrain from the constant use of any one drug, accessibility made it tempting to overindulge. Even as Allen skirted with addiction, his friends were not as cautious. He alone managed to avoid the future agony that drained the energy of Burroughs and Corso and several other close friends who became addicts during those days in Paris.

When Burroughs arrived in Paris, Corso was away working with Ansen on a German anthology of Beat poetry. He returned to a scene where drugs were readily available, and although he always blamed Burroughs for getting him hooked that first time, it wasn't to be the last. That winter they all made friends with a wealthy man named Jacques Stern. Stern was a victim of polio, a writer, and a book collector who came from a prominent family. He was also an addict and wealthy enough to buy not only whatever drugs he wanted, but to provide them for his new friends as well. There was always a box of cocaine available for someone to snort. Stern was generous by nature, and his supply of narcotics seemed to be unlimited.

Regular use quickly led to addiction for both Burroughs and Corso. It seemed more tragic for Corso because it triggered a rapid decline in his poetic output. He had been in the midst of one of his most creative periods, but as time passed, he focused more and more on his next fix instead of his next poem. In the years ahead, he would experience a collapse of his creative powers because of the drug habit he picked up in Paris. On the other hand, Burroughs was able to continue working during most of his addictions and sometimes was inspired by them. Bill also had the financial means to find treatment from time to time, something that Corso could not afford to consider.

As Corso was beginning his new life as an addict in Paris, Ferlinghetti was putting the first bright red copies of Gregory's book, *Gasoline,* in the window of his bookshop. Lawrence had admired Gregory's writing from the very beginning, but he thought that his work was not of uniform quality. He proved to be a tough editor and was much more critical and opinionated than many of his writers could appreciate. Ginsberg alone became the one writer who could publish whatever he wanted at City Lights, with or without Ferlinghetti's editorial agreement.

While working on the manuscript for *Gasoline,* Corso had learned that Lawrence was discerning about what he would publish under the City Lights imprint. Before the first book was out, Gregory began to send him poems for a second volume. It was then that Lawrence objected to a poem entitled "Power" that Gregory sent to him, with lines like "O joy to my human sparkle Power! / Joy to its march down the street!" Ferlinghetti refused to publish it because he said that it had an undertone of fascism to it. Corso considered "Power" to be one of his best works, so he was disappointed by Lawrence's opinion. "I am professing love; and I find that my love stems from humor and originality . . . I can condone no harm to man, but I can see with opened eyes the harm there be," he wrote to Lawrence. Even though he could be rude about other people's poetry, Gregory was always very sensitive to criticism of his own work. Before he sent poems to any publisher, he made certain that they were perfect by his standards, reworking them dozens of times if need be.

After hearing Corso read "Power" many times, Ginsberg had to agree with Gregory that it was one of his most important works. He wrote to Ferlinghetti asking him to reconsider his decision, but Lawrence had made up his mind and stood firm. His unwillingness to reexamine his opinion about that particular poem motivated Corso to look elsewhere for a publisher. When the time came to assemble his next book, *The Happy Birthday of Death,* Gregory had already found a more sympathetic ear in the person of James Laughlin at New Directions in New York City. From that moment on, Laughlin became Corso's publisher, patron, and friend.

For years, Ginsberg, in his unofficial capacity as everybody's literary agent, had been trying to interest New Directions in the work of his close friends. New Directions was well known as the publisher of avant-garde European and American writers like Ezra Pound, Hermann Hesse, Dylan Thomas, and William Carlos Williams, but it wasn't until the national press ran stories about the Beat Generation and the San Francisco Renaissance that Laughlin began to take notice of them. In May 1958, he published Lawrence Ferlinghetti's *A Coney Island of the Mind,* which became the biggest-selling book of poetry by any of the Beats. By the turn of the twenty-first century, over a million copies were in print. In addition to Corso and Ferlinghetti, New Directions became the primary publisher for Snyder, McClure, Creeley, and others associated within the Beat canon.

Since it had been so difficult to find editors who were open-minded and willing to take a chance on publishing the work of the Beats in the first place, Ginsberg had begun to encourage poets to publish their own magazines and books. If they were interested in his friends, he would work tirelessly with editors to help them collect poems to fill the pages of their magazines. In 1958 LeRoi and Hettie Jones put out the first issue of *Yugen,* a little magazine that would become seminal in spreading the work of the Beat Generation during its run of eight issues. They listed Philip Whalen, Diane Di Prima, and Allen himself among the contributors to their initial issue. Under the imprint of Totem Press, LeRoi and Hettie also published paperback monographs at a reasonable price.

The Joneses were not alone in the world of do-it-yourself publishing. After the University of Chicago censored them for publishing the first chapter of William Burroughs's *The Naked Lunch*, the editors of the *Chicago Review* decided to break away from their sponsor and publish their own magazine. Kerouac himself suggested that they call the new magazine *Big Table*. In 1959 their premier issue offered more episodes from *The Naked Lunch* as well as Kerouac's prose poem *Old Angel Midnight* and controversial work by Edward Dahlberg.

Seeking support whenever he could find it, poet John Wieners began to publish *Measure* magazine on a shoestring budget while he lived in San Francisco. Also working with limited funds, Diane Di Prima turned her idea for a poetry newsletter into reality. The result was ten years of *Floating Bear Newsletter*. Many of the writers who appeared in Diane's newsletter could also be found in Michael McClure's *Ark II Moby I* and Bob Kaufman's *Beatitude* that sprang up on the West Coast. These publications were the literary beginnings of an underground press movement that would grow throughout the sixties, all made possible by low-cost printing techniques like mimeo and ditto machines and writers willing to share their work for no profit.

Almost a year after *Howl* was seized by the San Francisco police, Gary Snyder's freighter docked in San Pedro, California. Toward the end of April 1958, he was back with his friends in the Bay Area and living once more in his little Marin-An cabin in Mill Valley. Over the next few months, he considered his cabin a home base for camping and hiking trips throughout the west. Several times during those months he invited Kerouac to visit him for another hike into the mountains, but Jack had become tangled in the web of his own fame and couldn't escape. Nothing would have pleased him more than to climb the hills with Gary, but by then he was beginning to suffer from physical problems brought on by his sedentary lifestyle and heavy drinking. Deep down he knew that he no longer had the strength to keep up with Gary.

The harsh criticism of Kerouac and the Beat Generation continued unabated. That was when articles with titles like "The Know-Nothing Bohemians" and "The Cult of Unthink" began to appear regularly in the press. Even the few reporters who were more sensitive to the Beat writers wrote articles like "Here to Save Us, But Not Sure from What." Kerouac had wanted only two things from the world. First, he wanted to earn a living through his writing, and second, he wanted to be recognized as a serious artist. Instead, all he seemed to reap was abuse.

As if harsh criticism of Beat writers wasn't enough, *San Francisco Chronicle* reporter Herb Caen used a word in his column that would stick to the group until their dying days. In October 1957 the Russians launched the Sputnik satellite and thus started the space race. It was the biggest story of the year, and everyone was talking about it, even the poets. In a North Beach bar one day, Caen happened to overhear poet Bob Kaufman playfully invent the word *beatnik*. Caen loved the sound of the word and used it in print for the first time on April 2, 1958. To Caen, the meaning of the word was obvious, because both the Beat Generation and Sputnik were "way out." It was exactly the kind of pejorative term that the press was looking for, and before long the phrase "Beat Generation" was replaced by the more disparaging label "beatnik." And so it wasn't long before the press dubbed Kerouac, the most prominent writer in the group, "The King of the Beatniks."

The press began to use the word to mean not just the few writers who had originally joined to form the Beat Generation, but also the myriad disenfranchised young people who were flocking to urban areas looking for more exciting, alternative lifestyles than the suburban conformity enjoyed by much of America in the 1950s. In the collective mind of the general public, the word *beatnik* became synonymous with *juvenile delinquent*. By the late fifties, some young people had begun to adopt the mannerisms and vocabulary of black jazz musicians. Men grew goatees, wore sandals, and played bongo drums, while women wore their hair long and straight, dressed completely in black, and adopted "cool" personas, snapping their fingers in lieu of clapping at performances.

None of these affectations had anything to do with Kerouac and company. Jack, maybe more than any of the others, believed he had little in common with this new trend. He was nearly a generation older than most of the people who were streaming into the bohemian districts in search of their own kindred spirits. He saw himself as a hardworking professional writer, not as a rebellious punk trying to avoid getting a job. The characters in some of Jack's books might include people who fit that mold, but to him, the quality of "Beat" was much more spiritual. He agreed with the press that these newcomers were just oddballs and troublemakers, and he objected to being identified with them. He seemed not to realize that many of them had taken to the road inspired by his stories and some of them sought to transform themselves into the characters in his books.

Allen Ginsberg took the opposite view. He regarded all the publicity generated by the press as an opportunity to be exploited. Although he never embraced the word *beatnik*, he never failed to identify himself and his friends as members of the Beat Generation. Through his experience in market research, he knew that a group of people would command more attention, more "shelf space," and possibly even more respect than a gaggle of individual writers competing for recognition. Lumping everyone into the same group, despite their divergent writing styles, was a good way to make a connection that even the press could understand. To Allen any writer was a candidate for membership in the Beat Generation.

In many ways, it was Ginsberg who solidified the structure of the group more than the press. If you became Allen's friend, you became a member of his group. It wasn't an exclusive category, all were welcome, but once the press labeled someone as Beat, it was impossible to break the connection.

Shortly after the coining of the term *beatnik* in the late fifties, the paths of the Beat Generation and what most of America believed to be beatnik culture began to diverge exponentially. In 1959 and continuing for several seasons, the beatnik stereotype was epitomized by a ditzy character on the television program *The Many Loves of Dobie Gillis*. Maynard G. Krebs, played by Bob Denver, became the quintessential beatnik in the eyes of most viewers. Maynard is still remembered by people of a certain age when conversations turn to the subject. The qualities that made Maynard memorable—laziness, insipience, sloppiness, lack of ambition, and a self-conscious jazz vocabulary—were a caricature that had little to do with the Beat Generation writers.

Popular comedian Louis Nye parodied Kerouac on national television in one of his skits. He ranted and raved in such a violent and mean-spirited manner, and distorted Kerouac's sweet, peaceful nature, that Jack never forgot the pain and humiliation he felt as he watched. Another popular television series called *Route 66* aired from 1960 to 1964. It featured two young men who wandered back and forth across the country in a Corvette sharing adventures, just like Sal and Dean in *On the Road*. It was an obvious rip-off of Kerouac's concept, two restless men searching for some meaning to their lives. They were modeled after Jack's ideal of nonviolent rebels who found it impossible to embrace American bourgeois conformity.

Chapter 14

The Threads Loosen

few days after Herb Caen's 1958 invention of beat-nikery, Neal Cassady was arrested in San Francisco for giving a small amount of marijuana to undercover policemen. It was no secret in the city that Neal was the model for Kerouac's *On the Road* character Dean Moriarity, and many suspected that the police had singled him out because of that notoriety. Whatever brought about his arrest, Neal was tried and harshly sentenced to five years to life for the possession and sale of two joints. Kerouac did not rush to his friend's defense, worried perhaps that the police spotlight might fall on him next. He began to avoid mention of Cassady in his letters and distanced himself from Neal. Even when Jack had the chance to visit Neal in San Quentin the following year, he chose not to go. His treatment of Neal became typical of his growing attitude toward many of his old friends. Over the next decade, Kerouac slowly with-drew from the people he had been closest to and retreated to a reclu-sive life with his mother and his liquor.

So it happened that by the time Snyder got back to San Francisco to share his old cabin in Marin County with his Reed College class-mate, Lew Welch, Neal was already on his way to prison. For the next nine months Gary played an active role in the literary scene around the Bay Area, with the intention of returning to Japan as soon as he could afford it. More than ever his writing alluded to Asian and Buddhist subjects combined with the inspiration he found in the serenity of the forest. In December, in response to Snyder's repeated invitations to visit, Kerouac wrote, "If you only knew how horrible it is to be 'famous' you wouldn't want it, in fact you don't want it. No wonder Hemingway went to Cuba and Joyce to France." In his midthirties, but sounding more like a bitter old man, Jack went on to reminisce about their hikes of only a few years earlier, "I was in love with the world through blue purple curtains when I knew you and now have to look at it thru hard iron eyes."

From Europe, Ginsberg wrote regularly to publishers like Grove and New Directions, soliciting their attention to Snyder's poetry. Now that Corso was being published, Allen regarded Gary as the next great unpublished poet who should have a book contract. Ginsberg and Corso were still living in the Beat Hotel in Paris but had been invited to Oxford in May 1958 to read their work there. On that occasion, Gregory created controversy by reading his poem *Bomb*. Corso took an unexpected position in the poem by refusing to denounce the obvious evils of nuclear annihilation. Instead, he delighted in a romantic fantasy about the atomic bomb in which he considered the device a poor, misunderstood creature. The students didn't get the tongue-in-cheek irony and were outraged by what they considered flippant remarks about the destruction of mankind. They jeered him and threw shoes at the podium.

Ferlinghetti, who visited the poets in Paris shortly after that reading, read Gregory's poem with considerable interest. It was just the type of playful poetry he liked, and he took a copy back with him, promising to publish it as a broadside. The poem was typed in the form of a mushroom cloud on one long sheet of paper, and thousands of copies were sold for a quarter each and tacked to walls in dorm rooms and apartments all over the country.

That summer in France, Allen, Gregory, and Bill were invited to several sophisticated parties where they met many of the great French intellectuals, Henri Michaux, Marcel Duchamp, and Louis-Ferdinand Céline among them. The Beat circle expanded as they toured extensively, but even though Allen was thoroughly enjoying himself in Europe, he felt that it was time to get back home. That summer he left France aboard the liner *Liberté* bound for New York, where he hoped to rekindle the flames of his romance with Peter Orlovsky.

Allen was crushed when Peter failed to meet him at the dock, but they hooked up within a few days. If only they could live together again, Allen promised, he would give Peter complete freedom to sleep with women whenever he wanted. Allen believed that a platonic relationship was better than no relationship at all, and secretly he nurtured a wish for the occasional opportunity of sex with Peter. Allen did not demand sexual fidelity, but he did want to be around Peter as much as possible. The arrangement of being friends without any sexual strings attached did not last very long, but initially the agreement seemed like a good idea and made it possible for Peter to live with Allen once more.

Jack's initial success with *On the Road* was followed late in 1958 by a sequel, *The Dharma Bums,* which also sold well for Viking Press. Kerouac's publisher wanted to capitalize on the public's interest by offering them more of the same. From their point of view, it made no sense to risk failure by challenging readers with anything more experimental. Over one twelve-day period, Jack typed the manuscript of *The Dharma Bums* on a long roll of paper, just as he had done with *On the Road.* He was delighted to find that he still had the physical stamina to undertake a marathon of writing and was pleased with his results.

On the personal front, things were looking brighter for Kerouac, too. He had met an artist by the name of Dodie Muller at Robert Frank's loft in New York and began a romance with her. He had dabbled with drawings before, but Dodie showed him various paint-ing methods, something that appealed to his creative nature. Though he never became proficient technically, painting came to occupy a good deal of his time over the next decade.

Soon after Allen returned to New York, he and Peter settled into an apartment on the Lower East Side. While Peter cleaned and painted the walls a bright white, Allen returned to work on his poem in memory of his mother that he had begun in Paris. In a man-ner reminiscent of Kerouac's spurts of creative composition, Allen worked on his manuscript for three days without pausing to rest. Occasionally, Peter brought him a cup of coffee or a bit of toast to keep him going. When he stopped writing, he had produced a fifty-eight-page handwritten manuscript for *Kaddish,* arguably his finest work. Into that one masterpiece he poured the entire story of his heartbreaking relationship with his mother as she gradually suc-cumbed to paranoid insanity.

Back in Paris after Ginsberg's departure, Corso and Burroughs had continued their heavy drug use unabated. Corso progressed from being an occasional user to being a full-blown heroin addict, a curse from which he would never fully escape, and Bill did his best to keep up with him. In midst of all the drugs and literature, Bill re-newed his acquaintance with Brion Gysin, who had just moved into the Beat Hotel, too. Bill had known Gysin in Tangier, but they did not become close friends until they met again in Paris. Strictly speak-ing, Brion was an American artist, but his parents were Canadian and Swiss, and he seemed more European than American. He was just then experiencing a series of visions of his own that would radi-cally change his life and his art. The paintings that were inspired by those visions intrigued Bill. With Gysin's paintings propped against the wall, Burroughs would stare at the surface of them as if he were in a trance. By concentrating on nothing else except the painted sur-face, he was able to induce visions of his own. It was a variation on scrying, a technique commonly used by fortunetellers who look into crystal balls to see the future. This intense observation gave Bill what he called a "port of entry" into a painting. Finding ports of entry in Gysin's paintings was a breakthrough moment for Bill and became the foundation for a lifelong friendship between the two men.

Until then, Burroughs had always found his inspiration in the use of a wide variety of drugs. He felt that it was an author's job to alter his consciousness and report on these alterations. This was not a rationalization for his drug cravings: he genuinely believed that altered consciousness was the only way to see the world in a fresh way. The visions he had while on drugs were much more interesting than his day-to-day life, so he sought source material there, in addition to enjoying the instant rush of adrenaline that they gave him. Drugs allowed him to enter a dream world that he preferred to inhabit, where he could push anything he wanted to the ultimate limits, unlike the world outside the mind, where everything had to be kept guarded and under control. Gysin's paintings gave him another source for inspiration.

Corso was not as interested as Burroughs in spending his time staring at the surface of pictures in lonely rooms, and so he went off on his own to visit Shelley's tomb in Rome. In Italy he discovered that Ginsberg had placed an ad in the *Village Voice* requesting donations to help bring Corso back from Europe. Gregory was both delighted and angered by that piece of news. He was embarrassed that people should think he was a charity case starving in Europe, but he also knew that he did need financial help if he ever wanted to get back to New York. Corso had always maintained a take-it-or-leave-it attitude toward money. Given a choice, he would always prefer to have it, but even in the depths of poverty, he wasn't financially responsible. While Allen was trying to raise his rescue boat fare, Gregory was in Monte Carlo gambling. He actually won three hundred dollars at the casino, more than enough for his passage home, only to lose every penny the next day. In the end, Allen was successful and raised enough money to provide for Gregory's transportation home.

During the fall of 1958, Jack Kerouac accepted several invitations to speak and read at schools like Brandeis and Hunter College. The Beat's growing notoriety made them highly sought after, and the speaking fees they were offered could be substantial. By then Ginsberg had given quite a few readings himself and found that it created a moral dilemma. Realizing that he might be influenced to write only what people would be willing to pay to hear, he decided that he would not accept money for his readings. Jack saw the fees as merely a way to support himself since he knew he would write only what he wanted to write anyway. He also believed that if he appeared on the college circuit, it might help to establish him as a legitimate writer and not just an indolent beatnik.

Unfortunately, Jack was reticent when it came to public appearances. The alcohol he needed to build up courage for a performance took a toll on his reputation. He was insulted when interviewers asked ludicrous questions that had nothing to do with the craft of writing. Reporters wanted to know about the media image of the Beat Generation and the beatnik lifestyle in general, all of which Jack disdained, because he was not a bohemian. Frequently, his wise but drunken answers were held up as further evidence of the Beats' wackiness. Kerouac had his supporters, but he was an easy target for those who set out to ridicule him. Occasionally, for the sake of friendship, Ginsberg accompanied him to offer moral support, but it caused a strain on their relationship as Jack began to see Allen as the source of his problems instead of as an ally. Their views, especially on political and social issues, had never been the same, but now their differences stood out. Jack became a fan of conservative commentator William F. Buckley and agreed with him that Allen was straying much too close to socialist viewpoints just for the sake of being controversial.

Unlike Kerouac, Allen Ginsberg welcomed the media limelight and thrived on center stage. He knew that public readings were opportunities for him to put his message before the public, to give exposure to his work, and—just as important—to introduce his audiences to the work of his friends. At his own readings, he read work by Kerouac, Corso, Creeley, Snyder, and Whalen as often as he read his own poems. Wherever possible he invited friends to join him onstage and read from their works, and he directed the speaking fees to them. When he read alone, he began to ask that his honorarium be given to the college library for the purpose of buying more volumes of contemporary poetry.

Corso's ship arrived from France just in time for Christmas, and he moved in with Ginsberg and Orlovsky on East Second Street. For years other friends like Bob Kaufman, Herbert Huncke, and Alex Trocchi also lived in the same cheap apartment building, often supported through Ginsberg's generosity. Unfortunately, many of the new arrivals spent more of their time taking drugs than writing, and the period proved to be unproductive for many of them.

One hardworking poet who lived in Ginsberg's neighborhood was Diane Di Prima, one of the few women to be recognized as a full-fledged member of the Beat Generation. She grew up in an Italian American family in Brooklyn, making her one of the few Beat poets actually raised in New York City. In the evenings, Diane was often found reading her poetry in Village coffeehouses, trying to get her work before the public. It wasn't long after Ginsberg's return to the Lower East Side that Diane began to publish and edit books herself. Her first book, *This Kind of Bird Flies Backward,* was printed by LeRoi Jones's Totem Press that same year and featured an introduction by Ferlinghetti.

Like many Beat writers in the fifties, Di Prima decided that if she could not get the major New York publishers to put out her books, she would do it herself. Ginsberg had used a mimeo machine to print his first publication while waiting to be "discovered," and Ferlinghetti had self-published his *Pictures of the Gone World,* so she was following a similar path. Before long, LeRoi joined her to edit a newsletter she named in honor of Winnie-the-Pooh's boat, *The Float-*

ing Bear. Publications like hers helped struggling writers get their own work out and were important as a means of keeping up with new work written by friends. *The Floating Bear* wasn't sold in bookstores; instead, it was simply sent out free through the post to anyone who wanted it, a true grassroots approach to publishing. Diane was unlike some of her male counterparts in that she never shied away from the Beat label. In fact, she used a hip vocabulary and proclaimed that she was a beatnik, playfully calling her autobiography *Memoirs of a Beatnik.*

We should think of the Beat Generation as a social circle created by Allen Ginsberg and his friends instead of as a literary movement. This will explain why so few women writers are identified with it, Di Prima being the exception. People are products of their times, and Ginsberg and his friends were no exception. They grew up in an era where men were called on to do important things and women were expected to support them in those endeavors. Many of the Beats saw women only as sex objects, providers, and mothers, and rarely did they believe that they could write as well as their male counterparts. They failed to examine their own prejudices and missed opportunities to discover some remarkable talent. Even though these men were avant-garde in many respects, the role of women was severely limited in their eyes.

Even if some of the women Allen knew were also writers, he didn't realize their work might be as notable as the efforts of his male friends. The simple truth is that Allen had few female friends to begin with, and he was surrounded almost exclusively by males. He didn't befriend women or seek them out; he sought out men. It wasn't that he hated women, but he did disregard them.

Only strong women who were extremely self-confident and self-assured, like Diane Di Prima, could break out of the "little-woman" mold that Allen and others put them into. It took years for many of the men of the Beat Generation to realize that the world was changing. Only then did they recognize that some of the women they had known were marvelous writers. Thirty years later, the Beat canon was expanded to include them, but it remains to this day a small subset within the larger circle.

Although many Beat writers treated women badly, Burroughs was arguably the worst. Some blatantly misogynist passages appear in Burroughs's books. He was quoted as saying that he regarded women as an alien virus that needed to be segregated from men. Ginsberg never hated women in the same way that Burroughs did, but he often overlooked or ignored them without realizing it. Since Burroughs and Ginsberg were gay, they tended to travel in a predominantly male world and were somewhat isolated from women who might otherwise have influenced them. Many of the references to women in Kerouac's novels also reflect the times and were blatantly chauvinistic. Certainly his personal life is fraught with examples of poor treatment of the women in his life, other than his mother. Although the Beats did have many loyal female advocates, these men were not role models when it came to gender equality.

With the arrival of Ginsberg and some of his friends back in New York City, Robert Frank and Alfred Leslie took the opportunity to make a movie with them during the winter of 1959. Originally, Frank planned to call his film simply *The Beat Generation,* using the title of a Kerouac play that Robert had excerpted for the movie. Later the name was changed to *Pull My Daisy,* otherwise, the title of a collaborative poem that Jack, Allen, and Neal had composed a decade earlier. For several weeks Robert shot black-and-white footage in Leslie's Fourth Avenue loft, operating on a shoestring budget. He concentrated on one scene from the play in which a bishop came to visit at the home of Neal and Carolyn Cassady. During the course of the bishop's visit, several friends arrived and their antics, both premeditated and spontaneous, cause chaos and turmoil in the house. The film featured Ginsberg, Orlovsky, Corso, Kerouac, David Amram, Larry Rivers, and a few others who improvised a day in the life of the Beat generation.

When the filming was over, David Amram composed a musical score for *Pull My Daisy* loosely based on the whimsical poem of the same name. Kerouac then narrated the previously silent footage after the film's editing was completed. It was risky because Jack's heavy drinking made his performance unpredictable, and the producers took the chance that he would be up to the task. After finishing the first take of his unscripted narration, Frank asked Kerouac to do it again. Even though multiple takes are standard practice in filmmaking, the request shocked Jack. He wasn't prepared to repeat what he had said, and in fact he didn't really remember the bulk of what he had improvised. For him it was a spontaneous, impromptu event and he had no interest in trying to recreate his extemporaneous monologue a second time. Robert Frank was able to mollify him and reluctantly Jack did try once more, but the first take proved to be the better one.

By the late fifties, not only film but the theater was undergoing radical changes. Judith Malina and Julian Beck, who had been friends of Ginsberg's since the subterranean days at the San Remo, finally found theater space of their own in the Village. Late in 1958 they opened the new home for their Living Theatre acting troupe on Fourteenth Street. Until then they had been performing wherever they could find an empty stage, even using their own living rooms for some productions. With the luxury of a permanent stage, they were able to produce many more plays, several of which were written by poets. That combination of poets and dramatists seemed to work well with the experimental nature of their productions. In fact the Living Theatre's first production was *Many Loves,* a verse comedy written by William Carlos Williams. Nontraditional plays were written by poets Michael McClure, Diane Di Prima, Frank O'Hara, and Philip Whalen and performed off-off-Broadway at the Living Theatre, where they attracted a steady audience over the years. Drama was yet another example of the ever-widening variety of activities that the Beats were beginning to influence.

Chapter 15

The Circle Widens

In response to the new demand for Beat writing, many publishers put out anthologies of Beat work. Most important of these was Donald Allen's collection, *The New American Poetry, 1945–1960,* which helped codify that generation of writers. Don Allen combined poetry by members of the Beat Generation with that of poets associated with both the San Francisco Renaissance and Black Mountain schools. This became the definitive collection of avant-garde postwar poetry and remained in print for the next fifty years. It helped define who and what "Beat" was all about. *The New American Poetry* influenced a younger generation of poets who looked to these poets for inspiration and example.

Some critics contrasted Don Allen's anthology with the highly popular *New Poets of England and America*, which appeared around the same time. That anthology, with an introduction by Robert Frost, focused on poets who were much more conservative and traditional in style and subject matter. Poems by Robert Bly, Thom Gunn, James Merrill, and Richard Wilbur filled the pages of that collection. It is interesting to note that no poets found their way into both anthologies. Clearly, a line was drawn between the academy and the iconoclasts, and it was impossible to cross from one camp to the other.

By the sixties, some of the Beats had become well known, even if those names were identified with foul language and antisocial behavior. It was impossible to believe that they would ever be embraced by the academy. Their audiences were mainly the young bohemian crowds who flocked to edgy urban neighborhoods looking for a new, less stifling lifestyle. Most middle-class Americans viewed the works of the Beats as obscene and irrelevant. Even though the Beats had intended to create a populist literature, it appeared as if the populace didn't want it. For incorporating the language of the streets in their works, they were scolded by the very people who used that language.

Frequently the publication of their work stirred strong emotions, as it did in the case against the *Chicago Review*. When the University of Chicago refused to allow the editors to publish work by Burroughs, Kerouac, and Edward Dahlberg, the editors formed *Big Table*. To raise money for the legal expenses incurred by the beleaguered publication, Ginsberg, Orlovsky, Corso, and Ferlinghetti all made trips to Chicago. *Time* magazine devoted a full page to the story, but instead of delving into the issue of censorship, which should have been of primary importance to them as a news magazine, *Time*'s reporter dwelt on some of the offbeat comments the poets made. "I'm crazy like a daisy" was one flip remark that Allen made, and it was repeated in the pages of *Time*. From that and similar experiences, Ginsberg learned that you could not joke with the press. In the future, he would take a more serious and businesslike approach to publicity.

It might seem contradictory to think that people who were defending their First Amendment rights would be ridiculed by the press, but many conservative observers considered the Beats a danger to society. In 1960, FBI director J. Edgar Hoover, speaking before the Republican National Convention, declared that "beatniks" were one of the three greatest threats to American security. The other two were communists and eggheads.

Even liberal intellectuals voiced their disapproval of the Beats, possibly jealous of the attention they were receiving. Shortly after Ginsberg, Corso, and Orlovsky returned from the *Big Table* benefit, the trio gave a reading at Columbia University. Diana Trilling, the wife of Allen's old Columbia professor, Lionel Trilling, and a proponent of many liberal causes, was in the audience that evening. In fact, Allen, proud to be back at his alma mater, took the opportunity to dedicate a poem to her husband. Diana reported on the evening's events in a *Partisan Review* article entitled "The Other Night at Columbia," in which she opened by saying that as soon as she arrived at the theater and took one look at the audience, she knew it would smell bad. Agitated by her analysis, Allen fired off an angry letter denouncing the article and tried to convince the Trillings that true intellectuals should support the efforts of younger writers instead of tearing them down. According to Allen, the avant-garde didn't need enemies from within.

The Columbia event was followed a week later by a reading at the Gaslight, a Greenwich Village coffeehouse that was much more in tune with the Beats. Appearing with Ginsberg and Corso that night was a new poet by the name of Ray Bremser. Bremser had recently been paroled after spending several years in a New Jersey prison. Like Corso, Ray had spent his time in jail reading, writing poetry, and educating himself. His poetry was designed to be the verbal equivalent of jazz, and his style appealed to the audience that night. LeRoi Jones, who had a deep interest in jazz himself, was there and became a champion of Bremser's work. He even acted as his guardian for a time when Ray was on parole.

Later that month Bremser joined Jones, Corso, Ginsberg, and Orlovsky on a reading tour to Washington, DC, where they read before appreciative crowds at Howard and George Washington universities. It was a worthwhile trip for Ray, who met Bonnie Frazer at one of the readings. Bonnie soon left school and married Ray; later she would write a memoir about their life together. Poets with jailhouse backgrounds like Bremser and Corso helped to further the public misconception that the Beats were nothing more than unschooled juvenile delinquents.

LeRoi Jones was one of only a handful of black writers who became associated with the Beat Generation, along with Bob Kaufman and Ted Joans. The reason for the lack of African American representation in the group was similar to the reason that few women were associated with them. Ginsberg simply didn't know many black writers in the forties and fifties. It was LeRoi Jones, in fact, who first approached Ginsberg after he had read *Howl,* a poem that influenced him a great deal. While Allen was still in Europe, he had received a fan letter from LeRoi that had been written on a long piece of toilet paper. The unusual stationary got Allen's attention and he began a correspondence with Jones, encouraging him to write and publish poetry. With Allen's blessing and the help of his wife, Hettie, LeRoi began a little magazine they called *Yugen.* It ran for only eight issues but proved to be influential in helping to disseminate the work of the Beats. Through magazines like *Yugen,* Ginsberg was able to become the great poetry advertiser of his age, as Ezra Pound had been in the 1920s. Allen funneled poems by his friends to young editors like LeRoi Jones and Diane Di Prima in New York City and Lawrence Ferlinghetti and John Wieners in San Francisco.

Wieners, a Bostonian living temporarily in San Francisco, was near the center of the thriving poetry scene there and was the editor of *Measure.* Like many other aspiring poets, he had attended Black Mountain College to study under Charles Olson, Robert Creeley, and Robert Duncan. From Black Mountain he had followed Duncan to San Francisco, where he had the freedom to pursue a more openly homosexual lifestyle than he could have in his old Irish Catholic neighborhood in Boston. Wieners, along with Michael McClure, Philip Whalen, Lew Welch, Lawrence Ferlinghetti, and Gary Snyder, often made the rounds of the poetry venues in North Beach. Many of them followed Kenneth Rexroth's example and read their poems to an accompaniment of jazz music, and a lively poetry-and-jazz fad swept the city temporarily. It was fun and made poetry more accessible to the public.

Through the combination of jazz and poetry, the poets were successful in transferring their readings from the sterility of the classroom into the neighborhood coffeehouses and bars. In San Francisco, David Meltzer and ruth weiss (who, like e. e. cummings, eschewed uppercase letters) excelled at the combination of poetry with jazz because they both had the musical ability to make their readings entertaining as well as thought provoking. Meltzer worked just down the street from City Lights at the Discovery Bookstore by day and wrote poetry by night. Ferlinghetti also did some excellent work with jazz early on, but soon came to believe that without cooperation and practice with the musicians, the readings were doomed to be little more than music interrupted by poetry.

Ferlinghetti was spending much of his time in his bookstore on the publishing end of his business during those days. New books were constantly issuing forth from City Lights's tiny basement office. City Lights would be the only small publishing company with origins in the Beat esthetic that managed to turn a profit and stay in business. Most of the other small press ventures and poetry magazines were short-lived, but City Lights managed to thrive through the dedication of Lawrence and his staff. In large part they survived due to the steady sale of their Ginsberg titles. Even after the more prestigious New York publishers tried to lure Allen away with the promise of higher royalties, he remained loyal to City Lights because he appreciated the fact that Ferlinghetti had defended *Howl* in court. Had the verdict gone against him, Lawrence might easily have lost his business, and Allen never forgot that. Allen's importance to City Lights also gave him leverage with Ferlinghetti. Repeatedly he tried to persuade Lawrence to publish the work of his friends, and over the years many of the people he discovered were published by City

Lights. Still, Ferlinghetti always exercised his own editorial judgment, and he elected not to publish books by Burroughs and Kerouac in spite of Allen's urging.

In 1959, after less than a year in California, Gary Snyder set off again for Japan, where he spent the next five years as a student of Buddhist meditation. He returned to the Daitoku-ji monastery in Kyoto where he studied under the master Oda Sesso Roshi. Gary was very much an expatriate and his first book, *Riprap,* was in fact edited and published in Kyoto by Cid Corman's Origin Press. In that book he collected some of his best poems written during his years of study and wandering.

On his recent trip back to America, Gary had met Joanne Kyger at a poetry reading, and the two made plans for her to visit him in Kyoto. To prepare herself for living abroad, Joanne moved into the East-West House in San Francisco to immerse herself in Japanese culture. An eccentric group of people had lived there over the years, including poets like Lew Welch, Philip Whalen, Albert Saijo, and Claude Dalenberg, to learn what they could about Asian culture and traditions.

In May 1959, the same month that Kyger took up residence in the East-West House, Ginsberg made his first jet flight to San Francisco, where he stayed with friends and used a desk at City Lights as his own office. In addition to giving some readings, he was there to try to secure Neal Cassady's release from prison. One day Allen gave a lecture for the inmates at San Quentin and he had the opportunity to read his own poetry in front of a class of convicts that included Neal. The prisoners loved Allen's work and cheered madly for him, but in spite of Allen's best efforts, Neal's term of five to life was not reduced.

It was also during this 1959 trip that Allen made a stop in Menlo Park to participate in an experiment that would radically change popular culture in America over the next decade. Always open to new metaphysical experiences, Ginsberg volunteered to take a psychedelic drug that Stanford University was then testing. Ever since Ginsberg had been introduced to drugs by Burroughs and Huncke during the mid-forties, he had remained interested in the hallucinations and distortions to perception that they induced. Following his Blake visions in the summer of 1948, he had methodically experimented with one drug after another, hoping to find something that would recreate the flash of revelation that he had experienced then. Occasionally, he came close to recreating the sense of epiphany he had felt when Blake's voice revealed the world's mysteries to him, but nothing duplicated it precisely. The Blake visions had occupied him for more than a decade by the time he got to Stanford, and he still believed that somewhere a drug existed that would give him instantaneous enlightenment.

Allen hoped that LSD-25, the drug being tested at Stanford that year, might produce the effect he was searching for. Although in the end this drug fell short of recreating his vivid Blake experiences, it did prove to be the most interesting that he had yet sampled. Certainly it led him into a part of his mind that he would never have discovered without chemical inducement. It proved to be one more powerful consciousness-expanding experience for him, but he realized it was not a replacement for true illumination. Ginsberg later learned that the experiments were secretly subsidized by the CIA, whose agents hoped that LSD could be used for interrogation purposes. It was ironic that the government first provided LSD to people who would later be arrested for using it.

Immediately after Allen's first dose of LSD, he signed up to take it again and began to recommend it to all his friends. He even wrote to his father, suggesting that Louis get someone at a college in New Jersey to administer it to him. The following year another writer began to work on a novel that was based on his own experiences working as an orderly in the clinic where Allen had received his first LSD.

That writer's name was Ken Kesey, and the book was *One Flew over the Cuckoo's Nest*. Kesey's own experiences with drugs would soon become legendary and would foreshadow the dramatic shift to the youth-oriented drug culture of the later sixties.

Gregory Corso found that his own drug use was not as experimental or controlled. Now truly hooked on heroin, he needed his daily dosage in order to survive, and it was becoming increasingly dangerous and expensive to buy narcotics in New York City. For that reason, he decided to return in June to Europe, where living as an addict seemed easier. He set out for Greece, only to be put off the boat in Genoa when the captain found out that Gregory's check for the voyage had bounced. From Genoa he navigated across Italy to Alan Ansen's apartment in Venice, and from there mapped out further European adventures.

It wouldn't be until September that Corso finally made it to Greece overland via France and Germany. For him, Greek and Roman culture represented the very apex of civilization and in the less expensive city of Athens, he could indulge his passion for the classics on a tight budget. The low cost of living in Greece made it more practical for him to survive on the occasional kindness of wealthier friends. He used all the Greek museums and archaeological sites as his classroom and continued his own private study of mythology and the ancients.

Ever since the spring of 1958, Jack Kerouac had been spending most of his time in the small Long Island village of Northport. With his royalty checks, he was able to put a down payment on a house and was comfortable living with his mother. The older Gabrielle Kerouac became, the more she suffered the effects of the harsh northern winters, so she asked Jack if they could return to Florida. Since she had sacrificed so much for him during her life, he agreed and packed up all their belongings for the move. While she went on ahead, Jack sold their house but began to have second thoughts about relocating.

As he waited for the closing on the sale, he bought another house in Northport not very far from the first. His mother would have to return for at least another winter.

Although Kerouac's alcoholism had been a growing problem, he believed that he could control it by himself. At home, even though he drank continually, he managed to keep himself in check. But whenever he left his mother's supervision, he found himself spiraling out of control on binges. He discovered that he couldn't go into New York without getting into arguments with people who wanted to pick fights with the "King of the Beats" and so he spent less and less time away from home.

With Ginsberg now on the West Coast and Corso and Burroughs in Europe, Jack was alone to face the barrage of New York reporters who dogged his heels and broke his spirit whenever he appeared in public. His old friend Lucien Carr was still in town, but his drinking problem was nearly as bad as Kerouac's and he was of little help. Even the talented John Clellon Holmes had escaped to the quiet town of Old Saybrook, Connecticut, where he found a place to live near his own mother.

Kerouac could not understand why the critics hated him so much. He wondered why success had been withheld from him for all those years. Now that people wanted to read his books, why were the reviewers putting him down? Why couldn't they see him as the great writer he knew himself to be? If he hadn't had a problem before, these recent disappointments would have driven him to drink anyway.

With Peter Orlovsky at the wheel, Allen planned a slow circuitous route east across the country. In San Francisco he had renewed his friendship with Robert Creeley and together the three of them headed for Creeley's home in New Mexico, stopping off like all good tourists to see the Grand Canyon. Allen had liked Bob ever since he first met him in 1956, but he had always been puzzled by his poetry. It was only after he had heard Creeley read his own work that he began to understand what Bob was doing on the page with syllables and words. In print, Allen had missed the point of the breath stops and the rhythms that were crucial to Creeley's oral delivery of his poems. After listening to him read during their trip, Allen was converted and became an ardent promoter of Creeley's poetry. After a brief visit, Bob began his job teaching school, and Allen and Peter drove slowly back to New York City.

Chapter 16

Cut-ups

Back in Europe, both Burroughs and Corso were dealing with serious drug habits. Bill had learned how to survive in the world by becoming invisible to the authorities. He usually managed to keep a low profile and avoided attracting attention. That had worked well ever since he fled Mexico, but now the French police called Bill in for questioning about some drug deals that had taken place in Tangier. As a foreigner, he knew that he was in danger of being deported, so he was nervous about any publicity. Eventually he would have to find a safer home than Paris, but for the time being he stayed on at the Beat Hotel. To protect himself in the short term, he thought it best to kick his own habit through the exercise of sheer willpower.

Burroughs had been through this before, so he knew exactly what to do. Realizing that he had to have help, he had asked a young Englishman named Ian Sommerville to take care of him as he went through the agony of withdrawal. He had met Ian in Paris at the Mistral Bookstore where he worked, and Ian had grown to love both Bill and his writing. Little realizing what it meant to watch someone go through withdrawal, Sommerville had agreed to stay with him for twenty-four hours a day as he kicked his codeine habit. Although Ian described it as one of the most frightening experiences of his life, he managed to stick it out and nursed Bill through the worst stages, keeping him under lock and key and providing him with food, water, and support.

As soon as that ordeal was over, Ian became Bill's lover for a brief period. Sommerville was the first person since Ginsberg with whom Burroughs had dropped his emotional guard. Even after the romance faded, they remained inseparable and Ian took on the role of personal assistant. He was instrumental in assembling Bill's writings for publication, just as Kerouac, Ansen, and Ginsberg had done with *The Naked Lunch*.

In the meantime, Burroughs's friendship with Brion Gysin was also growing. The two found that they had much in common, although unlike Sommerville, their relationship was platonic from the start. Gysin had his own room at the Beat Hotel where he worked on his paintings and art projects. One day while Gysin was cutting some cardboard with a matte knife, he accidentally sliced through a pile of newspapers that were lying underneath. When he looked at the shredded paper, he noticed that the words on one side of the cut lined up with words from another page on the other side of the cut. By chance, he read a few of the severed lines from these cut-up collages and found that they created intriguingly odd juxtapositions of words and phrases. Since the randomness of the resulting words interested him somewhat, he happened to mention it to Burroughs.

To Gysin the new text created by the accident was merely a curiosity, but to Burroughs it represented something much more. He immediately began cutting up columns of text and rearranged the sliced bits. To Burroughs's assiduous eye, the chance realignment of pages revealed the true meaning of the passages that had been cut up. It seemed that subliminal good fortune had enabled Bill to read between the lines of any text. He began to experiment with everything he could think of, from newspapers and phone books to his own letters and manuscripts. Each collage provided a new interpretation of the material. Bill found that text, especially political speeches, seemed to work best and nearly always exposed hidden intent within the messages. The combinations and permutations were unlimited through this process. The technique became what Burroughs would call the "cut-up method" and it was to occupy most of his creative energy for the next decade.

Burroughs was so excited by the discovery that he showed it to Gregory Corso and Sinclair Beiles, a writer from South Africa who was also staying at the hotel at the time. They too took up the knife, and within days the four of them had created enough interesting material to fill a book that they called *Minutes to Go.* Although Corso initially took part in the cut-ups, upon reflection he decided to distance himself from the method. He was not disposed to leave poetry to chance. Gregory's poems were all crafted perfectly. He spent months refining and reworking every word, so he did not want to concede creative control to luck. For him, as for many others, the cut-up method remained a novel parlor trick.

Working with the cut-up technique and the printed word was only the first step in a natural progression that led to other media. Before long, Burroughs began to cut up tape recordings and pictures, rearranging them into unexpected and intriguing collages of sound and sight. Ian knew quite a bit about tape recorders and was of considerable technical help. Each new format offered even more possibilities.

Future sociologists have traced later developments in the arts back to this process. For example, the use of increasingly short film clip montages by cinematographers and the use of rapid cuttings of sound bites by music producers that became commonplace later had their roots in Burroughs's cut-ups. Philosophically, Burroughs extended the process to himself and began to see his life as a cut-up, too. It was composed of seemingly unconnected, random events, but actually, it formed a pattern that made sense in the sum of its parts. Just walking down the street was a form of cut-up, if you stopped to consider the myriad distractions, interruptions, and nonsequiturs encountered along the way.

While Burroughs was using his Japanese reel-to-reel tape recorder to make his first audio cut-ups in Paris, media frenzy over the Beats was still high back in the United States. The private affairs of Beat poets seemed to be of more interest than their poetry, and such was the case in November when Ray Bremser appeared on a local Philadelphia talk show. He was asked about his opinion of drugs and he replied that he supported the legalization and the use of marijuana. It was a serious mistake for Ray, because technically he was violating his parole at the time, since he was not permitted to leave the state of New Jersey without permission. The authorities sent him back to Trenton State Prison for another six months in spite of widespread protests from the literary community.

Interest in Jack Kerouac as a personality also continued to grow, even if the majority of literary critics had not warmed to his writing. The same month that Bremser violated his parole in Philadelphia, Steve Allen was interviewing Kerouac on nationwide television. Jack made the long trip to the West Coast once more, but this time he traveled as a fully paid passenger instead of riding inside a boxcar as he had on earlier trips to visit the Cassadys. In Hollywood, Jack spent most of his ten days trying unsuccessfully to interest movie producers in adapting his work for the big screen. Then, with nerves calmed by alcohol, he appeared on *The Steve Allen Plymouth Show* only slightly tipsy. Nonetheless, he gave a spectacular reading, accompanied by Steve Allen on the piano. Kerouac had wanted to read from his unpublished book, *Visions of Cody,* but the directors insisted that he read from the popular *On the Road.* Without telling anyone, Jack read a bit from *On the Road,* and then turned to the back of the

172 / THE TYPEWRITER IS HOLY

book and read a few pages of *Cody*, which he had secretly inserted within the covers of *On the Road*. No one was ever the wiser.

Even with a sympathetic interviewer like Steve Allen, Kerouac couldn't escape the inevitable question about what it meant to be "Beat," and Steve also expressed curiosity about typing the manuscript on a long roll of paper. Those things were of little interest to Jack. He felt that how it was typed had little to do with the book; the scroll was only a tool that allowed him to type faster and get his thoughts onto the page quickly.

Kerouac's Hollywood stay was followed by a short stopover in San Francisco for the premiere of Robert Frank's movie *Pull My Daisy*. Jack showed up at the premier party so drunk and disheveled that the bouncer wouldn't let him in to his own party until someone inside recognized him. Although Jack had promised to visit Neal in San Quentin, he decided that he didn't want to see his old friend under those circumstances and so he deliberately missed the appointment. Then, in a manner reminiscent of Neal, Jack abruptly left town with two other writers, Lew Welch and Albert Saijo, in their Jeep. They made a beeline across the country and didn't stop until Jack was sitting at his mother's kitchen table in Northport.

After another stint in jail, Huncke was back on the streets, living in Ginsberg's building on East Second Street. The fact that Corso was in Europe made it easier for Allen to help, since Corso and Huncke didn't care much for each other. Perhaps the rivalry came because the two con men were usually fighting over Allen's support. He was an easy mark, but he didn't have all that much money to go around. During this period Huncke finally gave in to Allen's constant urging and began to compose short stories. Since the late forties Allen had encouraged Huncke to write down his reminiscences, but it wasn't until the early sixties that Herbert had written enough material for his first book. He had always enjoyed telling stories about the characters he knew from his days on Times Square. They were sensitive, honest portraits of people who, like Huncke himself, lived on the very fringe of society. Huncke's tales are the literary equivalents of Diane Arbus's photographs, which unsentimentally reveal people on the margins of society.

Ginsberg was a genius when it came to encouraging people who didn't believe that they had enough talent to write or express themselves. From time to time, as with Huncke, the results of his hectoring were wonderfully personal and creative. Within a few years, Diane Di Prima recognized the beauty of Huncke's prose and published his first book, *Huncke's Journal,* with an introduction by Ginsberg. Every story in the book displays Huncke's desire to be loved, no matter how unlovable he might act in his personal life, and each is infused with his deep respect for others.

In addition to Huncke, Ginsberg also encouraged other close friends like Alan Ansen, Peter Orlovsky, and Neal Cassady to write and publish their work. Ansen, who had always composed marvelous poetry, had never tried to find a publisher. Still acting as a benevolent agent, Allen contacted the Tibor de Nagy Gallery about Ansen's work. Through their association with Frank O'Hara, the gallery had established a tradition of working with both artists and writers, and in 1959 they put out Ansen's first book, *The Old Religion.* Although prominent among his contemporaries, Ansen has been virtually forgotten by students of the Beat Generation. In fact, he was left out of both the encyclopedic *Beat Culture* and the two-volume *The Beats: Literary Bohemians in Postwar America,* even though he was a wise counsel to many of the Beats on all aspects of literature. Corso, Burroughs, and Ginsberg, along with more traditional writers like W. H. Auden and William Gaddis, all turned to Ansen for editorial and linguistic help at one time or another. Ansen was fluent in eight or nine languages and read encyclopedically on a wide range of topics. That he spent much of his life in Italy and Greece and never returned to America perhaps obscured his importance.

Although New York was the biggest market for Beat publications, it was not the only hotbed of activity. In San Francisco, small presses like Auerhahn, Coyote, Haselwood, Measure, and White Rabbit proliferated. Even Jonathan Williams's Jargon Society Press, which became well known as the publisher for Black Mountain authors like Charles Olson and Robert Creeley, had its beginnings in San Francisco and published the works of several Beat writers. Bob Kaufman was a central figure in the group that published a mimeo newsletter in North Beach called *Beatitude*. They focused on emerging writers and for a brief while tried to produce a weekly magazine of what was current in San Francisco poetry. Few of them were commercially viable, but they all contributed to a grassroots effort to put new poetry before a wider audience.

As interest in the Beat Generation spread, San Francisco's North Beach and Los Angeles's Venice became the West Coast counterparts to Greenwich Village as havens for talented and aspiring writers. Some of the new arrivals worked hard and partied hard, while others only partied. In reaction to the growing public fascination with the new art and literature that was being created, North Beach was added to tourists' itineraries and so-called Beatnik Tours were promoted. On weekends busloads of tourists from around the country would descend on North Beach to stare at the crazy-looking, bearded freaks who recited their poetry to jazz music in the neighborhood's coffee shops. One enterprising bohemian retaliated by organizing a "Squaresville Tour" and drove a busload of beatniks to a department store to stare at the shoppers.

Although the majority came to gawk at the inhabitants, the small bohemian enclaves captured the imaginations of many others. Young people who wanted to escape their middle-class roots began to pour in. Their view of that scene was distorted by a media image of a Beat lifestyle that focused only on carefree, irresponsible behavior and ignored the whole intellectual basis for the group. Beat culture as it came to be outlined by the homogenizing influence of *Time* and *Life* magazines had very little to do with the Beat Generation. The rapid influx of people into North Beach, Venice, and Greenwich Village also destroyed the sense of community that had been built by earlier participants in the scene. So many new people flooded into those neighborhoods that the original small core of artists could not survive.

Among the waves of new arrivals came many who were not interested in the literature and art that had formed the foundation of the community spirit. They were interested only in being part of "the Beat scene." These people helped to dilute the serious, creative spirit that the artists tried to maintain. A shy, sensitive person, Jack Kerouac couldn't handle the endless stream of admirers who wanted to spend time with him, buy him drinks, and prey upon his creative energy. Michael McClure once said that he knew it was time to leave North Beach when he was approached on the street by a man completely attired as a pirate.

In January 1960, Lawrence Ferlinghetti and Allen Ginsberg flew to Concepción, Chile, to take part in a Latin American writers' conference. This was only the first of many international literary events that were to draw attention to the Beats, and their influence would grow outside the country over the next few decades. After the conference Ferlinghetti spent a few weeks traveling in Bolivia and Peru, but Allen decided to stay on for another six months to enjoy the exotic nature of the countryside and to escape from the intense media pressure back in the States.

Allen set his sights on finding a source for yage, the hallucinogenic vine that Burroughs had discovered a few years earlier. As he traveled into the most remote parts of the South American jungle, he enjoyed the total isolation. The experience reinforced his notion that a protracted period of seclusion might be beneficial for him both personally and creatively.

In February, Joanne Kyger left San Francisco to visit Gary Snyder in Kyoto. She had completed her orientation at the East-West House, where she had learned enough about Asian customs to get by in Japan. Once in Kyoto she and Gary were married. They had already agreed that it was the only acceptable way for her to stay in Japan for any length of time. Single women traveling with a man generally were not welcome because there were strict social rules against cohabitation. Joanne agreed that the easiest way around the prohibition was to get married. Although the rules were more rigid in Japan than in America, women in both countries had to play roles subservient to men. Perhaps the more rigid social structure of Japan was one of the things that Gary found culturally appealing. Like many of the other male members of the Beat Generation, it would take him a long time to adjust to feminist ideas of equality. For the time being, Joanne did the household chores while Gary studied.

Leaving Chile behind, Ginsberg journeyed to the headwaters of the Amazon on his quest. During his trip in the early fifties, Burroughs had described the terrifying visions brought on by yage, the drug that was locally known as "the death vine." Since Allen had always been fascinated by death, he wanted firsthand experience and hoped that he could locate a native shaman to administer it to him properly. Fresh from his LSD experience in California, Allen wanted to compare the visionary effects of both drugs. Finally, somewhere along the Ucayali River in Peru, Allen found a *curandero* (drug doctor) who agreed to preside over his preparation and ingestion of yage. During a series of sessions, Allen experienced some of the most frightening visions he would ever have. At times he feared that he would go mad or possibly even die on the spot, but in spite of the risk, he wanted to persevere and explore the mysteries of his mind. He believed his experience gave him clarity on universal essentials. He realized that he was and always had been dwelling in a living universe, that nothing was static. His near-death experience proved to him that death was essentially a natural progression in a circle of life.

With yage he was able to envision creation itself and witness God's power firsthand.

For Allen, drugs truly were an experimental means to an end. When Allen got drunk for the very first time back in 1943, it had been premeditated. He wanted to learn what the effects of alcohol would be on his mind and body. In his journal, he had documented the various stages from the first buzz, through tipsiness, to complete inebriation. It was all done methodically with a scientific curiosity. It was the same with yage and many of his later experiences with drugs. This was not the case with very many of his friends. Drugs for the majority of them might have been an "experiment" at first, but often that initial curiosity would turn into a source of pleasure, escape, and finally dependency. Critics of the drug culture of the later sixties, especially as promoted by Timothy Leary and his followers, point out correctly that using the word *experiment* is inaccurate. For many, taking drugs was nothing more than self-indulgence. Allen was earnest, however and did use drugs as a key to unlocking unknown recesses within the mind. Only once, while he had been in Paris with Burroughs and Corso, had he ever used drugs with enough regularity to verge on addiction. Allen's positive descriptions of drug-induced wonders encouraged many to sample them without considering the possible consequences.

No sooner had Ginsberg returned to New York from South America than Jack Kerouac set out from Northport on one of the last great adventures of his life. By the early sixties Kerouac had become depressed and was in despair about the attacks upon himself and his work by the critics. The screen adaptation of *The Subterraneans,* which resembled Jack's novel in name only, had just been released to bad reviews, some of which were directed against Kerouac personally.

By nature, Jack was a quiet, peaceful, nonviolent man, but when he drank, he became belligerent and verbally abusive. The combination of argumentative drunkard and quiet pacifist did not serve him well during the inevitable barroom fights he provoked, and he had found himself on the receiving end of some severe beatings. Finally, by 1960, he had begun to realize that his dependency on alcohol was an obstacle to both his mental and his physical well-being.

To this end, Kerouac secretly bought a train ticket to California, determined to hide out in Lawrence Ferlinghetti's remote cabin in Bixby Canyon along the rugged Big Sur coast. Once alone and removed from the temptation of the bottle, he believed that he would be able to kick his dependency on alcohol and save his own life. He had always been able to muster up the willpower to detoxify himself, at least for short periods of sobriety as he had on Desolation Peak. Weakened by many more years of heavy drinking, he was physically unprepared to deal with the delirium tremens that came with going cold turkey and he could not resist his body's unyielding demand for liquor. After only days in the Bixby cabin, Jack ended up back in North Beach stumbling from one bar to the next on another binge.

One of the very few rewarding experiences to come out of his West Coast trip was that Kerouac was able to spend some time in San Francisco with Neal Cassady, who had been released from prison in June 1960. Surprisingly, Neal did not hold a grudge against Jack for not communicating with him during his time in jail. In fact, it was with Neal's blessing that Jack became involved with Neal's most recent girlfriend, Jackie Gibson, and for a few short days he toyed with the idea of marrying her. Since most of his visit took place in a drunken haze, the wedding did not materialize.

On one peacefully sunny afternoon, Neal and his now ex-wife, Carolyn, enjoyed a reunion with Jack. Sadly, it was to be the last time that Carolyn would see Jack alive. She had met the handsome young writer only a decade earlier, and they had shared an intense love. By then, Jack had written a dozen books and gone on to achieve the fame that he had always longed for. By 1960 he had lost his youthful charm and rugged good looks and was quickly becoming a bloated alcoholic in the process of drinking himself to death. It was not how Carolyn wanted to remember him.

Remarkably, once he was back home, Kerouac the writer was able to distance himself from Kerouac the alcoholic, and he wrote about what it had been like to go through the trauma of withdrawal. The resulting novel, *Big Sur,* accurately depicted what he could not face in real life: the fact that he was drinking himself to death.

Chapter 17

Bitter Fruits

Following his crushing failure to sober himself at Big Sur, Kerouac gave up and never tried seriously to kick alcohol again. He spent the entire decade of the sixties moving with his mother from one house to another up and down the East Coast, always restless, always looking for a place to settle but never finding the peace that he wanted. He cut himself off from his friends, possibly feeling that his mother was right when she complained that they were a bad influence on him. The first thing he did at each new home was have a tall stockade built around his property. It was symbolic of the fence he built around himself during the last years of his life.

Rejected by the literary world that he once had dreamed of joining, bitter after the personal attacks from the press, and neglected by his friends who were embracing their own newfound fame, Jack simply disappeared. There were fewer and fewer occasions when he would allow himself to venture into New York City to visit his friends, and when they came to see him, he often hid from them, refusing to answer the door. Only when very drunk did he pick up the telephone and call some of his old pals. In the end, most of them grew tired of his late-night drunken ramblings and stopped answering the phone.

While Jack was typing up the story of his ill-fated trip to Big Sur in the autumn of 1960, Burroughs finally packed up and left Paris. Fearing that police surveillance would lead to his arrest, he moved to London to be closer to Ian Sommerville, who was attending school at Cambridge. In England, William met a young, good-looking man still in his teens, the scion of a distinguished family. Michael Portman soon became Burroughs's first true groupie. He was willing to do anything as long as he could be close to his idol. He patterned everything that he did after Burroughs, ominously learning to mainline heroin so that he could be just like Bill. Portman, who had grown up privileged and spoiled by his mother, acted as if everyone was born to defer to him. Burroughs must have been flattered by the idea of having an acolyte, because he and Portman were constant companions from the start. Ian Sommerville, who loved Bill but was no longer interested in him physically, was relieved when Michael Portman appeared on the scene and took the sexual pressure off their relationship.

Even if Portman found Bill's addiction something to emulate, Burroughs was determined to break his drug habit and went to see Dr. Dent for his second apomorphine cure. Once again it seemed to be effective, and Bill was reassured that even if he relapsed, this cure would always be there as a backup. In London, Burroughs set up headquarters at the Empress Hotel, where he continued to work long hours on his newest book, *The Soft Machine*. It was his first solo book based on the cut-up experiments that he had begun in Paris with Brion Gysin.

Burroughs also worked simultaneously on two other cut-up books. These were eventually published as *The Ticket That Exploded* and *Nova Express*. These challenging books formed a trilogy that has neither a beginning nor an end and can be read as a single work. Bill always maintained that all his books were indeed one book, but the content of these three works in particular overlapped one another. Burroughs repeatedly revised each of these books; they were continually in flux even after they were published. As a result, various editions of each book are noticeably different.

During this period Bill was to describe his life and work as a constant struggle against the agents of control, both good and bad. He felt that the police, the government, and the mass media were all agents bent on the sole purpose of controlling men. Through the cut-up technique, he found that he had discovered the secrets to their method of control and that by reassembling their words he was able to reveal their concealed agenda. In the examples that he selected to send to his friends, Burroughs did manage to provide proof that by cutting up texts, an observer can read between the lines.

By the end of 1960, Allen Ginsberg had already made his first trip from New York to Harvard University to visit a psychology professor named Dr. Timothy Leary who was administering psilocybin for experimental purposes. Leary was actively studying the alleged therapeutic benefits of that drug on the human mind, hoping to discover new treatments for mentally ill patients. Ginsberg and Leary hit it off at once, and soon the Harvard professor came to New York to share his psilocybin with several of Allen's friends, one of them being Jack Kerouac. These experiments were completely legal at the time and it wasn't until the 1970s that psilocybin was banned through the passage of the Psychotropic Substances Act.

Leary had originally wanted to test the drug on artists and writers so that they could describe the effects of the drug precisely, with greater sensitivity and expression. It soon became clear that the possibilities for the use of consciousness-expanding drugs extended far beyond the mentally ill. In Allen's East Second Street apartment, he and Leary began to make plans for what they called a psychedelic revolution. The two of them naïvely hoped the widespread use of these new drugs would help to change the world for the better. Allen thought that people who took hallucinogens would be less likely to start wars and that there would be less misery in the world. During Leary's initial visit, Kerouac took some of the psilocybin and pointed out that, "Walking on water wasn't built in a day." It was both a silly and a sage remark that Ginsberg quoted frequently.

By the end of 1960, Corso was back in Greece looking for his own version of inspiration and happiness. He had visited Athens briefly once before, and since drugs were both inexpensive and easy to come by there, he knew he could survive on a shoestring. He steeped himself in the Greek classics, visited several of the islands of Greek mythology, and continued to write beautiful poetry. On his earlier visit, Corso had experienced visions of his own on the island of Hydra. He headed back, hoping to relive those moments, only to discover that the visions would not return on demand. While he traveled, he kept in close contact with his new publisher at New Directions, James Laughlin. In addition to asking Laughlin for some occasional cash, he hoped that the publisher would want to follow *Happy Birthday of Death* with a new collection of his poetry. To encourage some positive feedback, he wrote, "I am coming very close to a wonderful intelligence."

Occasionally someone in the group would hear from Ray Bremser, who along with his new wife, Bonnie, was enduring difficult times in Mexico. They were both deeply involved with narcotics during that trip, and Bonnie had turned to prostitution to support her husband and baby daughter, Rachel. She described it all quite vividly in her own book, *Troia: Mexican Memoirs,* published several years later. Ray wrote less and less during his stay in Mexico, and finally was picked up by the Mexican police and deported to the United States. Tragically, he and Bonnie gave their child up for adoption and separated for the first, but not the last time.

LeRoi Jones remained in New York City, writing and publishing the works of other poets who had become close friends. In early 1961, with the help of bookman Ted Wilentz, Jones published his own first collection of poetry under the provocative title *Preface to a Twenty Volume Suicide Note.* That book, addressed to his children, was meant to be ironic and playful, yet revealing an internal struggle. He was a black American from a Newark ghetto searching for his own place in a white literary world.

That same year he and Diane Di Prima, with whom LeRoi was having an affair, founded the *Floating Bear,* printing the mimeo newsletter cheaply and mailing it out in exchange for postage. Issuing their own newsletter seemed like the perfect way to circumvent the staid New York publishing industry. Self-publication did not free them from other problems though; financial support and censorship hassles were still giant issues that they had to deal with. Late in the year, the FBI knocked on Jones's and Di Prima's doors, charging them with sending obscene material through the mail. Di Prima and Jones had made the mistake of publishing Burroughs's routine *Roosevelt After Inauguration.* A short skit of questionable taste, it was based on a dream Bill had remembered about Roosevelt appointing a cabinet composed of every freak and misfit he could imagine, from Jerk Off Annie to Pantapon Mike. An overzealous postal inspector spotted it and notified the authorities. They also found LeRoi's poem "The System of Dante's Hell" to be equally offensive and decided to censor the newsletter. Di Prima and Jones were called before a grand jury but were not indicted. Even though the court found the case against them to have little merit, the debts they incurred through legal fees were crippling. It was part of the deliberate strategy used by the Justice Department to harass American dissenters during the post-McCarthy era. The intention was to intimidate activists so that their fears would lead to self-censorship.

Throughout the early sixties, a handful of Americans were trying to work through the proper channels to decriminalize the use of certain drugs. Usually the only result was that it opened these activists up to more intense scrutiny by the government. For Ginsberg, who usually found challenges invigorating, the cause of legalizing drugs proved to be all-consuming and exhausting. Since many of the existing drug laws were written before the newest hallucinogens became common, many, like LSD, were not listed as controlled substances. Although Allen and others worked to keep it that way, Harry Anslinger, the first commissioner of the U.S. Bureau of Narcotics, wanted to expand the powers of his office by adding more substances to the country's list of illegal drugs. To that effect, laws were passed making previously legal substances illegal. Those laws automatically turned many casual drug users into criminals. Allen's involvement in the issue began to infringe on the time he spent writing poetry, so he made plans to escape.

With Burroughs, Ansen, and Corso already abroad, Ginsberg and Orlovsky sailed to France in the early spring of 1961. Corso had once more suggested that if Allen and Peter came to visit, he and possibly Burroughs might accompany them to India. Gregory longed to find his old girlfriend, Hope Savage, with whom he was still in love. She was reportedly wandering around Central Asia in search of enlightenment, but their chances of actually finding her among the hundreds of millions of people were slim. Ginsberg had been dreaming of going to India, too. He was captivated by exotic places, and wanted to distance himself from America's drug laws. India offered him an excellent opportunity to view a culture that handled drug issues with tolerance and whose gods were as colorful as his own visions of Blake.

Allen had been receiving a steady stream of letters from Gary Snyder, who was still deeply involved in his monastic studies in Japan. He was learning a good deal about Buddhist practice, and when he suggested that Allen hook up with him to travel to holy sites in India, it sounded perfect. Allen had been somewhat interested in Buddhism ever since Kerouac had introduced him to the concept of meditation nearly a decade earlier. Jack was by now in no shape to go on an arduous trip. He and his mother were living a quiet life in Orlando, and he seemed safe and protected there.

Gregory returned from Greece just in time to meet Ginsberg and

Orlovsky as they arrived in Paris, but they were all surprised to learn that Burroughs had just left the city. They were even more perplexed because Bill had been told several times of their impending arrival. Fortunately, Corso had a little money of his own put away, so they didn't have to depend on the few extra francs that he could have begged from Bill. The money came from Maurice Girodias, who had given Corso an advance on a novel, *The American Express,* which Gregory had written quickly in Greece. Girodias had decided that it was high time for the Olympia Press to cash in on the "beatnik" craze and he had commissioned Corso to write a book with "beat" characters. In just a matter of a few weeks, Corso dashed off a short novel, but it was too surrealistic and disjointed to command a large audience. Still, for the time being, both Girodias and Corso seemed pleased with the results and the initial orders.

In honor of the new novel, Maurice hosted a publication party in Paris that April for Gregory, and Corso began to talk about writing a sequel. He said he would devote more time and energy to it, admitting that the first book had been hastily slapped together. When anticipated sales did not materialize, the idea for a second book faded away.

The bohemian lifestyle at the Beat Hotel came complete with a new sense of sexual freedom that was not widespread in America during the early sixties. Peter and Allen organized sizable orgies in their rooms. In a group situation, Allen found that he had the opportunity to be intimate with Peter, which was all that he really desired. No one in their group of friends was monogamous, and several of the participants were bisexual. Sexual freedom did not really become widely accepted in America until the late sixties, along with the wider use of drugs.

After the Olympia Press book party, Allen and Gregory decided to visit Burroughs in Tangier on their way to India. Ginsberg had been a bit unsettled ever since Brion Gysin, who loved to gossip, had told Allen that Burroughs had actually fled Paris in order to avoid seeing him. That news shocked Allen because he regarded Burroughs as one of his oldest and closest friends. Even learning about that rejection did not stop Ginsberg from helping Gysin to edit Bill's manuscript for *The Soft Machine* while he was in Paris.

Allen considered his relationship with Bill philosophically. Later he came to realize that Bill was so obsessed by the cut-up method that he wanted to cut up and dismantle his own life. Burroughs had his own interpretation of what was happening. He believed— perhaps absurdly—that unconsciously he might actually be working as an agent of control over his own spirit. It was his plan to escape into a vacuum of silence, which he deeply believed was the only way to liberate himself in his battle against the forces of control. Old friends and memories would only slow that process, and his immediate goal was to sever all ties with his own past.

Allen wasn't aware of all that philosophy at the time, and so, analyzing himself as usual, he feared that he might have done something to offend Burroughs. He was determined to get to the bottom of this rift if he could. Why else would Bill break away from him and try to isolate himself? After a brief stop in southern France, Allen, Peter, and Gregory arrived in Tangier, where they found that Bill didn't even bother to welcome them at the dock. Uncomfortable moving into the same hotel as Bill, they checked into one a block or so away. At the time Bill was living in a room in the Villa Muniria, where Ian Sommerville and Michael Portman acted as personal bodyguards. They prevented anyone from getting close to Bill, and one or the other of them was always present, which made private conversations impossible. Allen was surprised that Bill accepted this cloistering and never considered that it might be Bill's idea in the first place. As the weeks passed, they all began to get on one another's nerves.

With Burroughs's lack of communication and his intentional distancing of himself from his old friends that summer, Allen spent more time with Paul Bowles, who had been living in Tangier for years. Since their first visit in 1957, Allen had grown to admire Bowles both as a writer and as a person. When Paul invited Allen to go along with him to Marrakech for a couple of weeks to see the giant open-air market that was held there in the summer, Allen jumped at the opportunity. He needed a break from Bill and his sycophants. The sights, sounds, and colors of the market were intoxicating, leading Allen to gradually forget his problems with Burroughs. He and Paul relaxed and enjoyed an endless supply of marijuana on the roof of Paul's apartment. Paul kept Allen spellbound with his stories about Ceylon, where Allen was planning to meet Snyder. Paul tried to discourage Allen's plan to travel through India on the cheap, by telling him that it was unhealthy to stay in anything but first-class accommodations. He said that the water was poisonous and that eating food sold on the street was lethal. Allen had no money and Peter received only fifty dollars a month as a VA benefit, so they had planned to travel on a very tight budget. Paul's information was discouraging.

By the time Allen returned to Tangier, he had resolved to confront Burroughs and find out what was behind his hostile attitude. Bill was a different person than when Allen had last seen him in Paris a few years earlier. He had no time for his friends and absolutely no interest in anyone else's work. He told Ginsberg bluntly that poetry—including Allen's—was dead and irrelevant. For that reason, he hadn't even bothered to comment on *Kaddish.* This wounded Allen more than anything else Bill could have said. Burroughs believed that his cut-up experiments had broken down the surface meanings of everything, and in the rearranged words, he was discovering basic and irrevocable truths.

While away, Allen had given surprisingly little thought to Peter Orlovsky, who was left behind in Tangier at the mercy of Burroughs and his new friends. Burroughs had never cared for Orlovsky, and to leave him with Bill while Allen traveled with Bowles seemed cruel. Peter had never spent much time with Burroughs before, and he had actually been looking forward to getting to know him better. For years he had listened to Allen praise his old mentor, but now he began to believe that Allen had been misguided. Being in the company of the "new" Burroughs was sheer torture for Peter. He was forced to listen to Burroughs and his sycophants pontificate on everything. Since none of them liked Peter, they ridiculed everything he said. To make matters worse, Peter found that there were no girls available for sex in Morocco. There were plenty of male prostitutes around to keep Burroughs happy, but women were cloistered in the Muslim world, and the few prostitutes available were much too expensive. By the time Allen returned from Marrakech, Peter was feeling lonely and morose. The two quarreled heatedly. Peter decided to set off on his own to explore the eastern Mediterranean.

Following his Moroccan experience, Ginsberg blamed Burroughs and the revelations of the cut-up for upsetting some of his most basic beliefs. Until this trip, Allen had agreed with Peter that love and human contact were the most important qualities in life. Through sex, they believed they could spread love wherever they went. But when Burroughs began to ridicule love, regarding it and words themselves as alien viruses, Allen lost the conviction of his own beliefs. Trusting Burroughs's opinion in everything, Ginsberg felt that he had to consider the possibility that Bill might be right. Furthermore, it shattered Ginsberg's self-esteem to hear Burroughs say things like, "Anyone who owns a pair of scissors can be a poet." *What would be the value of a poet's life if that were true?* he wondered.

Allen remained blindly loyal to his old friend. When Bill made fun of Orlovsky for loving women, another form of life that Bill considered alien, Allen could not bring himself to defend Peter. He stood by silently as Burroughs's new followers snickered. While Allen was away, Corso had not been supportive of Peter either and had joined in the abuse. Gregory told Peter that he had never liked Peter's poetry and thought it was just childish scribbling. Sinking to a new low, Gregory said that Allen took advantage of Peter and treated him as his prat-boy. Peter was humiliated. His spirit was broken. He was eager to escape the Moroccan madhouse four days after Allen returned.

On July 30, 1961, Orlovsky boarded the Gibraltar ferry on the first leg of his trip to Egypt. Whether their separation was to be temporary or permanent was unknown, but Peter needed time away from Allen and his patronizing friends. After Peter set sail, squabbles within the group became even more heated. During one exchange, Allen slashed Bill's shirt open with a hunting knife, violence that was totally out of character for Ginsberg. For anyone else, this visit would have been the end of their friendship, but in spite of his extreme disappointment with Burroughs, Ginsberg could not help but feel that Bill might actually have a legitimate point. Maybe poetry was dead after all.

Fortunately for Ginsberg's spirit, he and Gary Snyder had been mapping out an itinerary for their trip to India, and it gave them both something to look forward to. Allen was to meet Gary and Joanne Kyger in Ceylon around New Year's. From there they would go to the Indian subcontinent to visit as many sacred sites as they could. Since relationships in Tangier had been strained, Corso backed out of the trip. Burroughs remained unresponsive, ignoring Allen's request that he go along. Allen certainly didn't want Sommerville or Portman with them; it seemed unlikely they would leave Bill's side anyway.

Additional visitors arrived in Morocco just as the group was preparing to disband. Even before Peter left, Alan Ansen had sailed over from Venice to visit his old friends, and in August Timothy Leary dropped in for a one-day stopover on his way to a psychedelics conference in northern Europe. At first Burroughs was interested in Leary's ideas and experiments in spite of his preoccupation with cut-ups. He even agreed to go back to America with him in the fall to lead some discussions at Harvard. However, after Bill got to Cambridge and spent a few days with Leary, his opinion changed drastically. His interest faded. Leary's methods were highly unscientific, and Burroughs began to consider him an opportunistic fraud.

As the small group in Tangier went their separate ways, it was apparent that their relationships would never be the same again. Although no one knew it at the time, they would never again live together in that same communal way. It was to be the beginning of more independent lives for each of them. Despite their growing differences, they did not cease to be friends, but they would never again share the same day-to-day comradeship. Ginsberg remained the adhesive that held them all together as a group, because he was patient enough to put up with their individual foibles. For more than a decade they had been inseparable, and for the rest of their lives the Beat label bound them together. For the most part, however, their lives diverged from this point. They ceased to be kindred spirits.

For one last time in July 1961, while things were falling apart in Tangier, Kerouac had managed to slip off to Mexico City on a retreat of his own. There he busied himself reworking the manuscript of *Desolation Angels,* which he had begun a few years earlier. Back in Florida he tackled *Big Sur,* his most introspective book. Although Jack was not yet forty and would live until 1969, these were among the last major works he would complete. Discouraged by his inability to break his alcohol addiction on his own, he had given up trying.

Even as Ginsberg spent a few months wandering around Greece alone, he kept in touch with Kerouac by mail. His letters were tinged with the loneliness that he felt without Peter. Finally, Allen managed to track Peter down via American Express letters. They reunited in Israel. Peter had also missed Allen's company as he traveled alone around the Mideast, and so together they headed off to rendezvous with Snyder and Kyger. Logistics became a problem when they discovered that they could not travel directly from Israel into a Muslim country. So, after a long delay, they took a cheap freighter to East Africa and from there boarded another ship to India. In February 1962, they arrived in Bombay too late to connect with Gary and Joanne in Ceylon. Instead, they caught the next train for Delhi, where they all met up at last.

Chapter 18

Setting the Global Stage

The early 1960s brought a new period of Cold War tension. At times during the Kennedy administration, it seemed as if nuclear war was inevitable, especially at the time of the Cuban Missile Crisis in October 1962. In addition to Cuba, showdowns between the nuclear powers took place in Berlin and Southeast Asia.

As international tensions grew, some Beat writers began to take political stands, commonly in opposition to what looked like misguided U.S. policies abroad. Lawrence Ferlinghetti, who in spite of (or maybe because of) his service in the navy throughout the entire Second World War, was sympathetic to anarchist and pacifist politics. Early in Castro's regime he visited Cuba and came away impressed. When Ferlinghetti wrote to Kerouac about what he saw in Cuba, Jack, always politically conservative, replied, "I got my own Revolution out here in Northport—the American Revolution." As soon as Ferlinghetti returned to San Francisco, he wrote a poem that could have been addressed to Jack called "One Thousand Fearful Words for Fidel Castro." It called attention to some of the real dangers that

Castro faced, from the Mafia to the CIA, after he ousted the capitalist dictatorship from his country.

LeRoi Jones supported Castro by this time and philosophically was moving toward Marxism. Jones also had visited Cuba after the revolution, and the trip became a turning point in his life. He returned to America determined to become more active in political and social reform. From then on, he believed that it was not enough to write; some form of action was also necessary. It marked the beginning of his search for a radical politics that would lead him away from his white Beat friends and into the more revolutionary worlds of the civil rights and Black Nationalist movements of the late sixties. In his essay about his Cuban experiences, *Cuba Libre,* Jones began to question the role of a black writer in modern America.

As strife between the superpowers grew, some Beat writers became more politically active than they had been in the past. They followed a long tradition of writers from Homer to Blake to Keats and Shelley, who wanted poetry to bring about social, political, and cultural change. Some became champions of various causes—opposing nuclear proliferation, fighting censorship, and supporting environmental issues.

Even Burroughs, who remained aloof to politics and seemed to reject every suggestion that he take action, created works that are cautionary tales about what might become of the world if conditions continued as they were. Of the major Beat figures, only Kerouac seemed to remain steadfastly conservative. Many literary historians have suggested that Jack became more conservative as he grew older, but he had never been a liberal and really didn't shift to the right. It was the shift of his friends to the left that made Jack appear more reactionary. To others who misinterpreted his earlier politics, he appeared to have become radically more conservative.

Old friends like Burroughs who knew Kerouac well said that he always held "very traditional values, always was conservative." Although Burroughs and Corso were apathetic in their politics, they were more sympathetic to the spirit of the emerging counterculture than Kerouac was. But they were in Europe most of the decade, away from press scrutiny. During those years, they maintained their addictions, tried to keep low profiles, and took little interest in politics.

As with politics in the sixties, spirituality was another concern for many Beats, but not something that interested them all. Back in India in 1962, Gary Snyder led his tiny group on pilgrimages to see the Dalai Lama and a dozen other spiritual leaders. Although Gary and Joanne focused on the ethereal, Allen and Peter were much more interested in the material world. Wherever they went they sampled new drugs; they even managed to visit their first opium den, long one of Ginsberg's dreams. The four of them delighted in the diverse cultures of India.

In April, when Joanne and Gary returned to Japan, Allen and Peter decided to stop being tourists and instead settle down in India for a longer visit. They wanted to "go native" and blend into the fabric of the country. It made Allen happy to go unrecognized. Leaving Bombay, they rode a train a thousand miles across India to Calcutta, where they set up housekeeping in a cheap apartment in a run-down neighborhood. With no specific plans, they were determined to let the culture of India wash over them.

Peter began to take sitar lessons and dated a local Indian girl, much to the disapproval of the neighbors. Still fascinated by death, Allen hung out with the holy men on the banks of the Ganges a few days each week observing the cremation of bodies. As he watched the human flesh turn to ash, he realized that his body was nothing more than a shell that contained a spirit. He visualized humans as great wheels of meat being worn down by life. When the inevitable happened, and the wheel wore out, it was only natural that it be discarded. There was nothing to fear when death finally came, because the spirit had already left the body, he felt.

During March 1962, while Ginsberg and Snyder were still exploring the Buddhist monasteries in the foothills of the Himalayas,

Grove Press published Burroughs's *Naked Lunch* back in the United States, leaving off the initial article from the title. Even though it had been available in France for nearly three years, it was not going to get past the American censors without a battle. The following winter, bookstore owner Theodore Mavrikos was arrested in Boston for selling the book. Although being "banned in Boston" was good for sales, the editors at Grove, Dick Seaver and Barney Rosset, decided to fight the book's prohibition. It would take years for the courts to reach a final verdict, but eventually Burroughs's novel would be exonerated.

Widespread recognition came much more gradually to Burroughs than it did to Ginsberg and Kerouac. It may have been because some of his earlier books had been published under pseudonyms, because his cut-ups were difficult books for the average reader to understand, or because Burroughs was satisfied to remain anonymous and wasn't interested in any publicity, good or bad. All that began to change as the case against *Naked Lunch* worked its way through the judicial system with all the attendant press coverage.

In the summer of 1962 Burroughs was invited to take part in an international writers' conference held in Edinburgh, Scotland, along with three other Americans: Mary McCarthy, Norman Mailer, and Henry Miller. During the conference, there were some heated and widely publicized debates about the future of writing. It was there that Burroughs received genuine recognition for the first time. In particular, Mary McCarthy, whose novel *The Group* was then at the top of the best-seller list, championed his work and singled out Bill as the novelist of the future. On one panel dealing with government censorship, Burroughs explained his theory about censors and their secret agenda as agents of thought control. He went on to describe the importance of his fold-ins, a more recent variation of the cut-up experiments. The conference generated a lot of positive publicity about Burroughs and his work, and Grove Press rushed even more copies of *Naked Lunch* into print as a result. Soon he found himself to be a hot literary property.

By the time copies of *Naked Lunch* were hitting the shelves in America, even Jack Kerouac's mother was worried about her son's uncontrollable drinking. Gabrielle encouraged him to visit his old friend, John Clellon Holmes, who was still living in Old Saybrook. There, with John's help, she hoped that Jack could find a nice place for them to live. Even though she dreaded the cold northern winters, she believed that Jack's self-imposed isolation from his friends was causing him to drink more than ever now.

Kerouac took the overnight train from Florida to New England with the best intentions. He was determined to find a modest place for himself and his mother, but instead he ended up on yet another binge in Holmes's comfortable home. In the week he stayed there, he was too soused to venture out to look at real estate. Holmes and his wife felt pity for Jack, but they could not do anything to help him. When they tried to pry him out of his easy chair to look at a few places, he lost his temper and drunkenly demanded that a taxi drive him to Lowell, about sixty miles away. They did. In his old hometown, he visited with friends from his childhood, continued to drink, and then returned to Florida having accomplished nothing. Finally, by the end of the year, his mother was able to convince him to move back to Northport, Long Island, a town where Jack felt comfortable.

During the following years, Kerouac's production as a writer declined. Sadly, he continued to make a drunken spectacle of himself in public, even as many of his fellow writers were blossoming. Critics continually lambasted Jack and his writing, and the resulting pain weighed on him. The fame he longed for had come to Jack too late. He was sensitive to criticism and leaned on alcohol to help him through the bad times. The success of his friends made him feel even more bitter toward them.

While Ginsberg was in India, City Lights published *Kaddish,* the poem that is widely considered Ginsberg's masterpiece. It was the title poem of the fourteenth book in their Pocket Poets Series and the second Ginsberg book in what would become a long list of titles. In addition to being a successful publisher, Ferlinghetti was now famous as a poet in his own right. His *Coney Island of the Mind* was well on the way to becoming one of the most popular poetry books of the twentieth century. His brilliant lyrics and sharp wit made his poetry irresistible to tens of thousands of young people looking for inspiration.

By the end of 1962, Gregory Corso's second New Directions book, *Long Live Man,* was also in the bookstores. His own early fascination with death had turned into a joy in the human spirit with these poems, some of which sprang from his visionary experiences on the isle of Hydra. The larger New York publishers still wanted to publish poets from the Beat group.

That year Scribner's published Robert Creeley's breakthrough collection, *For Love.* It received warm reviews that pointed out the influence of jazz, Ginsberg, and William Carlos Williams on Bob's most recent work. Even Kerouac's old girlfriend Joyce Glassman published her first book, *Come and Join the Dance,* with Atheneum. Everyone Jack knew seemed to be thriving, which only contributed to Jack's bitter feelings toward the unfairness of the world in general and publishing in particular. For ten years he had carried his manuscripts around in his knapsack, begging for recognition, and he had been universally rejected. Now he believed that people were becoming successful on his coattails and he had yet to reap any real profit from his work, although publishers were tripping over one another to handle the work of other Beat writers. All that gave him new excuses to drink. To some of Jack's friends it was becoming clear that he was close to the end unless he could find a way to stop drinking and restore his health.

Late in the year, Allen and Peter moved from Calcutta to the most ancient and holy city in India, Benares. They tried their best to blend into their new surroundings, but they still attracted unwanted government attention. In January 1963, they received a visit from India's central intelligence police unit. Ginsberg had recently applied for an extension of his visa; that request had been denied and raised a red flag. The police wanted to know why Ginsberg wanted to stay in their country for such a long period. Typically, tourists came for a visit and then left; rarely did anyone except missionaries and social workers choose to settle down in India in those days. Allen had compounded his situation by opting to live in one of the city's poorest neighborhoods. The police assumed that if he wasn't a missionary, he certainly must be some sort of a spy, but they couldn't figure out whom he might be spying for. Allen had to go to Delhi to meet with some high government officials in order to plead his case, but the police harassment stopped only when Allen promised that he would leave India that summer.

Because he was broke and couldn't pay his own fare out, Ginsberg's promise was made possible by an invitation from Robert Creeley. In exchange for an airline ticket, Creeley asked Allen to speak at a poetry conference in Vancouver that summer. Reluctantly the Indian bureaucrats extended Allen's visa into the summer, but after the conference, if he wanted to return, he would need to get a new visa in New York. Originally Allen planned to return to India, but after the conference he decided against it.

For the two years that Allen and Peter had been living in India, Ginsberg had taken part in no political activity. Instead, he had preferred to sit and listen to the holy men who chanted and smoked ganja at the burning ghats. On one occasion he and Peter had marched in a peace demonstration to protest India-China border skirmishes, but that was the sole extent of their political involvement, and there was little for the government to fear from them. Ginsberg did note just how cruel these nationalistic skirmishes could become when Chinese restaurants in his neighborhood were targeted for vandalism and people who looked Chinese were beaten by mobs on the streets. But these were lessons that he would apply in the future.

As Allen was preparing to leave India, he received news that Timothy Leary had been fired from Harvard for the unscientific methods he used in his experiments, just as Burroughs had complained. Leary had become sloppy in his research, and in some cases had even distributed drugs to students without monitoring the results at all. Without documentation, his theories about drugs and their effects were of no use to the scientific community. By that time, Leary's mission had changed. He was now determined to expose everyone in the world to the extraordinary wonders of the new psychedelic drugs. Some of those drugs, such as LSD, were still legal, and that fact had begun to make America's drug police very nervous. It wasn't long before more drugs were added to the forbidden list and Leary himself became a target for investigation.

That summer on Ginsberg's way from India to Canada, he stopped off in Southeast Asia where he witnessed firsthand America's growing military buildup. Uncomfortable in that setting, he moved on to Japan where he had been invited to visit Gary and Joanne Snyder in their Kyoto home. Moving so quickly from the poverty and squalor of the Indian streets to the immaculate, affluent Japanese neighborhoods was yet another revelation for him. The contrast helped him put things about the material world into perspective.

During his Kyoto stopover, Snyder took Ginsberg with him to Buddhist meditation practice. There, for the first time, Allen was taught the rudiments of sitting straight and concentrating on his own breath to relax his mind. Finally he understood that it was essential to have a teacher to demonstrate proper meditation practice. In the past, he and Kerouac had only read about it, but in Japan he saw that a great deal of Buddhist transmission was only possible from teacher to pupil. He also realized that even though he had gone to Asia with no particular purpose in mind, he had managed to learn a great deal that would prove useful in later life.

On the train to Tokyo from Kyoto, Allen wrote a poem called *The Change* in his notebook. He lamented wasting ten years of his life searching for enlightenment through the expedient of drugs. It was clear to him now that drugs offered only a fleeting and inaccurate glimpse of what true enlightenment must actually be like. He promised himself that in the future he would use meditation as a means to self-education and self-awareness.

Spending nearly two years away had ended the intimacy between Ginsberg and some of his oldest friends. Even though Allen had tried to keep in touch with Kerouac and Burroughs via long letters from India, Jack and Bill had never answered. Jack lived increasingly in an alcoholic fog as he moved back and forth between Florida and the Northeast, continually looking for the perfect home and never finding it. He imagined conspiracies against him where there were none. Burroughs, engrossed in his various cut-up experiments with new collaborators like Sommerville, Portman, and Gysin, nearly lost touch with Allen altogether. The barriers Bill had set up to direct communication with Allen were still in place, but he wasn't sitting around wasting his time either. He continued to work industriously on cut-ups and even helped Sommerville perfect a dream machine, which was intended to disrupt normal brain patterns. All of his projects were carried out with scientific precision and directed toward the goal of outwitting the agents of control that he still believed ruled his actions.

Since he last saw Burroughs and Ginsberg in Morocco, Gregory Corso had traveled back and forth between Europe and America several times. On one of his trips to New York, he married a woman named Sally November. Corso was still addicted to heroin, and he found that it came to dominate his life as much as poetry ever had. As a result, his marriage did not last long and his resolve to create new verse began to weaken. By the time Allen got to Vancouver, Gregory was back in Europe, once more living off the kindness and generosity of others.

Chapter 19

A Culture Turned Upside Down

In Canada Ginsberg found that being thrown so rapidly back into Western culture was a beautiful shock to him. He couldn't stop himself from talking to everyone at the poetry conference about the basic things in life: love, the beauty of the human body, and especially about the importance of death and sex. Allen wanted to teach everyone what he had discovered, to communicate that everything in the universe had a time and a place. Allen advised that everyone was "happy in heaven on earth. Don't worry about nothing no more. Everything's coming true. All wars over and all hells vanished . . ." The students at the conference welcomed his impromptu lectures on free love, and many began to practice the Buddhist idea of "respect for all sentient beings" through his example.

The Vancouver conference and Allen's return from India in 1963 marked the start of a new era in his life. He was no longer embarrassed to discuss his true feelings about homosexuality, politics, drugs, death, or any other topic that he might have been hesitant to mention earlier in his life. His newly acquired openness led to sexual encounters with men and women alike, which was reassuring after his near-celibate stay in India. He wrote to Peter back in India, "I'm telling you the cold war's over, Hurrah! All we got to do is really love each other," echoing ideas Peter had long believed.

When the conference ended, Ginsberg and Philip Whalen drove down to San Francisco together, and once more Allen's time was immediately occupied by friends, both old and new. From that moment on, instead of trying to escape from the center of the storm of activity as he had in the past, Ginsberg began to enjoy and even revel in the frenetic pace of his new life. Although he had at first planned to return to India, once back in San Francisco he changed his mind and wrote to tell Peter. He saw that he had work to do in America and decided to stay in San Francisco for the next few months to take care of some business.

In addition to revising the proofs for his third City Lights collection, *Reality Sandwiches,* he also blocked out a period to work with Robert Frank. Although Frank's *Pull My Daisy* had not been a great commercial success, it remained the kind of film that interested Robert, and he wanted to do another. He asked Allen to write a film script for an adaptation of *Kaddish.* The project provided Allen with some much-needed cash, but eventually the backers of the film dropped out and it never progressed beyond the scriptwriting phase.

There was yet another urgent reason for Ginsberg to stay in San Francisco longer: he wanted to help Neal Cassady write his memoirs. Although Neal's book was not to be completed during his lifetime, it was published posthumously in 1971 by City Lights as *The First Third.* Following another separation from Carolyn, Neal had moved into the very same building that Robert LaVigne had once used as his studio. It was the place where Allen had seen and fallen in love with LaVigne's painting of Peter Orlovsky ten years earlier. Neal lived there with his girlfriend of the moment, Anne Murphy, and a group of people from the Midwest who were also practicing artists. Master printer Dave Haselwood lived there, as did Charles Plymell, a twenty-eight-year-old Kansas poet who knew the print trade as well. They were both close friends of fellow Kansan Michael McClure, who was often to be found around the house, too. Since the day they met, Allen had always liked McClure, but now he finally realized that there was even more to McClure's writing than he thought, and he began to describe him as a radiant poet. The entire group lived in the old Victorian house and shared everything, a precursor of the communal groups that would become much more common within a few years.

Ginsberg was fortunate to return to America in the early 1960s at the dawn of a new era of personal freedom, idealism, and experimentation. Young people in increasingly greater numbers were beginning to rebel against all types of conformity. They struggled to free themselves from middle-class expectations and social constraints of their parents' generation. By rejecting materialism, they hoped to find new ways to enrich their lives according to individual moral codes.

The interests of this new youth culture happened to coincide with Ginsberg's own ideas about the liberation of society. As a result, many young people looked to him and some in his circle for leadership and guidance. The Beat Generation aspirations were echoed in the next generation's search for greater personal freedom and liberty. Like the Beats, many young people adopted the use of drugs and marijuana and were seemingly less interested in alcohol. Some wanted to use drugs to explore and expand their consciousness, while others just wanted to get high. More people began to embrace the sexual revolution, which, aided by new methods of birth control, liberated women as well as men. Others looked for a spiritual basis to their lives in non-Western forms, finding value in Buddhist, Hindu, and other Asian teachings. More people became actively involved in finding ways to save the planet from self-destructive pollution and overdevelopment. Like Ginsberg, the younger generation also seemed intent upon questioning authority in all forms and believed that equal rights should finally be available to all people. These beliefs brought about a demand for the liberation of minorities, women, and homosexuals. Some saw that reform was needed in every area of government involvement. Nearly every young person listened to new forms of popular music, much of it coming out of San Francisco and England.

It would still be a while before the press began to call these young people "hippies" instead of "beatniks," but a universal change in consciousness was already in progress. Ginsberg, McClure, Di Prima, Ferlinghetti, and Snyder became some of the elder spokespersons for the counterculture of the later sixties. It is interesting to note that while the work of Beat writers such as Kerouac, Corso, and Burroughs became ever more popular during the next decade, they were never advocates for the social changes that were taking place.

For a few months following his return to the States, Allen lived in one of the extra rooms on Gough Street where he was able to record Neal's stories on a borrowed tape recorder. It had not been easy to get Neal to sit in one place long enough to do much work, and Allen found that the only way he could do it was to record Neal and transcribe his monologue later.

While Ginsberg was working and enjoying life in San Francisco, Peter Orlovsky's Indian visa expired; he made the long trip back overland through Persia and Europe. It took him months to get back to New York, but he didn't mind traveling alone. While in India he had become much too dependent on drugs, which were readily available, and his long trip across two continents with virtually no money forced him to curtail most of his drug use.

Ginsberg realized that the world was not going to change without political activism. He marched in his first political protest against the Vietnam War shortly after his arrival in California. Madame Nhu, the influential sister-in-law of South Vietnam's President Diem, was visiting San Francisco on a speaking tour and had denounced American liberals as a bigger threat to democracy than the communists. A handful of protestors, Allen among them, decided to picket outside her hotel. Those antiwar demonstrations, modest at first, grew to enormous proportions as America became tangled in the quagmire of Vietnam in the coming years.

Many of the Beat writers became directly involved in those protests, further reinforcing the connection between the Beats and the new American counterculture. For the next decade, most of the West Coast poets actively opposed the military incursion into Vietnam. Lawrence Ferlinghetti was involved from the very beginning, as were Michael McClure, Philip Whalen, Bob Kaufman, Diane Di Prima, and Charles Plymell. At countless marches and rallies in the Bay Area, their voices could be heard among the more youthful demonstrators in what became known as "the Movement." At the time, no one would have believed that the war would grind on until the fall of Saigon on April 30, 1975, leaving nearly a million and a half people dead in its wake.

At the end of 1963, Ginsberg flew back to New York to greet Orlovsky when he arrived from his journey halfway around the world. At a party celebrating their return to New York, they met Bob Dylan, a young folksinger from Minnesota who was making a name for himself in Greenwich Village nightclubs. Dylan had come to New York to pursue his music career, but a part of him was drawn there because he wanted to meet the poets and musicians he had read about, especially people like Woody Guthrie, Allen Ginsberg, and Ray Bremser. Poetry was important to Dylan; in fact, he even changed his name from Robert Zimmerman to Bob Dylan in honor of another great poet, Dylan Thomas. It was no accident that Dylan befriended Ginsberg. His friendship was something Dylan sought out. Many people who never heard of the Beat generation were to be indirectly influenced by them because of their effect on the new generation of singer-songwriters like Dylan. Before long, sales of Dylan's protest songs were far outstripping any poet's ability to reach an audience through the written or spoken word.

When he arrived from the West Coast, Allen found that many of the poets in New York were also becoming political and even revolu-

206 / THE TYPEWRITER IS HOLY

tionary. LeRoi Jones had become interested in drama through his association with Diane Di Prima's New York Poets Theatre. In January 1964, he opened his play *Dutchman* at the Cherry Lane Theatre. It received wide acclaim and won an Obie Award that year. Jones tried to show the racial bigotry he had experienced growing up in a black Newark neighborhood. It was a powerful story that illustrated what might happen if a mild-mannered black man ever found himself in an emotionally charged situation with a flirtatious white woman on a New York City subway.

Jones's writing and his life were in a transitional period, as was the civil rights movement itself. Many people were eager to put an end to racial prejudice and injustice, and some did not believe that the nonviolent tactics of Martin Luther King Jr. and his followers would ever achieve that goal. Jones was convinced that a more aggressive path had to be taken, and he became a strong proponent of the Black Power movement. As a black man in the white literary world, he was confused by what his role should be. In many ways he felt guilty that he had married a white woman and had surrounded himself with white friends. He came to believe that militancy and revolution were the only means by which African Americans could achieve true freedom from their oppressors.

Over the next few years, Jones turned his back on most of his former friends from his Beat past. He abandoned his white wife and children downtown and moved first to Harlem, where he set up a black arts program, and then back to his hometown of Newark. After the assassination of Malcolm X in 1965, Jones converted to Islam, remarried, and changed his name to Amiri Baraka. His experience as publisher and editor of *Yugen, Floating Bear,* and Totem Books came in handy in his new role as a coordinator of cultural programs for the African American community, and before long he had established a new activist press, Jihad Productions. Spirit House, the center for the arts that he established in Newark, played a major role in black cultural nationalism during the late sixties and early seventies.

Amiri's conversion to radical politics was so complete that he refused to remain in touch with many of his old white friends. He didn't believe that the nonviolent civil rights movement would ever achieve true equality between the races, and he became so militant that he wrote diatribes suggesting that killing police and whites might become necessary.

When William Burroughs came back to New York City for a brief visit in December 1964, he found that America had not yet changed enough to make him want to stay. He visited on assignment from *Playboy* to write a "return-to-St. Louis" style memoir. The trip gave Bill an opportunity to reconcile with Ginsberg, the first time they had seen each other since their heated disagreements in Tangier. Although beginning to moderate, the drug laws were still too harsh for Bill. He found out that Huncke had once again been arrested for possession and was doing another stint in prison. Bill had no desire to join him. After completing the article Burroughs returned to Europe. Although he visited his family and friends in America from time to time, it would be another decade before he would feel safe enough to live in the United States again with an active drug habit.

At the time of Bill's visit, the avant-garde art scene in New York was just about to break out of the established confines of museums and galleries and spring up in new venues all over town. Artists were beginning to do challenging, imaginative, and thoughtful work that moved from one discipline to another, and there was a widespread feel of something new in the air. At this point radical change was not to be confined to poetry and prose, as in the fifties. Now artists would mix those disciplines simultaneously with film, drama, music, and art to redefine what art could be.

Factions that were more conservative worried that art was spiraling out of control. They tried their best to maintain the status quo, repressing the new, experimental art forms wherever they could. Poets in the East Village came under attack as well. The Le Metro Cafe received a summons from the city for hosting what were termed "unauthorized poetry readings." The city fathers made a decision to crack down on poets who had become politically controversial. They planned to silence them by enforcing old cabaret laws that would tax the coffeehouses out of existence. Since the cafes sold nothing but coffee and bagels, they would not be able to pay the new taxes and therefore would have to close. The battle over the coffeehouses became a call to arms for many of the city's writers. Ginsberg teamed up with other poets, such as Paul Blackburn and Ed Sanders, to fight the city's strong-arm tactics. They organized a powerful grassroots coalition and won the battle, allowing the cafes to remain open. They learned that they could accomplish a good deal through mobilizing concerned citizens.

Next, the city tried to shut down underground theaters for showing "obscene" experimental films. Once again the poets joined in the fight against the ban. The debate sparked a good deal of publicity for art that was being created in bohemian quarters. Artists were just beginning to work in multiple disciplines and had invented something entirely new called "happenings." Happenings combined music, performance, art, and poetry into one giant transient event. These happenings led directly to both the Situation International and the Fluxus movements. With its genesis in happenings, performance art became widely accepted and continues today to influence popular culture as an art form in and of itself.

The legalization of marijuana was another issue of great importance to many poets including Ginsberg. Once again he and Ed Sanders teamed up as founding members of LEMAR, a group determined to end the country's archaic pot laws. Sanders, born in 1939, was nearly a generation younger than most of the Beat writers. He had come to New York from Kansas City, where he had been strongly influenced by the work of Ginsberg and Kerouac. While Allen was in India, Ed had been active politically and had spent some time in jail after his participation in a pacifist demonstration against the Polaris submarine. His first published poem, *Poem from Jail,* was written during his incarceration. Using both his youthful energy and his humor, he established the Fuck You Press and ran the Peace Eye Bookstore, both of which continued to rely heavily on the work of his Beat forefathers.

While Burroughs was writing his St. Louis article, the case of *Naked Lunch* finally came to trial in Boston. There, Norman Mailer, John Ciardi, and Allen Ginsberg testified on behalf of the book. Although a lower court found that the book was obscene, the ruling was overturned upon appeal, and the book was free to be sold, even in Boston. Like Ginsberg's *Howl and Other Poems, Naked Lunch* was proved in the courts to have redeeming social value.

While Ginsberg and Sanders enjoyed being in the center of all these controversies, many of their friends did not. By now, some of them had established their own careers and were pursuing their own interests. For the most part, the communal aspects of earlier Beat relationships had disappeared as they grew older. What had begun in the mid-forties as a group of friends sharing inexpensive apartments on the edge of the Columbia campus, had grown into a larger network of writers and friends now living in various parts of the world. The Beat Generation was not the same small, cohesive group it had once been.

Kerouac continued to have a difficult time. Having always been somewhat conservative politically and culturally, he did not embrace the dramatic changes that were starting to take place in society. As a founder of the Beat Generation, he was personally attacked by conservative critics for having helped create the youth movement. Because his books had broken new ground and revealed a side of American culture hitherto unreported, every ill that the old guard perceived was laid at his feet. His critics said that he was responsible for everything from juvenile delinquency to drug overdoses. As the war in Vietnam escalated, protests against government policies grew, but Kerouac failed to see any connection between himself and the demonstrators, even though his books had helped shape their convictions. In Kerouac's opinion, many of the young protestors were just lazy, pampered, and misguided troublemakers. Not being a rebellious person himself, he scoffed at the intellectual left that now seemed to be against all aspects of American society, but found that people like William F. Buckley, who had similar political views, did not embrace him in return.

In December 1965 Michael McClure's play *The Beard* debuted in San Francisco and became an underground hit. During the following year, the police raided performances of the play, repeatedly attempting to shut it down. They arrested several of the actors on obscenity charges and threatened to close theaters if performances continued. A decade earlier it had been *Howl* that had aggravated the California censors. Now *The Beard* had assumed that same role. McClure's play became a cause célèbre until the courts eventually ruled in his favor and charges against the play were dropped. Later, when the play finally premiered in New York City, it won two Obie awards.

The threat of government repression and intervention in the arts persisted and forced Ginsberg to take direct political action on several occasions. For this purpose, he founded a nonprofit organization that he called the Committee on Poetry, or COP for short. Originally, it was set up to help pay legal fees in cases such as the coffeehouse ban. All the money that Allen received from his poetry readings went directly into this foundation, and he supported himself on what little income was left. Later he decided to continue funding COP for the support of worthy causes and to fund individual poets in dire straits. Over the years, he was able to help dozens of down-and-out artists financially. The fund helped Lenny Bruce pay for his court battles; it also provided legal support to Ed Sanders when his Peace Eye Bookstore was raided by the police.

By the spring of 1964, Neal Cassady had begun to spend most of his time with Ken Kesey and his followers, known collectively as the Merry Pranksters. Kesey's book *One Flew over the Cuckoo's Nest* had become a national best seller and with his royalties, Ken was able to support his friends so that they were free to celebrate and work on projects of mutual interest. Like Ginsberg, Kesey had taken part in the Stanford experiments with LSD unaware that he was part of a CIA-financed study called Project MKULTRA. They tested the effects of drugs on humans for brainwashing purposes, but little did they realize that by administering these drugs to people like Ginsberg and Kesey, they would unwittingly help create the sixties counterculture.

Kesey's cabin in the pine forest near La Honda became a magnet for people who wanted to use psychoactive drugs. The Merry Pranksters set up elaborate sound and recording systems in the woods behind the house, and music blared from giant outdoor speakers twenty-four hours a day. Kesey had a charismatic personality that drew people to him, and Cassady was just one of dozens of creative friends. For a while Neal lived in the back of his car in Kesey's driveway, delighted to be with people who appreciated his enthusiasm for drugs and free love. The camaraderie that he shared with the Pranksters was in some ways a repeat of the life he had lived with his Beat friends.

With the proceeds from *Cuckoo's Nest,* Kesey paid for giant LSD parties that eventually became known as the Acid Tests. This happened at a time when LSD was still a legal substance. On several occasions, more than a thousand people would drop acid and dance through the night to the music of Kesey's favorite band, the Warlocks, an early name for a group led by Jerry Garcia that became more famous as the Grateful Dead. Ginsberg and McClure also became friendly with Kesey and could sometimes be found at his cabin in the hills above Menlo Park making the Beat-Prankster connection even stronger.

That summer of 1964 Ken and his Merry Pranksters left California for New York to promote Kesey's new book, *Sometimes a Great Notion.* For the trip, Ken refurbished an old 1939 International Harvester school bus, complete with a state-of-the-art sound system and motion picture cameras. The Pranksters decorated the bus with Day-Glo psychedelic designs and christened it *Furthur*. All they lacked was someone to drive it across the country, and it didn't take much coaxing from Ken to get Neal to do it. He took a two-week vacation from his job as a tire recapper and headed east via Houston and New Orleans. Cassady, whom the Pranksters nicknamed Sir Speed Limit, swallowed amphetamines by the handful, but somehow managed to keep the bus on course. That legendary trip was described in detail in Tom Wolfe's popular *The Electric Kool-Aid Acid Test*. In fact, that trip became a well-known metaphor for participation in the sixties counterculture in general: "You're either on the bus or off the bus."

When the troupe pulled into New York City, Jack Kerouac came to see Neal. They met at a party at an elegant Upper East Side penthouse late in June for what turned out to be the final time. It was an uncomfortable reunion for both of them. Jack was not sympathetic to the actions of Neal and the young Pranksters, blissed out on drugs. It was not the future that he had envisioned as he labored on his books during the forties and fifties. Neal had become a stranger to him, and they seemed no longer to have anything in common except history. Someone at the party had been using an American flag as a blanket and after Kerouac folded it and set it aside, he quietly sat on a sofa, barely taking part in the conversation.

Kesey's business finished, Cassady drove the bus out of the city with Ginsberg, Kesey, and the rest of the group aboard. They headed for Millbrook in Dutchess County, New York, where Timothy Leary had relocated when he lost his job at Harvard. Through the generosity of wealthy patrons, Leary had set up his own "research" center, the Castalia Foundation, on the giant estate of his benefactors. Ginsberg had come along to take a look at Leary's version of communal living, but he left disappointed. Leary seemed to have lost his altruistic ideals and ran his foundation as if it were his own private kingdom. While he was there Allen snapped pictures of everyone and said good-bye when Neal left the Pranksters to return to his job in California. Considering how much has been written about the Pranksters' trip, it is interesting to note that Neal traveled with them for only eleven days. Unfortunately, he lost his job at the tire factory when he returned a few days later than expected.

A few days before Cassady left on the bus for the East Coast, Gary Snyder had returned to California from Japan. He had been away for most of the previous eight years, ever since the Six Gallery reading. One of the first things he wanted to do was take a long-overdue backpacking trek into the Sierra mountains. He fell in love once more with that rugged country and decided that if he ever settled down, it would be the perfect location for a home. More practical considerations would have to come first before he could think about buying property. He had to find a way to support himself. In the fall of 1964, Gary ran some poetry workshops and taught English classes at the University of California, Berkeley. By year's end, he had returned to Japan for even more Buddhist initiation.

At the same time, Kerouac had given in to his mother's wishes. Together they moved from Northport back to Florida. They found a house in St. Petersburg to be near his sister, Nin, but just when they had settled in, Nin suddenly died of a heart attack, leaving Jack and his mother bereft. "Just when everything was going to be fine and good for us all," Jack's mother wrote. "My heart is broke. My only little girl gone." In the wake of her death, Jack became Gabrielle's only living relative. Even though it put pressure on him to take care of his mother as she grew older, it was an obligation he accepted without question. He was aware that Gabrielle had sacrificed everything for her children. He was willing to do the same for her.

Chapter 20

The Sixties

Etymologists are uncertain about exactly when the word *hippie* came into existence, although it is clearly a variation of the term *hipster,* which had been in use during the forties, in reference to devotees of jazz music. Many of the people that Kerouac wrote about in *The Subterraneans* were considered hipsters, people who were intellectuals, "cool," and "with it." In the public mind, the change from beatniks to hippies took place in the late sixties when reporters began to label the next generation of beatniks as hippies. The first time this happened in print was in Michael Fallon's September 5, 1965, article in the *San Francisco Chronicle,* when he stated that the Haight-Ashbury neighborhood was becoming "A New Haven for Beatniks." There was no overnight change in terminology, however, and it took years to complete the evolution of vocabulary from beat to hippie. The semantic change from Beat Generation to Hippie Movement technically ended the notion of the "beat" lifestyle, but hippie was a change in vocabulary only. There was no substantive change behind the newer term. By the early seventies the Beat Generation was over as far as the media was concerned, although the writers previously known as Beats would continue to be referred to as such for the rest of their lives. There was no abrupt end to the Beat Generation, just a slow melting into what was to come next. During the sixties Ginsberg's worldwide influence grew enormously as he reached his greatest level of fame and popularity.

In 1965 Allen was invited to a poetry conference in Cuba at a time when Americans were not permitted to travel there. Ginsberg felt that he needed to experience life in a communist country for himself, instead of reading about it theoretically. To get to Havana, he had to fly via Mexico City, since the United States did not allow even invited guests to fly there directly. Beat friends who had been to Cuba, including LeRoi Jones and Lawrence Ferlinghetti, had told him positive things about what was going on there. However, while he was in Cuba Allen witnessed both the good and bad sides of Castro's form of communism. When he spoke out against Castro's repression of a free press and the government's poor treatment of homosexuals, Allen inadvertently ruffled some important feathers. Before long, Allen's friends in Cuba were detained by the police for questioning, and Allen was deported to Czechoslovakia.

Once in Prague, Ginsberg decided to enjoy himself as a tourist and to refrain from public statements. A month or so later, his resolve to remain out of the spotlight was broken when thousands of students elected him King of the May during a citywide festival. That drew attention to Ginsberg once again, and the communist leaders began to realize that Allen and his views could not be tolerated. Both Cuba and Czechoslovakia had invited him to visit, believing that if he spoke out against capitalism, he must be on their side. But Allen was no ideologue; he could denounce the darker sides of both capitalism and communism, and he spoke out against injustice wherever he saw it. The Czech secret police charged him with being a corrupting influence. Again he was deported, this time to England.

When Ginsberg landed in London, the city was already bursting with the youthful enthusiasm that was turning England into the center of the popular-music world. The Beatles and the Rolling Stones had become famous, and Allen met members of both groups nearly as soon as he arrived. Coincidentally, Bob Dylan was also in town, so Allen spent as much time with him as he could. With the help of one of Dylan's friends, Allen and a group of poets decided to rent the Royal Albert Hall for a gigantic poetry reading. In addition to Ginsberg, the event featured Corso, Olson, Ferlinghetti, and a dozen others who read to an enthusiastic audience one evening in June.

While he was in Europe Ferlinghetti traveled to Paris to read at Jean-Jacques Lebel's International Festival of Free Expression. Even Kerouac visited Europe for one final time that summer, although he did not hook up with any of his old friends. At the request of his Italian translator, Jack had flown to Italy for an interview. While in Europe, he stopped off in Paris to trace some of his family's geneal-ogy at the French national archives. He did not make much progress with that, and Paris became just another drunken scene for him. As he described in his *Satori in Paris,* Jack was so wasted on this trip that no one wanted to associate with him.

Following Corso's rather poor performance at the Albert Hall reading, he retreated to Paris and tried to apply himself once again to both his writing and his independent study of geometry and hi-eroglyphics. For a while he made some progress, and this era marked one of the last productive periods of his life, before his addiction got the better of him. When Allen stopped in to visit Gregory on his way back to America, he could see that Gregory was in bad shape, but there was nothing to be done. Ginsberg had become much too busy to hang around and nurse his friends back to health as he once had done. For the next thirty years he would find himself increasingly overscheduled and unable to stop himself from pursuing what he came to think of as "the business of being Allen Ginsberg."

Ginsberg had made a commitment to take part in the Berkeley Poetry Conference that was coming up that summer. Old friends from all over the country were gathering for a giant writing confer-ence similar to the one that had brought Allen back from India a few years earlier. Robert Creeley, Robert Duncan, Charles Olson, and Lew Welch were all planning to be there and, like Vancouver, this conference proved to be a triumph. In addition to seeing old friends again, Allen was able to meet some younger poets who were just starting their careers. Ed Sanders attended, as did future close friends like Anne Waldman and Ted Berrigan. They represented the next generation of poets who found inspiration in the works of Beat Generation writers. It became a symbolic meeting at which the torch was passed to a younger group of writers. Allen was delighted to know that there was a continuation of the revolution in the arts that he and the Beats had begun.

While in California Ginsberg spent a few days with Cassady and Kesey, enjoying their company almost like old times. Unlike the anonymous visits of the past, however, by now they were all famous and the center of attention everywhere they went. Late that summer Ginsberg and Snyder escaped on a trip through the Pacific Northwest and British Columbia where they combined some poetry readings with camping and mountain hiking. In Portland they attended a Beatles concert where John Lennon called attention to Ginsberg in the audience. Fame made them leaders of the new movement that shared some of their common goals. Together many of the Beat writers would work to end the war, legalize drugs, and promote freedom of expression.

Back in the Bay Area, Snyder and Ginsberg also took part in the Berkeley Vietnam Day Committee's marches and teach-ins aimed at putting an end to the war. When the Hells Angels threatened to disrupt the demonstrations, Kesey sprang into action. He volunteered to host a party for the motorcycle gang with an eye on winning them over to the side of nonviolence. During that party, some Angels sampled their first LSD and as a result a somewhat shaky peace was made between the opposing factions.

In 1966, nearly a decade after Cassady had gone to jail for the possession of pot, Kesey was sentenced to six months in a work camp and three years probation for the same thing. Instead of giving himself up, Ken decided to fake his own suicide and disappear into Mexico. By then Kesey was not alone in his disagreement with government drug policies. Nearly everyone under the age of thirty thought that American drug laws were draconian and found it incongruous that the government continued to lump marijuana, widely considered harmless in comparison to alcohol and tobacco, together with addictive drugs like heroin and cocaine. From time to time Ginsberg tried to explain the nature of drug use through commonsense appeals, but the media would not listen to him. When he appeared before the U.S. Senate to offer testimony about the use of drugs, he was ridiculed by the popular press. Around college campuses, an iconoclastic, alternative press began to emerge in response to conventional news coverage. Most of those younger reporters favored more lenient drug laws, and they looked once more to the older Beat writers for guidance.

On his way back to New York, Ginsberg stopped to do a reading tour of the Midwest. It had been organized by Charles Plymell, his friend from San Francisco, who was soon to publish the first issues of *Zap Comix*, featuring illustrations by R. Crumb, a new type of cartoonist with a satirical, bitter edge. The Beats were once again fodder for the media, due in part to the rise of the youth culture. *Life* magazine covered Ginsberg's tour in detail in a nine-page story entitled "The Guru Comes to Kansas." Robert Frank traveled with Allen and documented the trip in his newest black-and-white film, *Me and My Brother*, a movie that was originally to be about Allen but ended up focusing on the dysfunctional Orlovsky brothers.

Ginsberg, who had just turned forty in 1966, became a leader of nearly every cause associated with the youth movement. Political issues dominated much of his time, time that he had previously devoted to poetry. The more prominent he became as a social activist, the less time he had for literary creativity.

As Ginsberg grew older he welcomed the role of teacher. Ever since he returned from India, he began every public appearance by chanting the Hindu mantra, Hare Krishna. Then he instructed his audience in how to sit for a few minutes of silent meditation. In 1966 A. C. Bhaktivedanta Swami Prabhupada, the leader of the International Society for Krishna Consciousness, popularly known as the Hare Krishnas, set up headquarters right in Allen's own neighborhood, now known as the East Village. When Allen went to greet him, he welcomed the old guru, telling him that he was relieved the "reinforcements had finally arrived."

Although Ginsberg never adopted Hinduism, he was deeply interested in its practices, especially in the use of *mudras* (hand gestures) and mantra chanting. He had already experienced the change in consciousness that occurs when a chant is repeated; he said it was the closest he would ever come to pure euphoria. He never pretended to be more than a novice to the Hindu religion, but his example led many Westerners to begin meditation practices of their own. It was still years before Ginsberg found his own Tibetan meditation teacher and adopted Buddhism as his personal spiritual path. In that choice, he joined the earlier example of Kerouac, Snyder, Kyger, and Whalen. Later Diane Di Prima, Michael McClure, Anne Waldman, and Peter Orlovsky would also follow.

Sexual liberation also absorbed many of the Beats. Gay rights were important, since several of the writers were homosexual, and the free-love movement intrigued them all. In his own neighborhood, Ginsberg met the people associated with Kerista, a commune that advocated free love. Kerista was only one of a number of bohemian communes that sprang up in the mid-sixties condoning and even promoting love between consenting parties regardless of sexual orientation or marital status. Many of these communes were revolutionary in terms of morality and equality between the sexes. Free love was something that Ginsberg and Orlovsky had been preaching for years, so they were attracted to these groups hoping that they would help spread the concept more widely.

When the police broke up the Kerista commune, several of their members wound up on Allen and Peter's doorstep. Barbara Rubin was one of them. She wanted to have children, and for a while she hoped that Allen would be their father, a suggestion that Allen resisted. In keeping with her commune philosophy, Rubin found an old, dilapidated farm in upstate New York and convinced Allen to purchase it as a bucolic getaway for himself and his friends. The "back to the land movement" was then in its infancy. Many people held the opinion that self-sufficiency was the way to create a better, more healthful life for themselves and ensure the survival of the planet. Although Allen had some misgivings about being a landowner, he agreed that having a refuge in the country might be beneficial.

By the mid-sixties many prominent members of the Beat Generation had begun new phases in their careers. Several were making their livings as teachers, educators, and lecturers. Teaching gave them the flexibility to continue their writing while also providing a steady income. Some became affiliated with colleges and were often invited to participate in international conferences and readings. Previously, as starving artists, they had been forced to hitchhike from place to place, but now they enjoyed the luxury of travel allowances and hotels provided by their sponsors. Having access to funding made things easier for the poets, but it also made them less dependent on one another. Slowly, over time, their major works began to appear in anthologies and, somewhat begrudgingly, some in the academy had to accept the fact that the Beats were established literary figures.

One distinct advantage of more widespread acceptance was their expanded opportunities for publication. Major publishers asked for work, and they were included in textbooks and collections both in America and abroad. As he had for decades, Ginsberg continued to promote his Beat friends. Whenever he was asked to read anywhere, he tried to get his friends invited with him. Ferlinghetti's City Lights Press became even more successful in the sixties and Ferlinghetti was able to publish new authors and titles. Whenever reporters stated that the Beat Generation writers were not committed to social and political causes or were disenfranchised from society, Ferlinghetti did his best to dispel that notion. He believed that a writer who was not committed to improving society was merely wasting his time. Lawrence was active in protesting the Vietnam War, and in December 1967 he was arrested at the Oakland Army Induction Center for trying to prevent young men from being drafted.

That same month Ginsberg was arrested in New York at the Whitehall Draft Board on similar charges. Although Ginsberg had been in Europe during the October 21, 1967, March on Washington described by Norman Mailer in his Pulitzer Prize–winning book, *Armies of the Night,* Allen's spirit and words were present. Poet and activist Ed Sanders led some of the one hundred thousand protestors in an exorcism of the Pentagon and read Ginsberg's "No Taxation Without Representation" to the crowd that assembled hoping to levitate the building into space.

As the demonstrations became more widespread in protest of the war, Jack Kerouac remained out of the fray. In April 1966, he moved with his mother to Hyannis, but a few months later, she suffered a massive stroke. Throughout Jack's life, Gabrielle had been the one person he could always count on; now she became completely dependent upon him. Jack was lucky to be able to fall back on his oldest friends in Lowell for help. Stella Sampas, the sister of his closest childhood friend, Sebastian, came to help him nurse Gabrielle. As a young girl, she had been in love with her older brother's handsome friend. Being able to help him rekindled her crush. In November Jack and Stella were married, thus relieving Jack of some of the pressure of caring for his invalid mother. In December the Kerouacs returned to live in Lowell, but like all his recent moves it proved to be temporary.

Gregory Corso had spent the better part of the year in Athens studying the wonders of the ancient world on his own. Greece was ideal for him for several reasons, among them the availability of drugs and the low cost of living. As the sixties wore on, Corso found himself spending fewer hours writing; he published less and less. He rationalized by saying that publishing one collection of poetry every ten years was sufficient. After his poor performance on the stage at the Albert Hall reading in 1965, Gregory lost his confidence to give public readings as well.

Burroughs was still living as an expatriate in Europe and had little more than a passing interest in the court case that culminated in the vindication of *Naked Lunch.* His time continued to be spent in private, where he worked in solitude through his worst addictions. In the past friends had always come to visit Burroughs, first in Texas and Mexico and later in Tangier; it had never been the other way around. Now his Beat friends were busy with their own careers; they did not take the time to visit him in his self-imposed exile. His earlier relationships continued to fade away.

Around the time of Jack's mother's stroke, Allen and Peter dropped in on him in Hyannis to surprise him as they passed through on their way to Gloucester to visit John Wieners. Instead of welcoming his old friends, Jack pretended to be his "Uncle Bill" and ran into his house to hide. Of course, they recognized him, but by that time, Jack wanted to have nothing to do with them. It was especially sad because it turned out to be the last time that they would ever see one another.

Kesey was tiring of his self-imposed exile in Mexico, so he returned incognito to attend a "trips festival" at San Francisco State College. Neal Cassady had been with him, but stayed behind in Mexico with new friends he had made there. After the festival, Ken gave himself up to the authorities and served a brief sentence. When he was released in November 1967, Ken returned to Oregon where he bought a house, farmed, and settled into family life.

Gregory Corso returned to New York in 1967 in hopes of settling down in Greenwich Village. By then he had a new, wealthy girlfriend, Belle Carpenter, and for a while he resumed writing. Since drugs still played a major role in his life, America was an expensive and dangerous place for him. When his relationship with Belle failed, he returned to Europe straightaway.

As the sixties progressed, American society was changing rapidly, thanks to generational upheaval. On January 14, 1967, Gary Snyder, Allen Ginsberg, Timothy Leary, Michael McClure, and Lawrence Ferlinghetti were on the stage at the San Francisco Human Be-In as representatives of an earlier generation. The festival, billed as A Gathering of the Tribes, took place on a beautiful sunny day in Golden Gate Park, and marked the start of what became known as the Summer of Love. It was the symbolic beginning of a period of new social consciousness, accented by a spirit of communal concern. If any one event marked the zenith of what we now call "the sixties," this was it. It was a short-lived utopian experiment, soon destroyed by a variety of forces. Within a year, members of the Haight-Ashbury community in San Francisco were memorializing the passing of the era with a "death of the hippie" event.

In the month following the Human Be-In, William Burroughs returned from Europe to take his nineteen-year-old son, Billy, to a government detox hospital in Lexington, Kentucky. He himself had once gone to the same clinic, and he hoped that his son would benefit from treatments there, too. While in America, Burroughs joined Ginsberg and Corso in New York for the inauguration of Timothy Leary's League for Spiritual Discovery, although his low opinion of Leary's methods hadn't changed much. Burroughs then returned to London to continue work with cut-ups involving sound and film recordings.

Gary Snyder was still not ready to settle in America yet, and he had returned to the monastery in Japan for additional training with his Roshi at Daitoku-ji in Kyoto. While Gary studied in Japan, his friend Robert Creeley accepted a position as a tenured professor of English at the State University of New York at Buffalo. Creeley was the first, but not the last, member of the group to embrace an academic career. McClure, Ginsberg, Snyder, Di Prima, Waldman,

Meltzer, Orlovsky, and even Burroughs and Corso would seek the security that teaching offered.

While the West Coast Beats were enjoying the blissful summer of love, LeRoi Jones, not yet Amiri Baraka, was badly beaten by the police during the violent riots that swept Newark in 1967. They charged LeRoi with gun possession and threatened him with prison. Later his conviction was overturned, but because of his race, his experience of the sixties was becoming radically different from that of other Beat writers.

Back in London in 1968, Burroughs enrolled in a two-month course in Scientology. Unconventional interests like this differentiated him from the other Beat writers. His belief in Willem Reich's orgone generator (a device intended to concentrate the invisible energy of the universe), his practice of psychoanalyzing his friends, his belief that poetry had been rendered meaningless through the cutups, and his most recent fascination with Dianetics all took him in unusual directions.

The founder of Scientology, L. Ron Hubbard, had believed that humans were eternal beings who had abandoned their true natures and could be healed through what he termed "auditing." The self-help aspect of Scientology and the belief that people were reincarnated from lives lived on other planets appealed more to Burroughs than the religious indoctrination that he had to endure during his course of initiation. His initial classes were followed by additional studies in the years that followed, but the Scientologists were not completely comfortable with Bill, realizing that he was not a true believer. Their use of repetitive "clearing" techniques were very similar to Burroughs's own beliefs about getting rid of his ugly spirits through writing about them and cutting up their messages endlessly.

Ginsberg was convinced that his purchase of the Cherry Valley farm would make an ideal retreat for friends like Kerouac, Huncke, Bremser, and Corso. Ray Bremser had been in and out of jail repeatedly; in fact, his first book, *Poems of Madness,* was published while he was behind bars. It was Allen's belief that Bremser and the others could benefit from living on the farm, where they were separated from their drug connections in the city. Over the next few years, the farm became his home base and a gathering place for many writers, filmmakers, and artists who needed a place to live. Unfortunately, the farm's countryside location did not make it more difficult for his friends to obtain drugs. Any addict worth his salt was resourceful enough to find whatever he needed locally, and their addictions continued unabated in spite of Ginsberg's attempts to the contrary.

The farm itself never became the self-supporting enterprise that Allen had envisioned; it survived only by regular cash infusions from Ginsberg. He found himself giving poetry readings even more frequently to support the farm that he was then too busy to visit. Over the years, it became too expensive for even Allen to support. Without skilled workers, the fields became overgrown, the barn collapsed, and the old farmhouse fell into disrepair.

One of Ginsberg's primary reasons for buying the farm had been to provide a place for Jack Kerouac to sober up. For what seemed like decades, Allen had heard Jack talk about finding a place in the country where he could live a more active life. There, in hermitlike conditions, he dreamed of restoring himself to perfect health, through hard manual labor, abstinence, and self-discipline. Allen bought into this unrealistic dream. Even though Allen wasn't enthusiastic about farming himself, he thought it would be a curative for Kerouac.

Chapter 21

The End of the Road

Early in 1968 Allen and Jack received the news that Neal Cassady was dead. No one was surprised that the cause was drug-related. When Kesey had gone underground in Mexico to avoid prison, Cassady and a group of Ken's Merry Pranksters had followed. Later, when Kesey decided to return and serve his time in prison, Neal had stayed behind. He had settled down with some artists in San Miguel de Allende and was living there with a new girlfriend, J. B. Brown. The facts were meager, J.B.'s accounts were inconsistent, and his death was shrouded in mystery. On the night of February 3, Neal had left his house to walk to the railroad station. The next morning he was found naked along the tracks, dead from what was thought to be a toxic mix of alcohol and barbiturates. Ginsberg wrote that he died "exhausted and feeling lone and lost."

It was a terrible shock to Allen, who mourned his old lover. He had become accustomed to the deaths of people he loved, first David Kammerer and then Bill Cannastra, Joan Burroughs, and his mother. By now, Allen had learned to accept these sudden and unexpected tragedies. In India he had learned that death was just another part of the natural order of things, but it was hard to always remember that lesson. Kerouac reacted in a completely different manner. He refused to acknowledge that his close friend had even passed away. He convinced himself that Neal was still alive and hiding out in Mexico for reasons known only to Neal. It was a way for Jack to protect himself from the awful truth that the man who had been his closest friend and muse was dead.

Later that year, leaders of the Youth International Party (Yippies), led by Abbie Hoffman, Jerry Rubin, and Ed Sanders, decided to demonstrate at the 1968 Democratic National Convention in Chicago. Because of widespread opposition to the Vietnam War, President Lyndon Johnson had decided not to run for reelection, and young people from across the country were mobilized in support of their candidate, Eugene McCarthy. *Esquire* magazine hired four writers to cover the story: Burroughs, Ginsberg, novelist Terry Southern, and the great French writer Jean Genet. They all agreed to go to witness what promised to be the largest antiwar demonstration in history, and they prayed that it would be nonviolent.

In spite of those hopes, the convention turned into a national embarrassment. Following harsh orders from Chicago's Mayor Daley, the Chicago police showed the demonstrators no mercy, beating and arresting them en masse. Burroughs wrote, "The police acted like vicious guard dogs attacking every one in sight." Every night the television networks covered bloody scenes of the police running riot. One day Ginsberg found himself and several hundred supporters trapped in a park surrounded by hostile police. He urged everyone to sit on the ground and remain calm while he chanted "Om" for hours on end. His patience paid off in that instance, and both the police and the demonstrators kept their composure. Once again he proved to himself that peaceful dissent was the correct approach.

The following month, a distant relative of Kerouac's, William F. Buckley Jr., invited poet-activist Ed Sanders to appear on his television program *Firing Line*. Buckley also asked Kerouac to appear at the same time, probably thinking that Jack would get along well with the hippies, since they generally regarded Jack as a hero. In truth, Kerouac had little in common with Sanders or his leftist politics and would not acknowledge that the Yippies and hippies were in any way his heirs, although he reluctantly said that they were basically "good kids." Being somewhat drunk during the interview, Kerouac summed up the Vietnam War as a Vietnamese "plot to get Jeeps into their country." By the late sixties, Jack had decided that he wanted no part of what he saw as the mischief of the Left.

That year Ginsberg began setting the poems of William Blake to the music that Allen composed on a rickety old pump organ in his Cherry Valley farmhouse. For quite a while, he devoted most of his spare time to that project; his own poetry was moved to the back burner. Putting Blake to music was an outgrowth of his own desire to be a rock and roll star. Every time he saw the Beatles, Dylan, or the Rolling Stones perform, he somewhat jealously realized that the poet's unaided voice was no match when it came to reaching large audiences.

Ed Sanders had experienced the same realization and had decided to join with Tuli Kupferberg and Ken Weaver to form a rock group they called the Fugs, after Norman Mailer's euphemism for "fuck." With music they influenced more people than Sanders could ever dream of reaching through poetry. On the West Coast, where the California sound was in full swing, the same thing was happening. When Michael McClure helped Janis Joplin write the lyrics to her song "Mercedes Benz," he had the pleasure of hearing his words broadcast around the world to millions. More people knew the lyrics to that song than knew all of his other poetry combined. His collaboration with Joplin might have been the beginning of a long musical partnership had Janis not died suddenly three days after she recorded their song.

Even Huncke was making a name for himself. After being released from jail once again in 1968, he appeared on *The David Susskind Show*. For a while, he enjoyed the media attention and it briefly helped to keep him out of trouble. The attendant publicity led to the publication of one of his stories in *Playboy*. As public interest in the Beats grew stronger, their books sold in increasing numbers.

While Gary Snyder and his second wife, Masa, were still living in Kyoto, their first son was born. By year's end, the little family had returned to America for good. Having been out of the country for so long, Gary was surprised to find interested readers eagerly waiting for him. In California he set to work on environmental issues almost immediately and won both a Guggenheim Fellowship and the Levinson Prize from *Poetry* magazine shortly after his return. The same year, while he was taking a long backpacking trip into the Sierras, one of his most important collections, *The Back Country*, was published. In that book, Snyder continued to combine his knowledge of Eastern culture and poetic forms with his experiences in the American West.

During the autumn of 1969, Allen was laboring over his Blake music in Cherry Valley when the telephone rang in the little farmhouse. It was a long-distance call from Florida bringing news of Kerouac's death. In the few years since Allen and Neal had last spent time with Jack, he had bounced back and forth between New England and Florida, always hoping to find the perfect place to live, but with no success. Most recently, Jack and Stella had taken his ailing mother back to St. Petersburg where the climate was easier on her. One day while watching television, Jack began to hemorrhage and spit up blood. It was October 20, 1969. Kerouac was forty-seven years old. He was rushed to a local hospital where he passed away early the next morning from cirrhosis of the liver, the alcoholic's death.

Kerouac's body was flown to Lowell, where he was buried in the Sampas family plot beside his boyhood friend Sebastian. Ginsberg, Holmes, Creeley, Corso, and Jack's first wife, Edie, made the trip to say good-bye to their once-close friend. At the funeral Stella told Allen that Jack's final years had been lonely ones, but to Allen, Jack's loneliness seemed to be self-imposed. Jack had isolated himself from his past, but Jack's former friends had also given up on him. Newspapers around the country took pleasure in headlining the death of "The King of the Beatniks," exactly the type of coverage that had broken Jack's heart ten years earlier. He died fully aware that the general public still thought of him as nothing more than a "beatnik," and not one of the country's great writers. Many of his books had already gone out of print and others would follow. Many thought that his work would soon be forgotten entirely. Stella stayed in Florida, where she continued to care for Jack's mother until Gabrielle's own death in 1973, at the age of eighty-eight. She had outlived all three of her children.

Chapter 22

Aftermath

The deaths of Kerouac and Cassady marked the final dissolution of the Beat Generation. Many of the central figures had not seen one another in the years immediately preceding their deaths. Some members of the once inseparable group had become estranged, but as long as Jack and Neal were still alive, there was always the possibility that they would get back together. Ginsberg had even bought his farm hoping that he could eventually lure them there for periods of rest and rehabilitation. That dream of one more happy reunion died with them.

Never again would the remaining members of the old gang assemble for more than a few days at a time. The older they became, the only excuses to get together were limited to "Beat Generation" conferences and the occasional memorial service. No longer was there any need to drive all night across the country to see one another, or to share crowded rooms in cheap Parisian hotels, or to gather to edit manuscripts in Tangier. Now, there were too many other obligations, and so the intimate camaraderie faded.

It would be easier to summarize the last days of the Beat Generation had all the writers drifted into obscurity, but that was not the case. At the end of the sixties, several of these writers were yet to do their best work, among them Snyder, Kyger, and Di Prima. The celebrity status that Burroughs and Ginsberg enjoyed grew ever larger. When Kerouac died, Ginsberg had not yet become a Buddhist and was still to organize a university poetics department that would train a new generation of writers. Burroughs was not yet a cult figure to the punks, yet another movement whose roots traced back to the Beat Generation.

Determining when a literary generation begins or ends is arbitrary. Was the Beat Generation born with the meeting of Ginsberg, Burroughs, and Kerouac in 1944, or with the murder of David Kammerer later that same year? Was the Six Gallery reading in 1955 the beginning, middle, or end of the age? Kerouac himself believed the era ended as early as 1949. Were the deaths of Cassady and Kerouac the final chapters, or did the end come later, after Ginsberg, Burroughs, and Corso were all gone? There is no tidy closure for this group, only the later years of each of the participants.

Following Gary Snyder's example, Philip Whalen decided to visit Kyoto and submitted to the discipline of a Buddhist monastery. By that time, Whalen was in his forties and had been writing poetry and prose for more than twenty years while he held down one odd job after another. In Japan he taught English and worked on his second novel, *Imaginary Speeches for a Brazen Head.* That book, like many of his subsequent works, blended his interest in Eastern religion with a Western sensibility.

When Philip returned to California, Dick Baker, a friend of his, invited him to drop in to the San Francisco Zen Center to sit and meditate without obligation to join. Before long Whalen made a commitment to Baker and took the vows of a Zen Buddhist monk. By the mid-seventies, he had been appointed head of Baker's Tassajara Springs retreat and remained in administrative positions at Buddhist centers for the rest of his life. In 1991 he accepted his final assignment as the abbot of the Hartford Street Zen Center in San

Francisco's Castro district, where he remained until his death in 2002.

Herbert Huncke never broke the cycle of addiction that gripped him for a good part of his life. He continued to write intermittently, gave readings sparingly, and lived most of his life in New York City. He tried unsuccessfully to keep away from trouble with the law, which often proved difficult. Ginsberg and others supported Huncke in his later life via a monthly stipend, but he did not need very much for his meager lifestyle. In spite of his hard life and self-inflicted wounds, Herbert managed to survive to the age of eighty-one and lived to see his selected works published just before his death in 1996.

Michael McClure was one of the first members of the group to establish his own identity as a playwright and poet outside the narrower confines of the Beat genre. After he won the censorship battle over his play *The Beard,* he continued working as a playwright and produced many more controversial dramas including *The Sermons of Jean Harlow & the Curses of Billy the Kid.* He never abandoned poetry, and his organic approach to writing remained firmly fixed on the principle that mankind must respect its environment or perish. Like Snyder, McClure has focused his attention on ecology, and his writing often warns against the destruction of the planet, the ultimate threat to mankind. His work is complex and has made use of both scientific knowledge and more primal beast language to convey information and emotion. Because of his skill as a playwright, performance has always been an integral part of his poetry. In the days since he worked with Janis Joplin, he has continued to collaborate with musicians to provide appropriate musical settings for his words. A few of his books, including *Scratching the Beat Surface,* have looked back on his Beat past, and his essays remain some of his best work from that period.

After the early success of *Go,* John Clellon Holmes's only "Beat" novel, he moved away from New York City. Jack Kerouac remained in close touch with him for a few years, by which time Holmes had perfected the essay form. One of the more frequent topics for his writing and teaching became the Beat Generation, which he and Jack had named so many years before. He spent most of his career as a professor at various universities and was working at the University of Arkansas in Fayetteville at the time of his death from cancer in 1988.

Possibly the most intellectual member of the Beat family was Alan Ansen. After he settled in Europe in the late fifties, he never returned to live in the United States. While helping Burroughs and Corso edit books, he had lived in Venice and later moved to Athens, where he devoted himself to encyclopedic reading and literary study. Occasionally he taught poetry or English and was active in the literary life of that city while publishing several volumes and eventually collecting much of his work in *Contact Highs*. Until Ansen's death in 2006, Ginsberg, Corso, and the rest continued to drop in to visit him whenever they were in Greece.

After more than fifty years in publishing, Lawrence Ferlinghetti and City Lights go on stronger than ever. Their backlist still reads like a who's who of twentieth-century literature. One of the secrets of City Lights' success has been Ferlinghetti's determination to avoid being pigeonholed as a Beat publisher. The publishing company has been dedicated to finding cutting-edge talent worldwide. While bringing important international and third-world literature to America, Lawrence remained committed to alternative politics. Friends sometimes joked that although the world changes, Ferlinghetti remains steadfast in his principles and in his art.

Financially Gregory Corso was not as fortunate as his colleagues were. His lifelong addiction to drugs and his lack of enthusiasm for all types of employment contributed to his continual lack of funds. Corso was always in debt to someone. Early in his career, he nearly became a professor at the University of Buffalo, the school where Gregory had been invited to teach a course on his beloved Shelley. His dream for an academic life was short-lived, because he was required to take an oath stating that he was not a communist. It was standard procedure at the time, and while Corso certainly was not a communist (in fact, he was not even interested in political issues), he felt that he had to refuse as a matter of principle. That "subversive" act prevented him from pursuing a professorship that might have afforded him the same financial security that it did for Snyder, Creeley, Holmes, and even Ginsberg. Corso came to rely on the generosity of friends and patrons for the rest of his life. That route turned out to be quite difficult at times, given Gregory's fiery disposition.

An addict like Huncke, Corso also suffered through several trips to jail and was held in a few psychiatric treatment centers following some of his most traumatic drug-induced breakdowns. He never wanted to admit that he was hopelessly addicted, but near the end of his life he did enroll in a methadone program. Even though he hated the program, it served to stabilize his dependency. As one of the younger members of the Beat group, he managed to outlive many of the other "daddies," as he liked to call them, before he succumbed to prostate cancer in 2001.

In the sixties Diane Di Prima moved to California to join the Diggers, a countercultural group dedicated to implementing a non-capitalist economic system. One of her most popular books, *Revolutionary Letters,* comes from her days of working with the Diggers and the Black Panther Party toward radical political and social reform. As the California scene changed from Beat to hippie, Diane assumed a leading role in the new movement. Like some of the other Beat writers, she also became a student of Tibetan Buddhism, studying with the same meditation teacher as Ginsberg. Eventually she became a teacher and lecturer and wrote dozens of books culminating with her memoir, *Recollections of My Life as a Woman.* That revealing autobiography tells the story of the first half of her career when she was the sole female voice among the New York Beats.

Even as a child, Joanne Kyger had written poetry. When she arrived in San Francisco intending to become a writer, the only thing she lacked was self-confidence. During her first years with the Beats, she wrote in secret, and her talent went unnoticed by the men around her. In letters and journals from India, Ginsberg frequently referred to Joanne only as Gary Snyder's wife, not even bothering to refer to her by name, even though they traveled together for several months. Allen wasn't aware that she was an excellent poet until years later, at which point he was somewhat embarrassed by his earlier lack of interest. In 1965, a year after she divorced Snyder, Joanne finally published her first book of poetry, *The Tapestry and the Web*. With each new publication her poetry has grown stronger. She edited her own notebooks, *The Japan and India Journals,* telling of her life on the road with Snyder, Ginsberg, and Orlovsky, but it was through her poetry that her talent was fully recognized.

Throughout the seventies, Peter Orlovsky made more use of the Cherry Valley farm than Ginsberg ever did. Even though he grew up in New York City, Peter had attended an agricultural high school where he learned to love farm life, the natural world, and hard manual labor. For many years he lived in the old broken-down farmhouse with his girlfriend and tried to cultivate the poor, rocky soil. Through it all Ginsberg continued to encourage Peter to write poetry, and in 1978 City Lights published his first and only book, *Clean Asshole Poems and Smiling Vegetable Songs*. Peter had many deep-seated problems. Like several of the others in the group, he was hooked on drugs and alcohol for many years. He also suffered through mental problems that became more pronounced as he grew older. For decades he toured with Ginsberg, accompanying him on banjo and reading his own poetry, but he became increasingly unable to function independently and was occasionally remanded to mental wards and halfway houses. Following Allen's death, the courts appointed a guardian for him, and he moved away from the city to a more peaceful life in his own house in a small Vermont town.

Beginning in the eighties, a rebirth of interest in the Beat Generation took place. Former spouses and girlfriends of the Beats began to publish memoirs and autobiographies themselves. These "minor characters," as Joyce Johnson described them in her book of the same title, captured all the excitement of the era. Many of Jack Kerouac's former partners, including Johnson, Edie Parker, and Joan Haverty, wrote books describing their relationships with Jack. Carolyn Cassady also published several books about her life with Neal and Jack, beginning with *Heart Beat,* a story that was turned into a mediocre Hollywood film starring Sissy Spacek and Nick Nolte.

Hettie Jones documented her own life with LeRoi Jones during the fifties in *How I Became Hettie Jones.* That book established her career as a writer and poet. Since the renaissance of interest in the Beats, several collections of writings by and about these women have also been issued. Those have been followed by collections focusing on black Beats, gay Beats, Beat films, and so on.

Chapter 23

Respectability

Shortly after his permanent return from Japan, Gary Snyder decided to settle on San Juan Ridge in the foothills of his beloved Sierra Nevada mountains. There, in 1970, with the help of a small group of committed Buddhist practitioners, he constructed his own cabin in the forest and christened it Kitkitdizze after a native plant. With local friends he organized a *sangha,* or meditation group, that met regularly at his home. There was some discussion then about Whalen, Welch, and Ginsberg settling nearby, but only Allen had the means to buy the acreage that adjoined Snyder's property. He dreamed of retiring there someday, so he built a small cabin on his land. In the end his schedule was far too crowded with reading dates to allow him time to get away, so in 1992 when he finally realized that he would never retire, he sold the place to Gary.

Even though poet Lew Welch loved the mountains, he couldn't afford to buy land. He did visit Gary as often as he could during the first year of Snyder's residence, but unfortunately Welch suffered from bouts of depression that were compounded by alcoholism. One day in May 1971 while visiting Snyder at Kitkitdizze, Lew walked off into the mountains with a gun, leaving behind a short suicide note. Despite a thorough search, no body was found, and Welch was never seen again.

As a Buddhist, Gary was able to put the tragedy in perspective. Using his practice as his anchor, he developed ties with the land and raised his family. His regard for ecology led him to become active in local environmental issues, and he was finally able to put ideology into practice on a grassroots basis. At Kitkitdizze he raised two sons in addition to writing dozens of books and teaching at the Davis campus of the University of California.

As the years passed, Gary became increasingly respected as one of the elder masters. His works were published to favorable reviews, and one, *Turtle Island,* won a Pulitzer Prize for poetry in 1975. After serving for several years on the board of the California Arts Council, he was inducted into the American Academy of Arts and Letters by the same people who had previously dismissed the Beats. In the short span of two decades, Gary and the Beats had gone from being considered little more than troublemakers to being respected peers in the academy.

William Burroughs returned to America from his self-imposed exile in 1974. He had lived abroad for nearly twenty-five years. Even though Bill had treated both Allen and Peter badly in the early sixties, Allen had never held a grudge. In fact, once someone had become Ginsberg's friend, Allen would never abandon him, no matter what he did. He didn't stop loving Kerouac when Jack called him a "dirty Jew," and he remained loyal to both Huncke and Corso even after they stole his treasured books and manuscripts. His relationship with Burroughs might have been shaken by the revelation of the cut-ups, but it was easy for him to restore his old affection for Bill. Once back in New York, Bill and Allen spent a good deal of their free time together talking, reminiscing, and making plans for the future. On rare occasions they gave readings together, but the limelight was not something that Burroughs craved as Ginsberg did. He continued to be content writing in the shadows, hidden behind his work.

Burroughs was the one major writer in the group who had re-mained something of an enigma throughout the sixties. Much of his published work was misunderstood and underrated, and even though he was sixty, some of his most productive years were still ahead of him. At Allen's urging, Bill had returned to America to ac-cept a temporary teaching position at City College of New York, and surprisingly, he found the intellectual climate in America changed for the better. He decided to stay. For the first time, he felt comfort-able and welcome in his own country.

Soon after Burroughs settled in New York City, he had a stroke of good fortune that would make it easier for him to stay in America. Ginsberg introduced him to James Grauerholz, a young man who was to become his lifelong adviser and friend. With James acting first as a lover and then as his editor, secretary, and agent, Burroughs was able to support himself as a writer for the first time. No longer did he have to wait on his ever-dwindling trust-fund checks.

He soon produced a new trilogy of books, the first volume being his *Cities of the Red Night.* It contained outrageous stories that began to make him popular with the emerging punk counterculture, which was intrigued by his alien view of the world. With money enough to pay his bills, Burroughs didn't much care where he lived, so after James moved to his home state of Kansas in the eighties, Burroughs decided to follow. Bill was still using heroin, and he hoped that by getting away from his connections in the city he might be forced to stay clean. In Kansas he entered a drug maintenance program and for the rest of his life he lived quietly near James in a small two-bedroom house on a little side street in the university town of Lawrence.

Even though he was a thousand miles away from New York, Bur-roughs didn't try to isolate himself as he had in the past. Thanks to Grauerholz's organizational skills, he was able to hire an office staff to assist him as he continued his habit of working long hours every day. Frequently he entertained visits from old friends, fans, and younger admirers, all of which James was able to arrange without disturbing Bill's writing schedule. When Burroughs passed away in 1997 at the age of eighty-three, he left behind a bookshelf filled with recent work.

In his later years, Allen Ginsberg became somewhat more palatable to the literary establishment. He was even asked to sit on the prestigious National Book Award Committee. In his capacity as judge he lobbied for the recognition of underappreciated Beat poets like Gary Snyder and Gregory Corso, but the top prize that year went to Mona Van Duyn. Believing Van Duyn to be a mediocre writer at best, Ginsberg publicly stated that the committee had missed their chance to give the award to a deserving genius and instead had picked someone "safe." He was never asked to be on the committee again.

In the early seventies, Ginsberg literally bumped into a Tibetan Buddhist lama, Chögyam Trungpa, on the street. It proved to be the beginning of a long relationship for both of them. Quite by accident Allen had found his own meditation teacher. For the first time in his life, Allen finally had someone to instruct him properly. He remained a serious practitioner and grew to favor meditation over drugs as a means of exploring the recesses of his mind. Through his Buddhist practice Allen was able to come as close as he ever would to recreating the experience of his Blake visions.

At the time they met, Trungpa was in the process of establishing the first Buddhist college in America in Boulder, Colorado, which he called the Naropa Institute after an eleventh-century mystic. Allen was flattered when Trungpa asked him to organize a poetics program at the school, and for the next twenty years, Ginsberg devoted himself to directing the department. Allen, along with codirector Anne Waldman, decided to name it in honor of his old friend, so it became the Jack Kerouac School of Disembodied Poetics.

Although he spent a lot of time in Boulder over the next twenty years, for Ginsberg there was no way that he could ever settle down anywhere. For the rest of his life he was constantly on the move, going from one speaking engagement to another. He summed up the irony of his exhausting pace in a short poem: "Put on my tie in a taxi, short of breath, rushing to meditate."

Ginsberg never considered his life of travel much of a burden. He was completely in his element on the road and rarely complained about his obligations until his health began to fail. He loved being a celebrity and blossomed in front of an adoring audience even when he overscheduled himself. During each performance he read, sang, chanted mantras, and instructed people in the proper technique of sitting meditation, adoring the professorial role he assumed.

In his official capacity as codirector of the Jack Kerouac School, he spent part of every year teaching in Boulder at little or no pay as a favor to Chögyam Trungpa. As an administrator, it gave Ginsberg the chance to bring all his friends to the writing program, and over the years he managed to invite each and every one of them. Following Trungpa's death in 1987, Ginsberg was hired by Brooklyn College to fill a chair in their English department, where he finally received medical benefits, a pension plan, and a good salary for the first time.

One day Ginsberg was delighted to learn that he was to be inducted into the eminent ranks of the American Academy of Arts and Letters. The "academy" as a monolithic group was something that he had often remonstrated and loved to disparage. Now that he was asked to join, he saw membership as a chance to change their conservative fabric from the inside. As part of that august fraternity he worked to bring in several members of his own circle and was instrumental in getting Creeley, Burroughs, Snyder, Ferlinghetti, and Baraka elected. His one failure in that respect was his inability to convince the esteemed group to admit Corso, the one poet after Kerouac who Allen believed contributed the most to contemporary literature.

During the seventies, Jack Kerouac's reputation had faded and many of his books had drifted out of print. Lack of appreciation for Jack's work was something that Allen could not tolerate, so he consciously and almost single-handedly began to revitalize interest in Jack's writing. Naming the English department at Naropa in honor of his friend was just one small example of his efforts on Kerouac's behalf. Everywhere he spoke, he talked about Kerouac's legacy as the chronicler of his generation.

When Kerouac died, his widow, Stella, had allowed the publication of his book *Visions of Cody*, which Jack's old girlfriend Joyce Johnson edited. Following the tepid sales and lukewarm reviews for that challenging book, publishers lost interest in bringing out any additional Kerouac titles, and Jack's agent, Sterling Lord, decided not to push for the release of any more of his unpublished works at that time. Unwittingly, their ban on new books helped fuel an aura that was to surround Kerouac from then on. Literary mavens speculated on the contents of Jack's vast archive, and some believed that all that was worth publishing had already been released, while others thought there were dozens of books to come, and some even believed that Stella had destroyed manuscripts. All of those assumptions proved to be false. When Stella died, the new executors began to press for the release of new Kerouac titles. More fiction, nonfiction, short stories, plays, and selections of journals and correspondence were issued. The legend surrounding Kerouac grew even more when a collector paid a record $2.4 million to purchase the scroll manuscript of *On the Road* at a highly publicized auction.

Chapter 24

Acceptance

In time Ginsberg's strategy to restore Kerouac's reputation paid off as a rebirth of interest began to take place, not just in Kerouac, but in the Beat Generation itself. Some critics believed that the assimilation of the Beats into the academy came about because they had "sold out" to the establishment, but that was certainly not true. Even in 1973, the year Ginsberg was first elected to the American academy, he was still persona non grata within his own country. The FBI maintained a thick Ginsberg dossier, and he was routinely stopped at the border for thorough searches. Occasionally he was denied visas to other countries and on one tour, he was barely able to secure a three-day pass to enter Canada. All that happened during the same year in which he won the National Book Award for *The Fall of America*. J. Edgar Hoover regarded Ginsberg one of the major threats to the country and at least once forged a failed plan to entrap Allen in a somewhat questionable and highly inept sting operation.

In 1974 one of the first officially sanctioned "Beat" reunions took place in Grand Forks, North Dakota. Corso, Ginsberg, Orlovsky, Ferlinghetti, Rexroth, Snyder, and Kenneth Patchen's widow, Miriam, took part in what was billed as the City Lights in North Dakota

Conference. In the years that followed, numerous reunions, conferences, and symposiums were held around the world, from Paris to China, on the subject of the Beat Generation, each one attracting larger audiences.

During the eighties, Ginsberg, in his position as director of the writing department at Naropa, introduced his classes to the wide range of literature of the Beat Generation. Many of his students became poets and educators and are grouped together under an entirely new category that has been labeled Postbeat Poets.

Never was there a larger gathering of the old guard than the one Waldman and Ginsberg organized to commemorate the twenty-fifth anniversary of the publication of *On the Road*. Designed to revitalize interest in Kerouac, that 1982 conference attracted nearly every Beat author, and they all assembled to honor the tremendous role that Kerouac's novel had played in American literature.

To celebrate the twenty-fifth anniversary of the publication of *Howl*, Ginsberg, Orlovsky, and Corso made a triumphant return to Columbia University. They read in the same auditorium as they had that night in the late fifties when Diana Trilling predicted that the audience would stink. By this time, Ginsberg was internationally lionized, and his poetry had become the subject of countless dissertations. His appearance indicated that even Columbia had at last begun to appreciate their most famous living poet-alumnus.

In June 1988, Ginsberg, Ferlinghetti, McClure, and Creeley got together one last time for the purpose of unveiling a memorial to Jack Kerouac in his hometown of Lowell. Local residents had finally decided to honor the man who had spent his whole life writing about their town. It was a milestone in the acceptance of the Beats, but even after that honor many people in Lowell still talked about Kerouac as the town drunk rather than as a literary hero. The granite memorial commemorating his words will outlive the memory of his alcoholism, and as with Edgar Allan Poe, Ernest Hemingway, and F. Scott Fitzgerald, Kerouac's accomplishments will eclipse his drinking habits.

By the end of the century, old age had finally caught up with all the central Beat characters. In April 1997, seventy-year-old Allen Ginsberg died suddenly from liver cancer. He was followed in death just a few months later by William Burroughs, who died at his little home in Kansas at the age of eighty-three. The last of the original "daddies" died in 2001, when Corso also succumbed to cancer.

Chapter 25

Postscript

The Beats of the forties and fifties were the catalysts who precipitated the more widespread social rebellion of the sixties and seventies. As a small group of kindred spirits determined to practice absolute personal freedom within a society governed by stifling conservative attitudes, they set an example embraced by the next generation. The period of general upheaval that we call "the sixties" might well have taken place without the Beat Generation, but it would have certainly had a different flavor and moved at a different pace. When the Beats first broke free of the status quo in life and art, they set the stage for the future.

The importance of any artist, group, or movement might best be measured by the influence that they exert on the subsequent culture. Therefore, the Beats certainly rank high among the most powerful groups of twentieth-century America. The original members of the Beat Generation developed their own visions for a new society as early as the mid-forties, and during the fifties and sixties, they worked to communicate those ideas via their literature to an ever-growing number of readers. At a time when the average American was content and wanted to enjoy postwar prosperity quietly, the

Beats sensed that an essential spiritual element was missing. They believed that the human condition had been damaged through the unleashing of the atom bomb. To them, that act proved that atrocities like the Holocaust were not isolated events, but something that any nation might be capable of, given the right circumstances. In America, society's outcasts—homosexuals, minorities, addicts, anyone who was different—might become the victims of the next pogrom. The Beats wondered why people found it so easy to ignore injustice. They began to fear that man might be headed for extinction unless drastic changes in social attitude and behavior occurred.

Ultimately, their vision of the importance of the individual was thoroughly consistent with what many believe to be the real American dream. They rejected the notion that personal success was dependent upon financial prosperity and instead defined a "better, richer, and happier life" in terms of spiritual growth and intellectual freedom. They looked back on the underlying principles expressed in the Declaration of Independence and the Constitution as the basis for this belief. The concept of equality, upon which the country had been founded, was critical. Life, liberty, and the pursuit of happiness were not to be translated into economic terms for them. These were ideals within the reach of everyone. The true Beat rebellion was against the notion that freedom, prosperity, and security had to come at the expense of humanity. Personal liberation for every person was, to them, paramount; social connectedness held less appeal.

The bitter paradox was that the Beats' own pursuit of liberty often came at the expense of others. Kerouac's inability to commit himself to anyone kept him from accepting responsibility for his only daughter, and his growing alcoholism blocked his ability to relate to people except through his writing. Ginsberg was frequently blind to the suffering of his friends as they struggled with their addictions, and his generosity often enabled people to make poor choices in their own lives. This frequently made them feel inadequate and lack confidence in their own abilities. Burroughs's reckless streak sometimes went too far, and he injured people close to him both physically and mentally. Joan died as a result, and Billy Jr. signed letters as "your cursed from birth son."

Burroughs's tendency to withdraw into a world of his own inspired wonderful books but made life difficult for others. Cassady never seemed to realize that his self-centeredness had dire consequences either. His family suffered from that selfishness just as much as the victims of the five hundred cars he boasted of stealing. Finding a balance between personal freedom and the common good has always been difficult. The Beats came along at a time when many minorities were suppressed by the majority, and they addressed those problems, but their devotion to individual liberty could not solve everything.

The ripple effect from the changes brought about by the Beats continues to grow. It is too late for their critics to halt those profound transformations, and it is equally impossible to return to the puritanical social structure that was in place before they came along. Today, the changes made by the new vision of the Beats has become irrevocably absorbed into our culture, and the great liberation movements of the sixties benefited by them.

There have been in the past and there will be in the future many who oppose what they believe the Beat Generation brought about, but society must accept the current state of affairs and go forward, evolving from that baseline. Once the Beats had upset the established order, American society could never return to the earlier conformist, stifling status quo.

Their questioning of traditional values in the postwar period led to a host of social revolutions during a time of conformity, prejudice, and artistic stagnation. More than anything, the Beats believed in the importance of the individual and brought with them a new appreciation for idiosyncrasy. That helped lead to widespread changes in all the arts, especially through the Beat Generation's victories over the censors. It was through their efforts that freedom of speech was once again restored to America.

Ginsberg, who created the Beat Generation himself, deserves the final word, for he was correct when he said that the jury is still out on the Beats. "Nobody knows whether we were catalysts, or invented something, or just the froth riding on a wave of its own. We were all three, I suppose."

Source Notes

Abbreviations used frequently in the notes include:

A.G.: Allen Ginsberg. J.K.: Jack Kerouac. W.S.B.: William S. Burroughs. C.C.: Carolyn Cassady. N.C.: Neal Cassady. G.C.: Gregory Corso. L.F.: Lawrence Ferlinghetti. L.C.: Lucien Carr. H.H.: Herbert Huncke. P.O.: Peter Orlovsky.

Note: Complete bibliographic citations are given in the bibliography. For purposes of brevity, general biographies that were consulted frequently are listed only in the chapter of their first reference.

Introduction

xiii *"I have seen some"*: Anthony Daniels, "Another Side of Paradise," *New Criterion* (Sept. 2007), pp. 12–17.

xiii *"They were drug-abusing sexual"*: Roger Kimball, *The Long March*, pp. 38–39.

xiii *"know-nothing bohemians"*: Norman Podhoretz, "The Know-Nothing Bohemians," *Partisan Review* (spring 1958), pp. 305–318.

xiv *"the cult of unthink"*: Robert Brustein, "The Cult of Unthink," *Horizon* (Sept. 1958), pp. 38–45, 134–135.

xiv *"the most irritable"*: Al Capp, *Li'l Abner, New York Daily News* (May 1964).

xiv Susan Cheever, *American Bloomsbury*, pp. 10–11.

xvi Lawrence Ferlinghetti, *A Coney Island of the Mind.*

xviii Definition of Beat Generation: *The Beat Generation: A Gale Critical Companion, Vols. 1–3;* William T. Lawlor (ed.), *Beat Culture: Icons, Life-*

styles, and Impact; Steve Allen Pontiac Show (Jan. 16, 1959); John Clellon Holmes, "This Is the Beat Generation," *New York Times Magazine* (Nov. 16, 1952), pp. 10–22.

xviii   *"American College Dictionary sent":* letter from J.K. to A.G. March 24, 1959, reprinted in Jack Kerouac, *Selected Letters 1957–1969,* pp. 191–192.

xviii   *Over the years:* W.S.B. (in) Allen Ginsberg, *The Book of Martyrdom and Artifice,* footnote, p. 38.

xix   Gregor Roy, *Beat Literature.*

xx   Gilbert Millstein, "Books of the Times," *New York Times* (Sept. 5, 1957), p. 27.

xx   Eugene Burdick, "The Innocent Nihilists Adrift in Squaresville," *Reporter* (April 3, 1958), pp. 30–33; John Ciardi, "Epitaph for the Dead Beats," *Saturday Review* (Feb. 6, 1960), pp. 11–13, 42; "Beatniks Just Sick, Sick, Sick," *Science Digest* (July 1959), pp. 25–26.

xx   *"This notion that to be hopped":* Podhoretz, ibid.

Interviews with Steve Allen, G.C., L.F., A.G., Philip Lamantia, Kaye McDonough.

Chapter 1: Friendship and Murder

1   *a vocabulary that he had honed:* Allen Ginsberg, *The Book of Martyrdom and Artifice,* pp. 31–34.

2   *Lucien was blessed:* Edie Kerouac-Parker, *You'll Be Okay: My Life with Jack Kerouac.*

2   *That fall, Columbia's:* Bill Morgan, *The Beat Generation in New York.*

3   *Ginsberg had grown up:* Bill Morgan, *I Celebrate Myself: The Somewhat Private Life of Allen Ginsberg.*

3   Ted Morgan, *Literary Outlaw: The Life and Times of William S. Burroughs.*

4   "Kammerer's Parents Prominent," *New York Times* (Aug. 17, 1944), p. 13.

5   Unpublished A.G. journal entries are from the collection of the Stanford University Library.

8   *"a spindly Jewish kid":* Jack Kerouac, *Vanity of Duluoz,* p. 211.

8   Details about J.K.'s life, here and throughout, come from several excellent sources, including: Ann Charters, *Kerouac;* Barry Gifford and Lawrence Lee, *Jack's Book;* Dennis McNally, *Desolate Angel;* Gerald Nicosia, *Memory Babe;* Tom Clark, *Jack Kerouac;* Barry Miles, *Jack Kerouac: King of the Beats;* Paul Maher Jr., *Kerouac: The Definitive Biography.*

12   Aaron Latham, "The Columbia Murder That Gave Birth to the Beats," *New York* (April 19, 1976), pp. 41–53.

Interviews with L.C., A.G., Tim Moran.

Chapter 2: The Lumpen World

13   *Columbia University did not:* Unpublished Lionel Trilling journal entries are from the collection of the Columbia University Library.

13   *"gotten away with murder":* A.G. to author. Aaron Latham, "The Columbia Murder That Gave Birth to the Beats," *New York* (April 19, 1976), pp. 41–53.

14   Edie Kerouac-Parker, *You'll Be Okay: My Life with Jack Kerouac.*

14   Ted Morgan, *Literary Outlaw: The Life and Times of William S. Burroughs.*

16   "The Night of the Wolfeans," Allen Ginsberg, *The Book of Martyrdom and Artifice.*

16   "The Last Voyage," Allen Ginsberg, *The Book of Martyrdom and Artifice,* pp. 401–409.

17   William S. Burroughs and Jack Kerouac, *And the Hippos Were Boiled in Their Tanks.*

17   *"if you continue going back":* Allen Ginsberg, *Snapshot Poetics,* p. 21.

18   *filthy windows:* A.G. letter to Diana Trilling (in) Allen Ginsberg, *The Letters of Allen Ginsberg,* pp. 393–397.

18   Bill Morgan, *The Beat Generation in New York* [and throughout].

19   *The Herbert Huncke Reader.*

20   Rob Johnson, *The Lost Years of William S. Burroughs.*

22   *as good as any pimp:* James Campbell, *This Is the Beat Generation,* p. 49.

Interviews with L.C., A.G., James Grauerholz.

Chapter 3: The Adonis of Denver

24   Details about N.C.'s life, here and throughout, come from several excellent sources, including: William Plummer, *The Holy Goof;* Tom Christopher, *Neal Cassady: A Biography, Vol. 1: 1926–1940;* David Sandison and Graham Vickers, *Neal Cassady: The Fast Life of a Beat Hero;* Carolyn Cassady, *Off the Road;* Neal Cassady, *Collected Letters 1944–1967.*

26   Rob Johnson, *The Lost Years of William S. Burroughs.*

26   *"a wild weekend":* Allen Ginsberg, *The Book of Martyrdom and Artifice,* p. 169.

26   *"Great Sex Letter":* N.C. letter to J.K., March 7, 1947, (in) Neal Cassady, *Collected Letters, 1944–1967,* pp. 17–19.

27 *"I have met a wonderful girl"*: N.C. letter to A.G. (in) Neal Cassady, *Collected Letters*, p. 47.

28 Details about W.S.B.'s life, here and throughout, come from several excellent sources, including: Ted Morgan, *Literary Outlaw: The Life and Times of William S. Burroughs.*

29 Jack Kerouac, *Windblown World: The Journals of Jack Kerouac 1947–1954.*

30 *"I gather that"*: A.G. letter to N.C. (in) Allen Ginsberg and Neal Cassady, *As Ever,* p. 153.

31 *"My conviction that"*: Neal Cassady, *Collected Letters,* p. 59.

32 *"It was decided that"*: Unpublished letter from Harry J. Worthing to A.G., Nov. 14, 1947, is from the collection of the Columbia University Library.

32 Bill Morgan, *The Beat Generation in San Francisco* [and throughout].

Interviews with C.C., A.G., Tim Moran.

Chapter 4: Insanity

34 Details about A.G.'s life, here and throughout, come from several excellent sources, including: Barry Miles, *Ginsberg: A Biography;* Michael Schumacher, *Dharma Lion: A Critical Biography of Allen Ginsberg;* Bill Morgan, *I Celebrate My Life: The Somewhat Private Life of Allen Ginsberg.*

34 *"If you had taken my advice"*: Allen and Louis Ginsberg, *Family Business: Selected Letters Between a Father and Son.*

35 John Clellon Holmes, *Go.*

35 Jack Kerouac, *On the Road.*

37 John Clellon Holmes, *Passionate Opinions,* pp. 53–55.

39 *"[He is] ready to sacrifice"*: William S. Burroughs, *The Letters of William S. Burroughs: 1945–1959,* p. 37.

41 Unpublished letter from Louis Ginsberg to Lionel Trilling is from the collection of the Columbia University Library collection.

42 Jack Kerouac, *Selected Letters 1957–1969.*

43 *"a big wheat farm"*: J.K. journal entry for April 23, 1949, published in *New Yorker* (June 22 and 29, 1998) and reprinted in Paul Maher Jr., *Kerouac: The Definitive Biography,* p. 197.

Interviews with L.C., A.G., H.H., Elbert Lenrow.

Chapter 5: The Subterraneans

49 Details about W.S.B.'s life, here and throughout, come from several excellent sources, including: Ted Morgan, *Literary Outlaw: The Life and*

Times of William S. Burroughs; Barry Miles, *William Burroughs: El Hombre Invisible;* Rob Johnson, *The Lost Years of William S. Burroughs;* Willie Lee [William S. Burroughs], *Junkie.*

46 *"The rest of the people":* Unpublished letter from A.G. to J.K., Nov. 14, 1947, is from the collection of the University of Texas Library.

48 *"Am leaving today":* Neal Cassady, *Collected Letters,* p. 129.

48 *original scroll version:* Jack Kerouac, *On the Road: The Original Scroll.*

50 Louis Ginsberg, *Collected Poems.*

50 *"no ideas but":* William Carlos Williams quoted in Allen Ginsberg, *Deliberate Prose,* pp. 334–341.

53 *"I have started":* A.G. letter to J.K. (in) Allen Ginsberg, *The Letters of Allen Ginsberg,* p. 58.

54 Joan Haverty Kerouac, *Nobody's Wife: The Smart Aleck and the King of the Beats.*

55 *"At first the mother":* Neal Cassady, *Collected Letters,* p. 252.

56 *"I first met Neal":* Jack Kerouac, *On the Road: The Original Scroll,* p. 109. *Jack Kerouac's Typescript Scroll of On the Road* (Christie's auction catalogue, May 22, 2001).

Interviews with L.C., C.C., A.G., Helen Parker, John Sampas, Carl Solomon.

Chapter 6: Literary Lives

58 William S. Burroughs and Allen Ginsberg, *The Yage Letters.*

58 John Clellon Holmes, *Go.*

58 Allen Ginsberg, *The Book of Martyrdom and Artifice.*

58 *"I read a letter":* A.G. letter to N.C. (in) Allen Ginsberg, *The Letters of Allen Ginsberg,* pp. 64–65. William S. Burroughs, *The Letters of William S. Burroughs: 1945–1959,* pp. 88–90.

60 William S. Burroughs, *Queer.*

62 *"Essentials of Spontaneous Prose":* (in) Jack Kerouac, *The Portable Jack Kerouac,* pp. 484–485.

63 Gregory Stephenson, *Exiled Angel: A Study of the Work of Gregory Corso.*

63 Details about G.C.'s life, here and throughout, come from several excellent sources, including: Kirby Olson, *Gregory Corso: Doubting Thomist;* Michael Skau, *"A Clown in a Grave": Complexities and Tensions in the Works of Gregory Corso.*

65 *"Why don't you just sketch":* Jack Kerouac, *Selected Letters: 1940–1956,* pp. 354–357. Jack Kerouac, *Selected Letters 1940–1956,* p. 364.

Interviews with A.G., James Grauerholz, John Clellon Holmes, James Laughlin, Sterling Lord, Carl Solomon.

Chapter 7: The Name of a Generation

72   *"I'm completely stuck":* Neal Cassady, *Collected Letters, 1944–1967*, p. 374.

73   *"October in the Railroad Earth":* Jack Kerouac, *Evergreen Review* (1957), pp. 119–136.

73   Jack Kerouac, *Maggie Cassidy.*

74   *"The smell of his work":* J.K. letter to A.G. dated Oct. 8, 1952, in the collection of the Columbia University Library.

75   John Clellon Holmes, "This is the Beat Generation," *New York Times Magazine* (Nov. 16, 1952), pp. 10–22.

76   *"I shall certainly":* Unpublished letter from J.K. to A.G., Oct. 8, 1952, in the collection of the Columbia University Library.

77   Allen Ginsberg, *Journals Early Fifties Early Sixties.*

78   Jack Kerouac, *The Subterraneans.*

Interviews with Alan Ansen, C.C., G.C., Sterling Lord.

Chapter 8: To the West Coast

81   Alison Lurie, *V. R. Lang.*

81   Gregory Corso, *An Accidental Autobiography.*

81   Gregory Corso, *In This Hung-Up Age, Encounter* (Jan. 1962), pp. 83–90.

81   Gregory Corso, "I Held a Shelley Manuscript," *Happy Birthday of Death.*

82   Gregory Stephenson, *Exiled Angel: A Study of the Work of Gregory Corso.*

82   Gregory Corso, *The Vestal Lady on Brattle.*

82   William S. Burroughs, *The Letters of William S. Burroughs: 1945–1959.*

83   Gina Cerminara, *Many Mansions.*

84   *"California is the only state":* Unpublished letter from A.G. to Eugene Brooks, July 15, 1954, is from a private collection.

84   Allen Ginsberg, *Journals Mid-Fifties.*

90   Deborah Baker, *The Blue Hand.*

Interviews with C.C., G.C., A.G., John Sampas.

Chapter 9: Nightmare of Moloch

91   Jean-Louis [Jack Kerouac], "Jazz of the Beat Generation," *New World Writing*, pp. 7–16.

93   *"He come near killing me":* W.S.B. letter to A.G. (in) William S. Burroughs, *The Letters of William S. Burroughs: 1945–1959*, p. 302.

94   Details about L.F.'s life, here and throughout, come from several excellent sources, including: Barry Silesky, *Ferlinghetti: The Artist in His Time;*

Larry Smith, *Lawrence Ferlinghetti: Poet-at-Large;* Neeli Cherkovski, *Ferlinghetti: A Biography.*

94 Lawrence Ferlinghetti, *Pictures of the Gone World.*

96 Allen Ginsberg, *Howl: Annotated Edition.*

96 Allen Ginsberg, *Howl and Other Poems.*

97 *"Most of my":* A.G. letter to Eugene Brooks dated Aug. 16, 1955, published in Allen Ginsberg, *The Letters of Allen Ginsberg,* p. 121.

97 Linda Hamalian, *A Life of Kenneth Rexroth.*

98 *"Whalen I think":* Unpublished letter from A.G. to Charles Olson, Feb. 18, 1957, collection of the University of Connecticut.

99 Lawrence Ferlinghetti and Nancy J. Peters, *Literary San Francisco.*

99 Warren French, *The San Francisco Poetry Renaissance, 1955–1960.*

100 William S. Burroughs, *Interzone.*

100 Jack Kerouac, *Tristessa.*

100 Jack Kerouac, *Mexico City Blues.*

Interviews with Ann and Sam Charters, L.F., A.G., Philip Lamantia, Michael McClure, Gary Snyder, Philip Whalen.

Chapter 10: The Six Gallery

101 *"amid much laughter":* Unpublished letter from A.G. to Robert La Vigne, Sept. 26, 1955, in the collection of the University of Texas.

101 *The Selected Letters of Allen Ginsberg and Gary Snyder.*

101 Allen Ginsberg, *Howl: Annotated Edition.*

102 Phil Lamantia and John Hoffman, *Tau and Journey to the End.*

102 Michael McClure, *Scratching the Beat Surface.*

102 Philip Whalen, *The Collected Poems.*

103 Gary Snyder, *Myths and Texts.*

103 Gary Snyder, "A Berry Feast," (in) *A Range of Poems.*

106 Jack Kerouac, *The Dharma Bums.*

107 *"an unidentified blonde woman":* "Woman Fights Off Rescue, Leaps 3 Stories to Death," *San Francisco Chronicle* (Dec. 1, 1955), p. 2.

107 Jack Kerouac, *Visions of Gerard.*

108 Details about Paul Bowles's life, here and throughout, come from several excellent sources, including: Paul Bowles, *Without Stopping;* Christopher Sawyer-Laucanno, *The Continual Pilgrimage.*

108 Quotes from William S. Burroughs letters are found in *The Letters of William S. Burroughs: 1945–1959.*

Interviews with Ann Charters, L.F., A.G., Philip Lamantia, Michael McClure, Shig Murao, Gary Snyder, Philip Whalen.

Chapter 11: Desolation and Loneliness

111 *"took a lot of peyote"*: Unpublished letter from A.G. to Charles Olson, Feb. 18, 1957, collection of the University of Connecticut.

112 Gary Snyder, *Mountains and Rivers Without End.*

113 Gregory Corso, *The Vestal Lady on Brattle.*

113 *"As I saw her coffin"*: Allen and Louis Ginsberg, *Family Business,* p. 52.

114 Details about Robert Creeley's life, here and throughout, come from several excellent sources, including: Ekbert Faas, *Robert Creeley: A Biography;* Martin Duberman, *Black Mountain: An Exploration in Community.*

114 Charles Olson, *The Maximus Poems.*

115 Details about Ed Dorn's life, here and throughout, come from: Tom Clark, *Ed Dorn: A World of Difference.*

115 Details about Kenneth Rexroth's life, here and throughout, come from: Linda Hamalian, *A Life of Kenneth Rexroth.*

116 Details about Bob Kaufman's life, here and throughout, come from: Mel Clay, *Jazz, Jail and God.*

118 *"Don't like San Francisco"*: Gregory Corso, *An Accidental Autobiography,* p. 9.

119 *"Why hasn't my name"*: Gregory Corso, *An Accidental Autobiography,* p. 8.

120 *"Japan of old"*: *The Selected Letters of Allen Ginsberg and Gary Snyder,* p. 8.

120 Allen Ginsberg, *Journals Mid-Fifties.*

120 Jack Kerouac, *Desolation Angels.*

Interviews with Alan Ansen, G.C., Gary Snyder.

Chapter 12: Censorship and Vindication

123 *"golden inspired period"*: *The Letters of Allen Ginsberg,* p. 169.

126 Details about *Howl* are from Bill Morgan and Nancy J. Peters, *Howl on Trial.*

126 *"You wouldn't want"*: Abe Mellinkoff, "Iron Curtain on the Embarcadero," *San Francisco Chronicle* (March 28, 1957).

129 *"Sura is a little too"*: Gregory Corso, *An Accidental Autobiography,* p. 36.

131 *The Selected Letters of Allen Ginsberg and Gary Synder.*

132 Barry Miles, *The Beat Hotel* [here and throughout].

Interviews with G.C., Helen Elliott, L.F., A.G., Sterling Lord, P.O., Helen Weaver.

Chapter 13: Fame

133 Jack Kerouac, "Aftermath: The Philosophy of the Beat Generation," *Esquire* (March 1958), pp. 24–26.

134 *"In God's name"*: Jack Kerouac, *On the Road*, p. 180.

135 Joyce Johnson, *Minor Characters*.

136 *"The fact is"*: Gilbert Millstein, "Books of the Times," *New York Times* (Sept. 5, 1957), p. 27.

136 Allen Ginsberg, *The Letters of Allen Ginsberg*.

137 *"a man belligerently"*: Robert Brustein, "The Cult of Unthink," *Horizon* (Sept. 1958), pp. 38–45, 134–135.

138 *"It isn't writing"*: Truman Capote appearing on the television program *Open End* with David Susskind.

139 Peter Orlovsky, *Clean Asshole Poems and Smiling Vegetable Songs*.

139 David Amram, *Offbeat: Collaborating with Kerouac*.

140 Allen Ginsberg and Peter Orlovsky, *Straight Hearts' Delight*.

142 Gregory Corso, *Gasoline*.

142 Gregory Corso, "Power," (in) *Happy Birthday of Death*.

142 "I am professing love": Gregory Corso, *An Accidental Autobiography*, p. 137.

144 *Big Table,* no. 1 (Spring 1959).

145 Marc D. Schleifer, "Here to Save Us, But Not Sure from What," *Village Voice* (Oct. 15, 1958), pp. 3, 9.

Interviews with David Amram, Alan Ansen, W.S.B., G.C., L.F., A.G., Sterling Lord, P.O.

Chapter 14: The Threads Loosen

149 *"If you only knew"*: Jack Kerouac, *Selected Letters 1957–1969,* pp. 167–168.

149 Gregory Corso, *Bomb*.

149 Barry Miles, *The Beat Hotel*.

151 Ed Adler, *Departed Angels: Jack Kerouac, The Lost Paintings*.

151 Allen Ginsberg, Unpublished *Kaddish* manuscript in the collection of the New York University, Fales Library.

152 Unpublished William S. Burroughs material is found in his archive at the New York Public Library, Berg Collection.

154 Diane Di Prima, *This Kind of Bird Flies Backward*.

155 Diane Di Prima, *Memoirs of a Beatnik*.

155 Brenda Knight, *Women of the Beat Generation*.

156 *Robert Frank: The Film and Video Work*.

156 Jack Kerouac, *Pull My Daisy*.

156 David Amram, *Offbeat: Collaborating with Kerouac*.

Interviews with David Amram, G.C., Diane Di Prima, A.G., H.H., Judith Malina.

Chapter 15: The Circle Widens

158   Donald M. Allen, *The New American Poetry: 1945–1960*.

158   Donald Hall, Robert Pack, and Louis Simpson, *New Poets of England and America*.

159   *"I'm crazy:"* (in) "Manners and Morals," *Time* (Feb. 9, 1959), p. 16.

159   Dave Hoekstra, "Sputnik 1 Begat Beatniks," *Chicago Sun-Times* (March 18, 2007).

160   Diane Trilling, "The Other Night at Columbia, A Report from the Academy," *Partisan Review* (Spring 1959), pp. 214–230.

161   Amiri Baraka, *The Autobiography of LeRoi Jones/Amiri Baraka* [here and throughout].

161   Hettie Jones, *How I Became Hettie Jones*.

162   David Meltzer, *San Francisco Beat*.

Interviews with G.C., A.G., Ted Wilentz.

Chapter 16: Cut-ups

170   Sinclair Beiles, William Burroughs, Gregory Corso, and Brion Gysin, *Minutes to Go*.

171   Jack Kerouac, *Visions of Cody*.

172   Herbert Huncke, *The Evening Sun Turned Crimson*.

173   Herbert Huncke, *Huncke's Journal*.

173   Alan Ansen, *The Old Religion*.

173   Lawrence Lipton, *The Holy Barbarians*.

175   "Squaresville U.S.A. vs. Beatsville," *Life* (Sept. 21, 1959), pp. 31–37.

175   G. B. Leonard, "The Bored, the Bearded, and the Beat," *Look* (Aug. 19, 1958), pp. 64–68.

175   Allen Ginsberg unpublished South American journals in the collection of Stanford University Library.

176   Joanne Kyger, *Japan and Indian Journals, 1960–1964*.

179   Jack Kerouac, *Big Sur*.

Interviews with Alan Ansen, Carolyn Cassady, L.F., A.G., H.H., Michael McClure.

Chapter 17: Bitter Fruits

182   Robert Greenfield, *Timothy Leary: A Biography*.

182   Allen Ginsberg, *Journals Early Fifties Early Sixties*.

183   Bonnie Bremser, *Troia: Mexican Memoirs*.

183   LeRoi Jones, *Preface to a Twenty Volume Suicide Note*.

184   William S. Burroughs, *Roosevelt After Inauguration*.

185 Deborah Baker, *The Blue Hand.*
186 Gregory Corso, *The American Express.*

Interviews with A.G., Barry Miles, P.O., John Sampas.

Chapter 18: Setting the Global Stage

192 Lawrence Ferlinghetti, *One Thousand Fearful Words for Fidel Castro.*
193 LeRoi Jones, *Cuba Libre.*
194 Gary Snyder, *Passage Through India.*
194 Allen Ginsberg, *Indian Journals.*
197 Robert Creeley, *For Love.*
197 Joyce Glassman, *Come and Join the Dance.*

Interviews with Robert Creeley, A.G., John Clellon Holmes, Joanne Kyger, P.O., Gary Snyder.

Chapter 19: A Culture Turned Upside Down

201 *"happy in heaven"*: Unpublished letter from A.G. to L.F., Aug. 5, 1963, in the collection of the University of California, Bancroft Library.
201 *"I'm telling you the cold war's over"*: Unpublished letter from A.G. to P.O., Aug. 16–17, 1963, in the collection of the University of Texas.
202 Allen Ginsberg, *Reality Sandwiches 1953–60.*
202 Unpublished script of *Kaddish* in the collection of Stanford University.
207 William S. Burroughs, "St. Louis Return," (although not published in *Playboy,* it was picked up by) *Paris Review* (Fall 1965), pp. 50–62.
208 Ed Sanders, *Poem from Jail.*
209 "The Boston Trial of *Naked Lunch,*" *Evergreen Review* (June 1965), pp. 40–49, 87–88.
210 Michael McClure, *The Beard.*
212 Tom Wolfe, *The Electric Kool-Aid Acid Test.*
213 *"Just when everything"*: Gabrielle Kerouac to Stanley and Anne Twardowicz, (in) Jack Kerouac, *Selected Letters 1957–1969,* p. 383.

Interviews with Ray Bremser, A.G., Timothy Leary, Michael McClure, Jonas Mekas, P.O., Ed Sanders, Ted Wilentz.

Chapter 20: The Sixties

214 Michael Fallon, "A New Haven for Beatniks," *San Francisco Chronicle* (Sept. 5, 1965).
215 Allen Ginsberg unpublished Iron Curtain journals in the collection of Stanford University.

218 Barry Farrell, "The Guru Comes to Kansas," *Life* (May 27, 1966), pp. 78–90.

221 Norman Mailer, *Armies of the Night.*

223 William S. Burroughs Jr., *Cursed from Birth: The Short, Unhappy Life of William S. Burroughs, Jr.*

Interviews with Gordon Ball, L.F., A.G., Timothy Leary, Michael McClure, Rosebud Pettet, John Sampas, Ed Sanders, Anne Waldman.

Chapter 21: The End of the Road

226 John Bryan, "The Death of Neal Cassady," *Open City* (Feb. 16–22, 1968), pp. 5, 8.

226 Ken Kesey, "The Day After Superman Died," *Esquire* (Oct. 1979), pp. 42–64.

226 *"exhausted feeling lone":* Unpublished letter by A.G. to Elbert Lenrow, Aug. 24, 1968, in private collection.

227 *"The policed acted":* Burroughs's account of the scene is from an unpublished manuscript dated Aug. 27, 1968, now found in the library of the University of North Carolina, Chapel Hill.

229 Herbert Huncke, "Alvarez," *Playboy* (Oct. 1968).

229 Joseph Lelyveld, "Jack Kerouac, Novelist, Dead. Father of the Beat Generation," *New York Times* (Oct. 22, 1969), p. 47.

Interviews with Gordon Ball, L.F., A.G., Michael McClure, John Sampas.

Chapter 22: Aftermath

232 Philip Whalen, *Imaginary Speeches for a Brazen Head.*

233 Michael McClure, *Scratching the Beat Surface.*

234 Alan Ansen, *Contact Highs.*

235 Diane Di Prima, *Revolutionary Letters.*

235 Diane Di Prima, *Recollections of My Life as a Woman.*

236 Joanne Kyger, *The Tapestry and the Web.*

237 Carolyn Cassady, *Heart Beat.*

Interviews with C.C., H.H., Michael McClure, Philip Whalen.

Chapter 23: Respectability

238 *The Selected Letters of Allen Ginsberg and Gary Snyder.*

239 Gary Snyder, *Turtle Island.*

240 William S. Burroughs, *Cities of the Red Night.*

242 *"Put on my tie":* Allen Ginsberg, *Cosmopolitan Greetings.*

Interviews with A.G., James Grauerholz, Peter Hale, Bob Rosenthal, Anne Waldman.

Chapter 24: Acceptance

244   Allen Ginsberg, *The Fall of America.*
244   Michael Vadnie, "7 'Beat' Poets Appear at 'City Lights in N.D.,'" *Grand Forks Herald* (March 19, 1974), p. 20.

Chapter 25: Postscript

248   *"better"*: Jim Cullen, *The American Dream: A Short History of an Idea That Shaped a Nation.*

Selected Bibliography

Adler, Ed. *Departed Angels: Jack Kerouac, The Lost Paintings*. New York: Thunder's Mouth Press, 2004.

Allen, Donald M. *The New American Poetry: 1945–1960*. New York: Grove, 1960.

Amburn, Ellis. *Subterranean Kerouac*. New York: St. Martin's, 1998.

Amram, David. *Offbeat: Collaborating with Kerouac*. New York: Thunder's Mouth Press, 2002.

Ansen, Alan. *Contact Highs*. Lincoln, NE: Dalkey Archive, 1989.

———. *The Old Religion*. New York: Tibor de Nagy Gallery, 1959.

———. *William Burroughs: An Essay*. Sudbury, MA: Water Row Press, 1986.

Ark II Moby I (1956).

Baker, Deborah. *The Blue Hand: The Beats in India*. New York: Penguin, 2008.

Ball, Gordon. *'66 Frames*. Minneapolis, MN: Coffee House Press, 1999.

Baraka, Amiri. *The Autobiography of LeRoi Jones/Amiri Baraka*. New York: Freundlich, 1984.

The Beat Generation: A Gale Critical Companion, Vols. 1–3. Detroit: Thomson Gale, 2003.

Beatitude, nos. 1–23 (1959–1976).

"Beatniks Just Sick, Sick, Sick," *Science Digest* (July 1959).

Beiles, Sinclair, William Burroughs, Gregory Corso, and Brion Gysin. *Minutes to Go*. Paris: Two Cities Editions, 1960.

Big Table, no. 1 (Spring 1959).

Black Mountain Review, nos. 1–7 (Spring 1954–Autumn 1957).

"The Boston Trial of *Naked Lunch*." *Evergreen Review* (June 1965).

Bowles, Paul. *The Sheltering Sky*. London: John Lehmann, 1949.

———. *Without Stopping*. New York: Putnam, 1972.

Bremser, Bonnie. *Troia: Mexican Memoirs.* New York: Croton Press, 1969.

Bremser, Ray. *Poems of Madness.* New York: Paperbook Gallery, 1965.

Brustein, Robert. "The Cult of Unthink." *Horizon* (Sept. 1958).

Bryan, John. "The Death of Neal Cassady." *Open City* (Feb. 16–22, 1968).

Burdick, Eugene. "The Innocent Nihilists Adrift in Squaresville." *Reporter* (April 3, 1958).

Burger-Utzer, Brigitta, and Stefan Grissemann, eds. *Frank Films: The Film and Video Work of Robert Frank.* New York: Scalo, 2003.

Burroughs, William S. *Cities of the Red Night.* New York: Henry Holt and Co., 1982.

———. *Interzone.* New York: Viking, 1989.

———. *The Job: Interviews with William S. Burroughs.* New York: Grove, 1970.

———. *Junkie.* New York: Ace, 1953.

———. *The Letters of William S. Burroughs: Volume I: 1945–1959,* edited by Oliver Harris. New York: Viking, 1993.

———. *Naked Lunch.* New York: Grove, 1962.

———. *Nova Express.* New York: Grove, 1964.

———. *Queer.* New York: Viking/Penguin, 1985.

———. *Roosevelt After Inauguration.* New York: Fuck You Press, 1964.

———. *The Soft Machine.* Paris: Olympia Press, 1961.

———. "St. Louis Return." *Paris Review* (Fall 1965).

———. *The Ticket That Exploded.* Paris: Olympia Press, 1962.

Burroughs, William S., and Allen Ginsberg. *The Yage Letters.* San Francisco: City Lights, 1963.

Burroughs, William S., and Jack Kerouac. *And the Hippos Were Boiled in Their Tanks.* New York: Grove Press, 2008.

Burroughs, William S. Jr. *Cursed from Birth: The Short, Unhappy Life of William S. Burroughs, Jr.* New York: Soft Skull Press, 2006.

Campbell, James. *This Is the Beat Generation,* Berkeley, CA: University of California Press, 1999.

Capp, Al. *Li'l Abner. New York Daily News* (May 1964).

Cassady, Carolyn. *Heart Beat.* Berkeley, CA: Creative Arts, 1976.

———. *Off the Road: My Years with Cassady, Kerouac, and Ginsberg.* New York: William Morrow, 1990.

Cassady, Neal. *Collected Letters, 1944–1967.* New York: Penguin, 2004.

———. *The First Third.* San Francisco: City Lights, 1971.

Cerminara, Gina. *Many Mansions.* New York: Sloane, 1950.

Chapman, Harold. *The Beat Hotel.* Montpellier, France: Gris Banal, 1984.

Charters, Ann, ed. *The Beats: Literary Bohemians in Postwar America.* Detroit: Gale, 1983.

Charters, Ann. *Beats & Company.* Garden City, NY: Doubleday, 1986.

—————. *Kerouac: A Biography.* San Francisco: Straight Arrow Books, 1973.

Cheever, Susan. *American Bloomsbury.* New York: Simon & Schuster, 2006.

Cherkovski, Neeli. *Ferlinghetti: A Biography.* Garden City, NY: Doubleday, 1979.

—————. *Whitman's Wild Children.* Venice, CA: Lapis Press, 1988.

Christopher, Tom. *Neal Cassady: A Biography, Vol. 1: 1926–1940.* Vashon, WA: 1995.

Ciardi, John. "Epitaph for the Dead Beats." *Saturday Review* (Feb. 6, 1960).

Clark, Tom. *Ed Dorn: A World of Difference.* Berkeley, CA: North Atlantic Books, 2002.

—————. *Jack Kerouac.* New York: Harcourt, Brace, Jovanovich, 1984.

—————. *Robert Creeley and the Genius of the American Common Place.* New York: New Directions, 1993.

Clark, Walter Van Tilburg. *The Ox-Bow Incident.* New York: Random House, 1940.

Clay, Mel. *Jazz—Jail and God.* San Francisco: Androgyne, 2001.

Corso, Gregory. *An Accidental Autobiography,* edited by Bill Morgan. New York: New Directions, 2003.

—————. *The American Express.* Paris: Olympia, 1961.

—————. *Bomb.* San Francisco: City Lights, 1958.

—————. *Gasoline.* San Francisco: City Lights Books, 1958.

—————. *Happy Birthday of Death.* New York: New Directions, 1960.

—————. "In This Hung-Up Age." *Encounter* (Jan. 1962).

—————. *Long Live Man.* New York: New Directions, 1962.

—————. *The Vestal Lady on Brattle.* Cambridge, MA: Richard Brukenfeld, 1955.

Creeley, Robert. *For Love.* New York: Scribner's, 1962.

Cullen, Jim. *The American Dream: A Short History of an Idea That Shaped a Nation.* New York: Oxford University Press, 2004.

Daniels, Anthony. "Another Side of Paradise," *New Criterion* (Sept. 2007), pp. 12–17.

Di Prima, Diane. *Memoirs of a Beatnik.* New York: Traveller's Companion/Olympia, 1969.

—————. *Recollections of My Life as a Woman.* New York: Viking, 2001.

—————. *Revolutionary Letters.* San Francisco: City Lights, 1971.

—————. *This Kind of Bird Flies Backward.* New York: Totem, 1958.

Donleavy, J. P. *The Ginger Man.* Paris: Olympia Press, 1955.

Duberman, Martin. *Black Mountain: An Exploration in Community.* Garden City, NY: Anchor, 1973.

Ehrlich, J. W., ed. *Howl of the Censor.* San Carlos, CA: Nourse, 1961.

Faas, Ekbert. *Robert Creeley: A Biography.* Hanover, NH: University Press of New England, 1998.

Fallon, Michael. "A New Haven for Beatniks." *San Francisco Chronicle* (Sept. 5, 1965).

Farrell, Barry. "The Guru Comes to Kansas." *Life* (May 27, 1966).

Ferlinghetti, Lawrence. *A Coney Island of the Mind.* New York: New Directions, 1958.

——. *One Thousand Fearful Words for Fidel Castro.* San Francisco: City Lights, 1961.

——. *Pictures of the Gone World.* San Francisco: City Lights, 1955.

Ferlinghetti, Lawrence, and Nancy J. Peters. *Literary San Francisco.* San Francisco: City Lights/Harper Row, 1980.

Floating Bear, nos. 1–38 (Feb. 1961–summer 1971).

French, Warren. *The San Francisco Poetry Renaissance, 1955–1960.* Boston: Twayne, 1991.

Gide, André. *The Counterfeiters.* New York: Vintage, 1973.

Gifford, Barry, and Lawrence Lee. *Jack's Book.* New York: St. Martin's Press, 1978.

Ginsberg, Allen. *Allen Verbatim,* edited by Gordon Ball. New York: McGraw-Hill, 1974.

——. *The Book of Martyrdom and Artifice,* edited by Juanita Lieberman-Plimpton and Bill Morgan. New York: Da Capo Press, 2006.

——. *Cosmopolitan Greetings.* New York: HarperCollins, 1994.

——. *Deliberate Prose: Selected Essays, 1952–1995,* edited by Bill Morgan. New York: HarperCollins, 2000.

——. *The Fall of America.* San Francisco: City Lights, 1972.

——. *The Gates of Wrath.* Bolinas: Grey Fox, 1972.

——. *Howl and Other Poems.* San Francisco: City Lights, 1956.

——. *Howl: Annotated Edition.* New York: Harper & Row, 1986.

——. *Indian Journals.* San Francisco: Dave Haselwood/City Lights, 1970.

——. *Journals Early Fifties Early Sixties,* edited by Gordon Ball. New York: Grove, 1977.

——. *Journals Mid-Fifties,* edited by Gordon Ball. New York: HarperCollins, 1994.

——. *Kaddish and Other Poems.* San Francisco: City Lights Books, 1961.

——. *The Letters of Allen Ginsberg,* edited by Bill Morgan. New York: Da Capo Press, 2008.

——. *Reality Sandwiches: 1953–60.* San Francisco: City Lights, 1963.

——. *Snapshot Poetics.* San Francisco: Chronicle Books, 1993.

——. *Spontaneous Mind,* edited by David Carter. New York: HarperCollins, 2001.

Ginsberg, Allen, and Gary Snyder. *The Selected Letters of Allen Ginsberg and Gary Snyder,* edited by Bill Morgan. Berkeley, CA: Counterpoint, 2009.

Ginsberg, Allen, and Louis Ginsberg. *Family Business: Selected Letters Between a Father and Son,* edited by Michael Schumacher. New York: Bloomsbury, 2001.

Ginsberg, Allen, and Neal Cassady. *As Ever.* Berkeley, CA: Creative Arts Book Co., 1977.

Ginsberg, Allen, and Peter Orlovsky. *Straight Hearts' Delight.* San Francisco: Gay Sunshine, 1980.

Ginsberg, Louis. *Collected Poems.* Orono, ME: Northern Lights, 1992.

Glassman, Joyce. *Come and Join the Dance.* New York: Atheneum, 1962.

Gogol, Nikolai. *Dead Souls.* New York: Vintage, 1997.

Green, Michelle. *The Dream at the End of the World.* New York: HarperCollins, 1991.

Greenfield, Robert. *Timothy Leary: A Biography.* New York: Harcourt, 2006.

Hall, Donald, Robert Pack, and Louis Simpson. *New Poets of England and America.* Cleveland: The World Publishing Co., 1965.

Halper, Jon, ed. *Gary Snyder: Dimensions of a Life.* San Francisco: Sierra Club Books, 1991.

Hamalian, Linda. *A Life of Kenneth Rexroth.* New York: Norton, 1990.

Haverty Kerouac, Joan. *Nobody's Wife: The Smart Aleck and the King of the Beats.* Berkeley, CA: Creative Arts Book Co., 2000.

Hoekstra, Dave. "Sputnik 1 Begat Beatniks." *Chicago Sun-Times* (March 18, 2007).

Holmes, John Clellon. *Go.* New York: Scribner's, 1952.

———. *Nothing More to Declare.* New York: Dutton, 1967.

———. *Passionate Opinions.* Fayetteville, AR: University of Arkansas Press, 1988.

———. "This Is the Beat Generation." *New York Times Magazine* (Nov. 16, 1952).

Huncke, Herbert. "Alvarez." *Playboy* (Oct. 1968).

———. *The Evening Sun Turned Crimson.* Cherry Valley, NY: Cherry Valley Editions, 1980.

———. *The Herbert Huncke Reader,* edited by Ben Schafer. New York: William Morrow, 1997.

———. *Huncke's Journal.* New York: Poet's Press, 1965.

Jean-Louis [Jack Kerouac], "Jazz of the Beat Generation," by Jean-Louis. *New World Writing.* New York: New American Library, 1955.

Johnson, Joyce. *Minor Characters.* Boston: Houghton Mifflin, 1983.

Johnson, Rob. *The Lost Years of William S. Burroughs.* College Station, TX: Texas A&M University Press, 2006.

Johnson, Ronna C., and Nancy M. Grace, eds. *Girls Who Wore Black: Women Writing the Beat Generation.* New Brunswick, NJ: Rutgers, 2002.

Jones, Hettie. *How I Became Hettie Jones.* New York: Dutton, 1990.

Jones, LeRoi. *Cuba Libre.* New York: Fair Play for Cuba Committee, 1960.

———. *Dutchman and the Slave.* New York: William Morrow, 1964.

———. *Preface to a Twenty Volume Suicide Note.* New York: Totem, 1961.

"Kammerer's Parents Prominent," *New York Times* (Aug. 17, 1944).

Kerouac, Jack. "Aftermath: The Philosophy of the Beat Generation." *Esquire* (March 1958).

———. *Atop an Underwood: Early Stories and Other Writings.* New York: Viking, 1999.

———. *Big Sur.* New York: Farrar, Straus, and Cudahy, 1962.

———. *Desolation Angels.* New York: Coward-McCann, 1965.

———. *The Dharma Bums.* New York: Viking, 1958.

———. *Doctor Sax.* New York: Grove Press, 1959.

———. *Jack Kerouac's Typescript Scroll of On the Road* (Christie's auction catalogue, May 22, 2001).

———. *Maggie Cassidy.* New York: Avon, 1959.

———. *Mexico City Blues.* New York: Grove, 1959.

———. "October in the Railroad Earth." *Evergreen Review* (1957).

———. *On the Road.* New York: Viking, 1957.

———. *On the Road: The Original Scroll.* New York: Viking, 2007.

———. *The Portable Jack Kerouac,* edited by Ann Charters. New York: Viking, 1995.

———. *Pull My Daisy.* New York: Grove, 1961.

———. *Sartori in Paris,* New York: Grove Press, 1966.

———. *Selected Letters: 1940–1956,* edited by Ann Charters. New York: Viking, 1995.

———. *Selected Letters: 1957–1969,* edited by Ann Charters. New York: Viking, 1999.

———. *The Subterraneans.* New York: Grove, 1958.

———. *The Town and the City.* New York: Harcourt, Brace and Co., 1950.

———. *Tristessa.* New York: Avon, 1960.

———. *Vanity of Duluoz.* New York: Coward-McCann, 1968.

———. *Visions of Cody.* New York: McGraw-Hill, 1973.

———. *Visions of Gerard.* New York: Farrar, Straus, and Co., 1963.

———. *Windblown World: The Journals of Jack Kerouac, 1947–1954.* New York: Viking, 2004.

Kerouac-Parker, Edie. *You'll Be Okay: My Life with Jack Kerouac,* edited by Tim Moran and Bill Morgan. San Francisco: City Lights, 2007.

Kesey, Ken. "The Day After Superman Died." *Esquire* (Oct. 1979).

———. *One Flew over the Cuckoo's Nest.* New York: Viking, 1962.

———. *Sometimes a Great Notion.* New York: Viking, 1964.

Kimball, Roger. *The Long March.* San Francisco: Encounter Books, 2000.

Knight, Brenda. *Women of the Beat Generation.* Berkeley, CA: Conari, 1996.

Korzybski, Alfred. *Science and Sanity: An Introduction to Non-Aristotelian Systems and General Semantics.* Lancaster, PA: International Non-Aristotelian Publishing Co., 1933.

Kyger, Joanne. *Japan and Indian Journals, 1960–1964.* Bolinas, CA: Tombouctou, 1981.

———. *The Tapestry and the Web.* San Francisco: Four Seasons Foundation, 1965.

Lamantia, Philip, and John Hoffman. *Tau and Journey to the End.* San Francisco: City Lights, 2008.

Latham, Aaron. "The Columbia Murder That Gave Birth to the Beats." *New York* (April 19, 1976).

Lawlor, William T., ed. *Beat Culture: Icons, Lifestyles, and Impact.* Santa Barbara: ABC CLIO, 2005.

Lawrence, D. H. *Lady Chatterley's Lover.* New York: Grove, 1959.

Leary, Timothy. *Flashbacks.* Los Angeles: Tarcher, 1983.

Lelyveld, Joseph. "Jack Kerouac, Novelist, Dead; Father of the Beat Generation." *New York Times* (Oct. 22, 1969).

Leonard, G. B. "The Bored, the Bearded, and the Beat." *Look* (Aug. 19, 1958).

Lipton, Lawrence. *The Holy Barbarians.* New York: Julian Messner, 1959.

Lurie, Alison. *V. R. Lang.* New York: Random House, 1975.

McCarthy, Mary. *The Group.* New York: Harcourt, Brace and World, 1963.

McClure, Michael. *The Beard.* New York: Grove, 1967.

———. *Lighting the Corners.* Albuquerque, NM: American Poetry Book, 1993.

———. *Scratching the Beat Surface.* San Francisco: North Point Press, 1982.

———. *The Sermons of Jean Harlow & the Curses of Billy the Kid.* San Francisco: Four Seasons Foundation/Dave Haselwood, 1968.

McNally, Dennis. *Desolate Angel.* New York: Random House, 1979.

Maher, Paul Jr., ed. *Empty Phantoms: Interviews and Encounters with Jack Kerouac.* NY: Thunder's Mouth Press, 2005.

Maher, Paul Jr. *Kerouac: The Definitive Biography.* Lanham, MD: Taylor Trade, 2004.

Mailer, Norman. *The Armies of the Night.* New York: New American Library, 1968.

"Manners and Morals." *Time* (Feb. 9, 1959).

Measure, nos. 1–3 (Summer 1957–Summer 1962).

Mellinkoff, Abe. "Iron Curtain on the Embarcadero." *San Francisco Chronicle* (March 28, 1957).

Meltzer, David. *San Francisco Beat.* San Francisco: City Lights, 2001.

Miles, Barry. *Ginsberg: A Biography.* New York: Simon and Schuster, 1989.

———. *The Beat Hotel.* New York: Grove, 2000.

———. *Jack Kerouac: King of the Beats.* London: Virgin, 1998.

———. *William Burroughs: El Hombre Invisible.* New York: Hyperion, 1993.

Miller, Henry. *Tropic of Cancer.* New York: Grove, 1961.

Millstein, Gilbert. "Books of the Times." *New York Times* (Sept. 5, 1957).

Morgan, Bill. *The Beat Generation in New York.* San Francisco: City Lights, 1997.

———. *The Beat Generation in San Francisco.* San Francisco: City Lights, 2003.

———. *I Celebrate Myself: The Somewhat Private Life of Allen Ginsberg.* New York: Viking, 2007.

Morgan, Bill, and Nancy J. Peters. *Howl on Trial.* San Francisco: City Lights, 2006.

Morgan, Ted. *Literary Outlaw: The Life and Times of William S. Burroughs.* New York: Holt, 1988.

Nabokov, Vladimir. *Lolita.* Paris: Olympia Press, 1955.

Nicosia, Gerald. *Memory Babe.* New York: Grove, 1983.

Olson, Charles. *The Maximus Poems.* New York: Jargon/Corinth, 1960.

Olson, Kirby. *Gregory Corso: Doubting Thomist.* Carbondale, IL: Southern Illinois University Press, 2002.

Orlovsky, Peter. *Clean Asshole Poems and Smiling Vegetable Songs.* San Francisco: City Lights, 1978.

Phillips, Lisa. *Beat Culture and the New America: 1950–1965.* New York: Whitney Museum/Flammarion, 1995.

Plummer, William. *The Holy Goof.* Englewood Cliffs, NJ: Prentice-Hall, 1981.

Plymell, Charles. *The Harder They Come.* Santa Barbara, CA: Am Here Books, 1985.

Podhoretz, Norman. "The Known-Nothing Bohemians," *Partisan Review* (Spring 1958).

Roy, Gregor. *Beat Literature.* New York: Monarch Press, 1966.

Sanders, Ed. *Poem from Jail.* San Francisco: City Lights, 1963.

Sandison, David, and Graham Vickers. *Neal Cassady: The Fast Life of a Beat Hero.* Chicago: Chicago Review Press, 2006.

Sawyer-Lauçanno, Christopher. *The Continual Pilgrimage.* New York: Grove, 1992.

Schleifer, Marc D. "Here to Save Us, But Not Sure from What." *Village Voice* (Oct. 15, 1958).

Schumacher, Michael. *Dharma Lion: A Critical Biography of Allen Ginsberg.* New York: St. Martin's Press, 1992.

Silesky, Barry. *Ferlinghetti: The Artist in His Time.* New York: Warner, 1990.

Skau, Michael. *"A Clown in a Grave": Complexities and Tensions in the Works of Gregory Corso.* Carbondale, IL: Southern Illinois University Press, 1999.

Sloman, Larry. *On the Road with Bob Dylan.* New York: Bantam, 1978.

Smith, Larry. *Lawrence Ferlinghetti: Poet-at-Large.* Carbondale: Southern Illinois University Press, 1983.

Snyder, Gary. *The Back Country.* New York: New Directions, 1968.

———. *Mountains and Rivers Without End.* Berkeley: Counterpoint, 1997.

———. *Myths and Texts.* New York: Totem/Corinth, 1960.

———. *Passage Through India.* San Francisco: Grey Fox, 1983.

———. *A Range of Poems.* London: Fulcrum, 1966.

———. *Riprap.* Kyoto: Origin Press, 1959.

———. *Turtle Island.* New York: New Directions, 1974.

Southern, Terry, and Mason Hoffenberg. *Candy.* Paris: Olympia Press, 1958.

Spengler, Oswald. *The Decline of the West.* New York: Knopf, 1926.

"Squaresville U.S.A. vs. Beatsville." *Life* (Sept. 21, 1959).

Stephenson, Gregory. *Exiled Angel: A Study of the Work of Gregory Corso.* London: Hearing Eye, 1989.

Steve Allen Pontiac Show, Jan. 16, 1959.

Suiter, John. *Poets on the Peaks.* Washington: Counterpoint, 2002.

Theado, Matt, ed. *The Beats: A Literary Reference.* New York: Carroll & Graf, 2001.

Trilling, Diane. "The Other Night at Columbia, A Report from the Academy." *Partisan Review* (Spring 1959).

Tytell, John. *Naked Angels: The Lives and Literature of the Beat Generation.* New York: McGraw-Hill, 1976.

Vadnie, Michael. "7 'Beat' Poets Appear at 'City Lights in N.D.'" *Grand Forks Herald* (March 19, 1974).

Whalen, Philip. *The Collected Poems.* Middletown, CT: Wesleyan University Press, 2007.

———. *Imaginary Speeches for a Brazen Head.* Los Angeles: Black Sparrow, 1972.

Wolfe, Tom. *The Electric Kool-Aid Acid Test.* New York: Farrar, Straus and Giroux, 1968.

"Woman Fights Off Rescue, Leaps 3 Stories to Death." *San Francisco Chronicle* (Dec. 1, 1955).

Yeats, William Butler. *A Vision.* New York: Macmillan, 1937.

Yugen, nos. 1–8 (1958–1962).

INDEX

About the Author

BILL MORGAN is a writer and archival consultant who has written and edited dozens of books on the Beat writers, including the acclaimed biography *I Celebrate Myself: The Somewhat Private Life of Allen Ginsberg* (Viking Press). In addition, he has served as the archival consultant for nearly every member of the Beat Generation. He lives in Vermont with his wife and is currently working on two new books: *The Letters of Jack Kerouac and Allen Ginsberg* and *The Letters of William S. Burroughs: 1959–1997.*

Printed in the United States
by Baker & Taylor Publisher Services